ROBBO

ROBBO

THE GAME'S NOT OVER TILL THE FAT STRIKER SCORES

John Robertson

MY
AUTOBIOGRAPHY

BLACK & WHITE PUBLISHING

First published in the UK in 2021
This edition first published in 2022 by
Black & White Publishing Ltd
Nautical House, 104 Commercial Street, Edinburgh EH6 6NF

A division of Bonnier Books UK
4th Floor, Victoria House, Bloomsbury Square, London, WC1B 4DA
Owned by Bonnier Books
Sveavägen 56, Stockholm, Sweden

This book is a work of non-fiction, based on the life, experiences and
recollections of the author. The author has stated to the publishers that the
contents of this book are true to the best of his knowledge.

The publisher has made every reasonable effort to contact copyright holders
of images in the picture section. Any errors are inadvertent and anyone who
for any reason has not been contacted is invited to write to the publisher so
that a full acknowledgement can be made in subsequent editions of this work.

A CIP catalogue record for this book is available from the British Library.

ISBN (PBK): 978 1 78530 392 0

1 3 5 7 9 10 8 6 4 2

Typeset by Iolaire, Newtonmore
Printed and bound in Great Britain by Clays Ltd, Elcograf S.p.A.

www.blackandwhitepublishing.com

To Dad, Mum, my brothers and sisters:
I hope I made you proud.

And to Sally, none of this would have been
possible without your love, guidance and care.
Thank you so, so much x

Contents

'Scoring Goals for Fun'

A Foreword

I was absolutely delighted when Robbo asked me to write this foreword for his book. I was fortunate to play and work with many great players over my career, but rarely have I seen such an out-and-out goalscorer as the wee man. I gave him his debut in February 1982 when I simply could not leave him out of the squad. He was scoring goals for fun for the reserves and he was one of a crop of great young players I had coming through. I gather it was an important night for him when he came on at Tynecastle that Wednesday evening, because it gave him his only chance to play alongside his brother Chris.

From then he was a virtual fixture in my team as his goals continued right through the last three months of the season. The thing I liked about him was that he was a listener and he got good advice from Sandy Jardine and myself as well as the seasoned strikers like Jimmy Bone then Sandy Clark. He showed real spirit on the field and was a handful for every defender. He scored a lot of instinctive goals inside the box, but he had the ability to score from all distances. He struck the ball well and he was always dangerous when he came into the box from the left side. So often when I saw him there, I knew it would be a goal as he curled the ball into the keeper's top left-hand corner. In many ways, it was a signature goal from Robbo.

He was a delight to have around the squad with his enthusiasm and determination to win. It was all the more obvious when we played against Hibs who used to give him dogs abuse. We told him to just go out there and shut them up by scoring, which he did on twenty-seven occasions. I am sure they were glad to see the back of him when he left Hearts.

In the dressing room, he was a great influence and very popular. He was an intelligent guy, too, and seemed to be able to conjure up an answer to everything. We used to call him 'Ceefax', which was the go-to place at the time to find out anything you wanted. Later on that night if anyone was watching the TV, I'm sure they would see Ceefax scoring goals. He was that kind of guy.

It is a long time since he trotted out at Tynecastle every other week, but I have followed his career and it does not surprise me that he has made a decent life out of the game. I am sure he has a story or two to tell and I imagine the book will sit on the shelf of every Hearts fan, but maybe not every Hibee! I am just pleased to have played a part in his career as he did so well in mine.

Alex MacDonald
former player/manager
of Heart of Midlothian FC

'A Joy to Watch Him'

A Foreword

I first remember John Robertson, along with Gary Mackay and Dave Bowman, signing for Hearts when Bobby Moncur was manager in 1980. Bobby was delighted they chose Hearts, having been in big demand from a lot of other clubs.

Not long after joining, I remember one particular game, a friendly at my home town Lauder, when Bobby Moncur officially opened their new changing facilities. It was a mixture of first team and youth players taking part. All three played in that game, but I witnessed first hand what John was all about as he scored a good few goals. I'm sure John could tell you the exact amount as he didn't earn the nickname 'Ceefax' for nothing, but I knew from that day that John was destined for a great career.

Having supported the club myself, I watched John's development under Alex MacDonald and Sandy Jardine, where he learned a lot playing with experienced strikers such as Jimmy Bone and Sandy Clark. It was a joy to watch him score on a regular basis, particularly against our derby rivals Hibs – and he must have given them nightmares when they saw his name on the team sheet.

On returning to Hearts as manager in 1995, I had the task of changing the club's fortunes since the previous two seasons had involved going to the last game to survive in the Premier League. Changes were inevitable, as a lot of great players were coming to the end of their careers, but John played a major part in us being back challenging at the right end of the table and contesting cup competitions again. I remember a game at Easter Road where I left John on the bench. We were losing, and John went on and scored. I turned to Billy Brown and said, 'I'll never leave him out against Hibs again.' Lesson learned!

I often get asked about the best players I've worked with and I've been fortunate to work with some very good ones in my time as manager. I have always said that John was the best striker, not just because he was a great finisher, but also because I admired how clever he was coming up against mostly big defenders. Their strength was never a problem to him; his awareness to find enough space to allow him to set himself to have an opportunity to score or lay on a chance – that was a great asset he had.

The 1998 Cup Final victory was a fitting end to John's Hearts playing career. It was great to see him get the winner's medal he so badly wanted after some disappointment in the past. No one deserved it more.

It's a privilege to be asked to write this foreword for a true Jambo legend and a pleasure to know him so well.

Jim Jefferies
Former manager of
Heart of Midlothian FC

1

Little Gifts From God

The date 20 February 1962 may not be the most well remembered by any Hearts fan in the footballing calendar. But in relation to what you are about to read over the following chapters it was an important day. For had it not been for a tragic occurrence on that day then the story about to unfold would never have happened and the life of John Grant Robertson would never have been lived. And if that hadn't happened then Jimmy Wardhaugh's record League tally of 206 goals would still be standing, Hibernian FC would have not suffered fifteen years of footballing torment and the Hammer of Hibs moniker would never have been bestowed. So how did all that happen?

John Robertson and his wife Janet were expecting child number six, having given birth to three girls, Moira, Marilyn and Jan, and two boys, George and Chris. The hope was that another boy would even up the family dynamics and that would have been the end of the Robertson brood. Janet had agreed with her husband that once this baby had arrived, she would return to hospital a few months later for a hysterectomy. This decision had been agreed with the family physician and a tentative timescale of six months after the safe arrival of the newest Robertson was put in place for the procedure.

A baby boy arrived on 20 February, but it was here that fate dealt a cruel hand. The baby was a good weight but was tragically delivered stillborn, and the speculation was that the umbilical cord may have tangled round preventing proper breathing during delivery.

As the natural grieving took place over the next months, it was decided to postpone any thoughts about the hysterectomy until such time as John and Janet had time to think clearly and decide what was best. It was years later and after a few discussions with the family doctor that they finally decided it was probably time to go ahead with the operation as their youngest son Chris was now approaching six and it would be big ask to have another child.

As Janet went for her appointment, the doctor had some surprising news. She was pregnant once again and would be expecting a child in September or October that year. Had the procedure taken place at any time in the previous twenty-four months, then John Grant Robertson Jnr and his little sister Heather, who arrived in February 1966, would never have seen the light of day.

Janet, from the moment of their arrival, always proclaimed them as her little gifts from God and that they had arrived for a reason. What that reason was she was not so sure but something told her that these two were special and that something lay in wait for them.

By this time, the Robertsons had moved from the bustling closes of Edinburgh's Royal Mile to the new, sprawling but countryside setting of the city's latest council estate at Meadowfield, where terraced houses, three storey high flats, new shops and schools were all being built as the city started to expand outwards. Parsons Green Primary and Portobello High School would provide the education for the extensive Robertson clan as well as all the other local kids arriving in the new estate.

Number 36 Meadowfield Drive, a three-bed end terraced house with the added bonus of a side garden, was the new abode where the family would thrive and grow. Right opposite was the biggest front garden in the whole of Edinburgh ... the Queen's Park! It was not the finely spruced and cut tourist side of the park, however, this was just a big hayfield with long grass that led up to a large copse of trees which was not much use for anything other than escaping the attention of your parents and any other suspicious glares from the adults.

All that changed in the early 1970s as Edinburgh Council decided that they needed to provide proper facilities for Meadowfield and Willowbrae residents by completely digging up the park's huge fields in order to provide two play areas, a nine-hole pitch and putt golf course and a new full-size football pitch for Parsons Green Primary School to use for their matches.

The football pitch was last on the agenda and would not be ready for another two years, but the creation and landscaping of the golf course greens and tee areas meant that suddenly there were some pretty decent sized flattish areas available for impromptu games of football ranging from 1 versus 1 to full scale Scheme versus Scheme which, on a Sunday, could be up to twenty-a-side.

This is where the three Robertson brothers would start to hone their skills alongside their friends and school pals as the new council estate started to produce players that would play at all levels of football over the coming years, with several going on to play at professional level and even represent their country.

2

The Field to Mr Brown's Boys

The field was the place all the local kids played, and I was lucky from an early age that I was part of a good football-mad group of players from the streets of Meadowfield. Jaz Graham, Edo Cochrane, Ian Hood, Scott Cowan, Paul and Tam Madely were just a few who would find the best places in the 'scheme' to play football. Mostly it was in the square where we would use the residents' council clothes poles as goalposts with the added bonus that their clothesline when pulled tight provided a crossbar.

More often than not we were chased as the locals did not share our love of the beautiful game. For them, it meant their washing getting battered by various footballs. They also had to endure the constant self-commentating as we imagined ourselves to be the players and heroes of the day and dreamed we were performing in the Scottish Cup or the FA Cup at Wembley.

The games were either Knockout – which was one goal for the win. When you scored, you progressed through to the next round, then played on until the final two players were left and the winner crowned (frustrating if six or more players had started!) – Crossie – which was straightforward crossing and finishing – or Long Bangers which was 1 versus 1 with the goals about thirty yards apart.

We used a mix of footballs. Normally they were light plastic balls with the names of all the top teams embossed on them, which usually lasted as long as it took to hit the nearest rose bush or prickly hedge. Then there was the Wembley ball, a strong rubber-based ball that could repel the thorns of the roses for a bit longer and, if caught quickly, could be repaired with a hot poker to smear rubber over offending thorn hole. And finally there was the prized and rarely seen Philly – the king of all balls of the 1960s and 70s – all leather, pretty much indestructible and as close to a real match ball as you could get. Once the field was opened up, these balls miraculously started to appear more and more frequently as we played in this new thorn-free environment.

It was on Sundays that the real characters arrived at the field as the older generations of the Meadowfield area strutted their stuff in the 'take-ons'. These were fifth or sixth year secondary school pupils, guys who played Saturday amateurs and junior players past and present and there were also some handy dads who had played the game at some level.

The age range was from sixteen to forty-five and the numbers at times were incredible as they split into teams of Old versus Young, Meadowfield versus Willowbrae or the frighteningly tough Willowbrae/Meadowfield versus Northfield/Piershill, the two schemes being separated by the busy Willowbrae Road which formed the natural border to both territories.

I used to watch my brothers George and Chris take part in these games. There was always a wager of one or two pints and it was full throttle stuff with fifteen to twenty a side being normal and they all gave it everything. It's fair to say that no prisoners were taken as the games got into full swing.

Being around nine years old at this time, I was not allowed anywhere near the games, other than spectating, even if a player was waiting for a 'cock' or a 'hen' – the method used to decide who played for who. George would explain it was no place for a bairn and, despite my plea that I didn't think Melbourne Thistle (George) or Rangers (Chris) would be best pleased, I had to make do with spectating.

Then my chance came when one Sunday, the opposition came with three more players and, despite the best efforts of the Meadowfield team to speed up their pals and try to get them to play, we were still left two short.

'Absolutely no way!' was still the message from my elder siblings and, despite being 10–5 down at half time (10 half time, 21 the winner having been agreed) I had to sit and watch. Eventually, after going 14–5 down, my brothers relented and told me I could play but with strict instructions to stand as close to the goalposts as possible and if anyone came near me to scuttle off the pitch as they would get it in the ear from my mum if anything happened to me.

Now, I would like to say that I played a major part in the victory that followed, but I suspect that it was to do with the arrival of two handy older players. But we did, in fact, end up winning 21–19 and the reason I know is that I scored my first ever goal of any note. As Chris ran through, the keeper (1 of 15 on a rotating basis) came out to block him and he rolled it to me. I was standing at the post as instructed and just popped it in.

I don't recall getting another touch the whole game and, given some of the menacing glares I was getting from the opposition, I think that was probably just as well. I was so happy and could not wait to get home and tell my dad, but this, however, was quite forcibly taken out of the equation by my two big brothers as they could not and did not want to explain to our parents that their youngest had been playing in a full-blooded local rival game against full grown adults. They knew that would land them up to their necks in it. But I didn't care that much. I had scored, I had enjoyed scoring, I needed more and I knew the perfect place . . . the school playground.

Parsons Green Primary School looked over the field and was built on the slope of Paisley Drive – this meant the playground was split into three natural fenced-off playgrounds, with steps up to the top two. The top playground was commandeered by the Primary 7 classes, the middle by Primary 6 and the bottom tier was for Primary 4 and 5, and the games became more structured the older you got.

At that time the best player in the school was Jaz Graham who was in Primary 6 and, being friends with him, he invited me – when I was only in P4 – to play, again on the strict instructions that I stayed near the goals. Happy enough with that, I proceeded to pop in a few goals over the days and weeks that followed and this knack of scoring, and the manner of popping them in, got me my first ever nickname, which would stay with me till I reached Tynecastle.

West Ham had a small but prolific striker that played at the time called 'Pop Robson' and given my way of scoring goals, the closeness of the surnames and my small physique, I was christened 'Pop' Robertson. Not the worst of nicknames.

I had made good friends with another boy who had recently started playing in the bottom playground and recommended him to Jaz as there was always an odd number in our games. The boy remains one of my best pals to this day – Dave Bowman.

Bow and I had been firm friends for a couple of years when one afternoon, and after several visits to the Robertson household, my dad asked Dave if he wanted him to walk him home as it was getting quite late. Bow said his dad was coming to collect him at a pre-arranged time and that he was due any minute now. Within a few minutes the door went. I answered it and naturally said, 'Hello, Mr Bowman' (as I had met him several times) and ushered him into the lounge. On seeing him, my dad's face went chalk white. He then introduced himself and asked if 'Andy' would like a drink? Getting the desired answer, he immediately produced a bottle of his favourite tipple and he and Mr Bowman started talking away.

Eventually, and a few drams later, Bow and his dad left. As the door shut, my dad came in with the biggest grin ever, clipped me round the ear and said, 'You didn't tell me your pal's dad was Andy Bowman!'

I said I didn't know who his dad was – it was just his dad.

'Just his dad! Just his dad!! Jesus, that guy is the legendary half-back for Hearts who won League and Cup trophies for them. He's one of my heroes and you never even told me you met him!'

That was when I realised for the first time that my dad was a Hearts fan. He then, like Bow and I, became firm friends with Andy.

Bow and I first started playing serious football in Primary 5 and we turned out for the Primary 6 B team on occasions and more than held our own, but it was not until we moved into Primary 6 that it really started to take off.

Before I started playing at school, my dad, who worked in McKinley's Brewery, had been asked by a colleague, Frankie Baton, if I wanted to play in his son's newly formed boys club team, Broomhall Saints. That was an easy yes and I was asked to play in a friendly at the Gyle pitches. It took two buses to get there, one to Haymarket and one out to the Gyle, and took just under two hours, but we arrived, and I played in the thirty minutes each-way game, scoring eleven in a 12–1 win. After that performance, Frankie wanted to sign me and arrangements were made to get me to training the following week. However, little did he know that my dad had already made a decision that I was not travelling two hours across the city three times a week there and back – or rather, he wasn't! What neither of us knew was that the game had been scouted by a top juvenile club that was now interested in speaking to my dad.

Parsons Green had two teachers who taught the Primary 6 and 7 age groups, Mrs Glennie and Mr Brown, and they taught the last two years of school before secondary. Mr Brown also took the school football team, and I was in his class.

Mr Brown was a fantastic teacher and a real old gentleman, always immaculately dressed in classic tweed jacket, wool trousers and brown brogues, and he always spoke in a calm and reassuring voice. Honour and fair play were always his priority and, as you were representing the school, any bad language was frowned upon. He really was a wonderful man.

He had seen me playing occasionally and would call me out every Friday and discuss the Primary 7(A) team and the Primary 6(B) team. In the warm-up games, the B team would regularly beat the older side but Mr Brown would not play any of the younger players up a level as he wanted everyone in last two years to play at their own age group.

Primary 6 did not have a league format and all the games were friendlies until the Edinburgh School Board Cup competition started, and that is where we would excel.

Every Friday morning, Mr Brown would send me off with a handwritten note to tell the Primary 6 and 7 players who had been selected for the following day's fixtures and what the arrangements were. The formation of both teams were the same, 3-4-3, and one substitute would be selected who would always come on at half time without fail. The captain would make that decision and for nearly two years our team was virtually the same, subject to illness or injury.

Kenny Jack

Gregor Russell   Ian Hood   Murdo McIver

Rob Atkin   Dave Bowman   Scott Cowan

Eddie Cochrane   John Robertson   Billy Aitken   Kenny Kivlin

This side were about to embark on an incredible two years of school football that would see them bring success back to Parsons Green Primary School, success that they had not seen since the late 1960s and early 70s when my older brothers George and Chris had played in successful league-winning sides.

School Board Cup 1975

The School Board Cup was to be my first success at school level and the side above went through the competition as follows (my goals are in brackets):

Round 1: Parsons Green 14–0 Dumbryden Primary (6)
Round 2: Parsons Green 11–0 Fernieside Primary (5)
Round 3: Parsons Green 3–3 Broughton Primary (1)
Round 3 replay: Broughton 2–7 Parsons Green (3)
Quarter-final: St Joseph's Primary 1–2 Parsons Green 2 (1)
Semi-final: Balgreen Primary 1–2 Parsons Green (2)
Final: Sighthill Primary 3–5 Parsons Green (3)

As the scores show, the first two rounds were very uneventful, as we were pretty decent on our home pitch and moved forward with ease. Round three was a different story and it took a late goal from Dave Bowman to salvage an undeserved draw and we thankfully showed our true ability in the replay away from home.

In the quarter final, our hosts scored with last kick of the game, but then we got the draw we knew would be toughest tie of the lot: Balgreen at Warriston. The semi-final – Parsons Green versus Balgreen at Warriston – was the Hampden Park of primary school football, where all semi-finals and finals were played. It was a huge deal for us.

Balgreen were generally known to be the top Primary 6 side in the capital so we were under no illusions about the task we had in front of us. I managed to give us an early lead before Gary Mackay pulled one back just after half time, but it was to be our day and I managed to head the winner three minutes from time to give us a surprising, rather than a shock, win and set us up for a rollercoaster of a final against Sighthill.

The final was a midweek match at Warriston where it seemed every teacher, pupil and parent turned up and it was just a dream world for any player. It was a game worthy of the attendance as three times Sighthill went ahead, only to be pegged back twice by myself and also an 'Edo' Cochrane lob. With only a couple of minutes to go, it was anyone's game. Then I had a shot crash off the bar for Billy Aitken to calmly stroke it home and my personal task of completing my hat-trick came shortly after as we caught Sighthill on the break to secure the school's first-ever Edinburgh Primary School trophy.

Tartan Boys Club

As mentioned earlier, my dad – much to his workmate's disappointment – had decided that travelling to the other end of Edinburgh was not an option, so it was decreed that local boys club Tartan Boys would be my first team as they were based at Peffermill Primary School, a five-minute bus journey or a twenty-minute walk away. They only had an under-12 team, and as I was still ten, this would also get me 'toughened up'.

The season turned out to be successful.

We finished up as follows in the league and cup, with my goals again in brackets:

Edinburgh Federation League East/North

Old Kirk Colts 2–4 Tartan Boys Club (2)

Tartan Boys Club 24–1 Jim's Boys Club (7)

Tartan Boys Club 7–1 Granton Boys Club (3)

Beechwood Boys Club 0–15 Tartan Boys Club (3)

Broomhall Saints 0–11 Tartan Boys Club (5)

Tartan Boys Club 2–1 Salvesen Boys Club (2)

Edina Hibs Boys Club 1–2 Tartan Boys Club (2)

Tartan Boys Club 15–0 Broomhall Saints (5)

Tartan Boys Club 17–0 Jims Boys Club (9)

Granton Boys Club 0–15 Tartan Boys Club (2)

Tartan Boys Club 15–0 Broomhall Saints (5)

Salvesen Boys Club 1–2 Tartan Boys Club (1)

Tartan Boys club 5–0 Edina Hibs Boys Club (3)

Tartan Boys Club 12–0 Beechwood Boys Club (6)

We played fourteen, won fourteen, drew none, lost none and our twenty-eight points meant we were pitched into a play-off with the South/West winners, Stockbridge Boys Club, at Double Hedges pitches near Liberton. Like the School Cup final, I was again fortunate enough to grab a hat-trick in a 3–2 win to ensure the overall title was ours. More joy was forthcoming in the cup competition as we beat Moredun 7–2 (2), Pilton 5–1 (2), Broomhall Saints 13–0 (5), and Salvesen 5–2 (2), before Stockbridge once more fell victim to us in the final 6–0 (3). Two medals and sixty-nine goals was my reward for my first year at a boys club and one of the victims, Salvesen, were about to come calling.

This double, plus the School Board Cup, was my first contribution to the Robertson trophy cabinet that already looked like a jeweller's shop thanks to Chris and George's exploits. Nonetheless, at last my medal count was up and running and, more importantly for myself, I had discovered I could score goals, I liked scoring goals and I wanted to score even more! After all, I had a hard act to follow: my big brother Chris had just signed for Rangers and he was the best Edinburgh-born schools striker for many a year. I wanted to emulate him and one day sign a schoolboy 'S' form for a professional club and these were my first steps to hopefully achieving that.

3

The Invincibles

As I moved into my final year at primary school, little did I know that it would turn out to be one of the most remarkable campaigns in the school's history.

Parsons Green had won the league only twice previously and, surprise surprise, my elder siblings had both been in those teams. It would take something special to eclipse that.

We flew out of the blocks and Peffermill, St Francis, Towerbank, Prestonfield, Lismore and Craigmillar were all put to the sword fairly easily before the first big crunch game of the season arrived in the shape of Greendykes away, played at the bottom pitches at the Jack Kane Centre just along from their school.

Unusually it was played on a Thursday afternoon at 2 p.m. as they could not get a pitch arranged on the Saturday morning. Instead of their normal football team teacher who could not get away from class, they were coached by the janitor who, as was the way, would also referee the match as they were playing at home. Normally the home team coach/teacher refereed, but Mr Brown never did due to his age. Now, to say that the janitor was slightly biased would be putting it mildly as Greendykes, who had a strong side led by Keith Wright (Dundee, Hibs) and Joe Malcolm, gave as good as they got. But with a brace from myself in the last ten minutes (or so we thought) we looked as if we had done enough to keep the points and head back up to Meadowfield Drive with our one hundred per cent record intact. However, well over time, Greendykes 'scored' a goal that to this day Kenny Jack and our defence claimed went two yards wide – there were no nets – and despite our muted protests, the 'goal' stood.

Another five minutes ensued and we now thought the 'janny' was at it, so it was no real surprise when he awarded them a penalty that was at best dubious. When duly converted by Keith Wright, the final whistle was blown immediately!

Injustice was a word we could barely spell never mind understand but we were mightily aggrieved and even the Greendykes lads were suitably embarrassed at the day's events. However, as usual, Mr Brown simply told us to shake hands, give three cheers to the opposition and three cheers to the ref who was, by now, halfway back to their school.

Our one hundred per cent record was gone but we knew we just had to knuckle down and get on with the job in hand. Craigentinny and Brunstane were beaten, albeit by only two goals each, as we battled to keep our lead in the table. The second half of our fixtures saw us reel off ten straight wins, scoring 107 goals with the loss of only thirteen. In most leagues, that should and would have won the title, but not this year. Although not as prolific, Greendykes had matched our tally of victories (conspiracy theorists in our team thought the janny might have had a say!), which meant quite simply it was a last day shoot-out for the title. Again, this would be played midweek, but as our fortress, Duddingston, was not available, it would be played at Craigentinny instead.

Now, a league title decider with only a handful of parents on a Thursday afternoon seemed a bit of an anti-climax, but this was the situation, and Greendykes would have the advantage of the ref, but on this occasion it was their teacher and not the infamous janny.

Keith Wright struck first, and they led at half time, but Bill Aitken quickly drew us level and it was up for grabs again. I then put us ahead with ten minutes to go and the excitement, tempo and nerves went up a notch or two. To their credit, Greendykes threw everything at us but, led by our captain Dave Bowman, we held on as both teams physically collapsed at the end of the game. We had done it. We had won the league and although we did not realise it at the time, we remained unbeaten which must have been extremely tough on the Greendykes lads as this was their only defeat of the season.

They were to get their revenge though as both teams had eased into the semi-final of the Inspectors Cup and, despite our best efforts, they deservedly beat us 3–2 and went on to lift the trophy, winning the final by a handful. Our school received its third winner's pennant and it went up in the gym alongside the other two previously won. I had managed a little personal milestone in matching my older brothers. It's amazing what a bit of motivation can do!

Parsons Green League Results 1975/76

Peffermill 0–9 Parsons Green (4)   Parsons Green 11–4 Peffermill (6)

St Francis 1–14 Parsons Green (8)   Parsons Green 15–0 Peffermill (7)

The Invincibles

Towerbank 0–8 Parsons Green (6)   Parsons Green 5–1 Towerbank (3)

Prestonfield 1–12 Parsons Green (7)   Parsons Green 14–1 Prestonfield (8)

Lismore 1–7 Parsons Green (0)   Parsons Green 10–1 Lismore (2)

Craigmiller 0–5 Parsons Green (3)   Parsons Green 6–0 Craigmiller (3)

Greendykes 4–4 Parsons Green (2)   Parsons Green 2–1 Greendykes (1)

Craigentinny 2–4 Parsons Green (3)   Parsons Green 6–0 Craigentinny (3)

Brunstane 4–6 Parsons Green (2)   Parsons Green 11–0 Brunstane (5)

Niddrie 1–14 Parsons Green (9)   Parsons Green 9–3 Niddrie (5)

Final League Standings
Parsons Green P20 W19 D1 L0 Points 39

Greendykes P20 W18 D1 LI Points 37

We scored an incredible 178 goals that 1975/76 season and only conceded twenty-six. Despite that, we only won the league with a goal ten minutes from time in the final game, but I swear that for the first time ever Mr Brown gave a little leap of joy when the final whistle had gone and we had won the pennant. It was a discreet celebration before dusting himself down and displaying that wise old owl smile. He was a proud man that day and rightly so. We had become Mr Brown's Invincibles, a fitting tribute to one of the nicest gentlemen I have ever come across.

4

Salvesen Boys Club

1975–76

My performances for Tartan Boys Club had caught the attention of Salvesen Boys Club, and my dad had decided that going to play for them in the Juvenile League was a step up from the Federation and would improve me as a player. The bonus was that despite a long bus journey out to the Calder Road and Broomhouse Primary School, I would be doing this trip with my best pal Dave Bowman twice a week.

I would be joining up with a team brimful of talent and was looking forward to seeing just where I was in terms of my progress. Like Parsons Green, it was going to be an amazing season.

Attitude, behaviour and sportsmanship were at the forefront of the club's values and the quality of training was a big step up from Tartan Boys Club. We were taken down to England for a pre-season tournament that saw us come home with the silverware and ready for the season ahead. The threat would come from other well-established boys clubs in the city. Edina Hibs, Tynecastle, North Merchiston and Stockbridge, in particular, were threats but we were confident in the talent we had at our disposal.

Little did I know that eight of our team would all turn professional upon leaving school and one, Kenny Morrison, would turn down approaches from north and south of the border in order to follow a career in accounting.

It was tough start to the league, facing Tynecastle and North Merchiston away, but we sneaked 2–1 and 1–0 victories before hammering Edina Hibs, Edinburgh Sparta and St Bernards before coming out ahead in a ten-goal thriller against Stockbridge. We also saw off Longstone and Currie Hearts with ease to reach the halfway stage at the top and unbeaten.

We started the second half of the season by seeing off St Bernards, Currie and Longstone again with relative ease before North Merchiston and Sparta were also dispatched. And with other teams beating each other, this left us well clear at the top of the league and champions-elect. The target now was to see out the season unbeaten, a rare feat in the Edinburgh Juveniles set up, such was the quality. When Longstone were again hammered, it left us three tough matches against Stockbridge, Edina Hibs and Tynecastle to finish with and keep our one hundred per cent record. I managed a hat-trick in a 5–2 win in the first of the games before notching the only goal as we beat Edina at the Jewel (their first home defeat) and one more as we beat Tynecastle to achieve another Invincibles-style league victory.

We had also reached the final of the Bobby Parker Scottish Cup after defeating Tynecastle (1–0), Whitburn (2–0), Edina Hibs (4–0), St Andrews (8–0), before finishing off St Bernards at a packed City Park, 3–0 in the final. A single goal in every round plus five in the semi had made sure I had contributed to this cup run. As was the way, we also won the Alexander

Shield, the Parsons Peebles Trophy and County Cup before Stockbridge beat us 3–2 in the Lawson Cup final as we were eventually vanquished.

It was another stunning achievement and whetted my appetite for more goals. This team was something special and would in a few years' time see Ian Westwater, Dave Bowman, Gary Mackay and myself sign for Hearts; Jimmy Doig, Carlo Crolla, Gordon Byrne and David Clark sign for Hibs and, as mentioned previously, our sweeper Kenny Morrison turn down offers galore. It truly was a remarkable side and a privilege to play for them with so many great players.

The 1975/76 League Results

Tynecastle 1–2 Salvesen (1)	Salvesen 3–1 Tynecastle (1)
Merchiston 0–1 Salvesen (0)	Salvesen 6–1 N Merchiston (3)
Edina Hibs 0–1 Salvesen (1)	Salvesen 6–2 Edina Hibs (3)
E Sparta 0–10 Salvesen (4)	Salvesen 14–0 E Sparta (5)
St Bernards 0–4 Salvesen (2)	Salvesen 10–0 St Bernards (3)
Stockbridge 4–6 Salvesen (3)	Salvesen 5–2 Stockbridge (3)
Longstone Hearts 1–12 Salvesen (6)	Salvesen 20–0 Longstone Hearts (8)
Currie Hearts 0–6 Salvesen (2)	Salvesen 11–2 Currie Hearts (2)

The league win was an incredible effort and the following year this team would sweep the board, winning every single trophy on offer, with a couple of league defeats thrown in, but would write their name in the history books. I was, however, not destined to be part of it.

5

Edinburgh Schools Select

As my scoring exploits continued so did my chances of gaining selection to represent Edinburgh Schools in the prestigious Wilson Scottish Cup. After the two trial games held, Dave Bowman and I were selected alongside several other Salvesen teammates to try and secure a trophy that Edinburgh had an outstanding record in and had been won previously – surprise, surprise – by my older brother Chris. On the odd occasion the *Pink News*, the Saturday sports edition of the *Evening News*, covered the schoolboy or Juvenile scene, my scoring exploits were always preceded by, 'John Robertson, younger brother of Rangers starlet, Chris'. Chris teased me endlessly about this.

Edinburgh played their home games at Warriston – they had immaculate pitches with pristine orange nets for the representative games and ordinary nets for domestic cup ties. The pitch was always roped off, so it gave you the feeling of a big match occasion every time you arrived to play.

In the first round we saw off Dumbarton Schools 11–0 and I got six. We followed up with a 10–0 demolition of Fife where another two goals came my way. Local rivals Leith were dispatched 5–0 in the quarter-finals as two more were added to my personal total before Dundee arrived in the capital for the semi-final. They shocked us with a first-minute goal and held us to 1–1 before three goals, including a brace from yours truly in the final ten minutes, saw us reach the final and a two-legged contest against Glasgow RC Schools.

A packed Warriston saw Gary Mackay give us the lead from the penalty spot and despite constant pressure led by future Celtic player Ronnie Coyle, we held firm and travelled west a week later with the most slender of advantages. In the second leg, strikes from Gary Mackay and George Milligan seemed to have us well in command but this time they showed their attacking teeth and two goals within minutes saw the game all square on the day and Edinburgh only one ahead. To be honest, I had been poor all game but such is the life of a striker I managed to score four minutes from time and clinch the trophy for Edinburgh. It was a hugely satisfying win, not least because I was once more keeping pace with my big brother and nemesis Chris!

6

School to Scotland

The transition from primary to secondary was quite scary. For most kids, suddenly arriving at the 'Big School' was somewhat forbidding to say the least. It was slightly eased by the fact we were in the annexe for the first two years and not the massive tower block that symbolised Portobello High School.

We were joined by various lads from other primary schools and it became pretty clear that we had a large base of players for the teachers to assemble their first-year squad from going forward. Most of the Parsons Green lads were selected alongside players from Greendykes and Duddingston. We embarked on what would be a successful season that would see us come up against plenty of fellow boys' club friends and foes as we started on the trail of success once more.

As expected, due to our success at primary level, seven of the Parsons Green team made the fourteen-man squad and were bolstered by the Brunstane powerhouse Graham Wood, a fearsome midfield player along the lines of Dave Bowman. With these two in control of midfield, we were stronger than most sides, with Tynecastle's Gary Mackay, Kenny Morrison, Alan

Crawford and Jimmy Doig proving the main obstacle on our route to success.

Portobello, despite having many pupils going directly to clubs on leaving school, had a massive rugby tradition as one of the house leaders, Mr Cuthbertson, was dominant in rugby coaching. So, for many years, first and second year pupils had no choice but to only play rugby as football was not allowed for the first two years. It was only thanks to continued success of the lads in the fourth, fifth and sixth years that they eventually allowed the first two years to play football in the leagues.

Our teacher and coach at first year level was Phil Sinclair, a PE teacher who was also a fine basketball player for the dominant Murray International Metals team. He was very laid back in style, but also competitive, and it rubbed off on us as we swept to the league title with only one defeat to Tynecastle on the way. We beat them at home, then two draws in their other matches saw us clinch the title. We then added the League Cup and Edinburgh five-a-side trophy. Tynecastle went on to win the Scottish Cup that year as they knocked us out at the quarter-final stage. It was a bit of revenge for them for our domestic success and it was merited as they were an excellent side.

The following year saw it swing, and as Tynecastle took the title we won the League Cup. Once more, however, they went on to claim the Scottish Cup. Both teams showed tremendous quality and Edinburgh football was flying as the standard of player was high.

The entry into the third year again saw success for both sides as we won the league and Tynecastle the cup, with no success for either in the Scottish Cup that year. But with the quality on show it was no surprise that we went into the Regional Scottish

Schools in a confident mood as we felt that as a squad Edinburgh would take some beating.

Seven of the Tynecastle squad were selected, with only David Bowman and myself making it from our side. Such was the strength going forward, with Gordon Byrne leading the line superbly, I wasn't required to play in any of the games until later on. Being a younger member of the squad this was to be expected and it wasn't until five minutes before the end of the semi-final against Glasgow away that I was given the call. That in itself was a drama.

My dad had always knocked it into us that we had to have our boots spotless and that as the tools of the trade we had to make sure they were ready and in good condition at all times. I had played the previous day for Salvesen and had not bothered to clean them as I thought I had no chance of playing, having not had a sniff in the previous four rounds which Edinburgh swept through with ease. As I'd guessed, I was not part of the starting line-up, and, as I stripped, I took my boots out. They were still caked in mud, but, to my horror, one of the studs had sheared off and the screw part was sticking out like a spike. I knew right away that when the ref came to check my boots there was no way he was going to miss it.

As I had not been playing, and the likelihood was that again I would not play as I hadn't even had a substitute appearance, I just shrugged it off as no big deal. When the ref turned up, I just showed him my Adidas Samba trainers and said I had blisters from new boots and could not wear them.

All was well, and I sat on the bench with the other five squad members as play raged on and with the game locked at 0–0 with less than five minutes to go, you can imagine my shock and then embarrassment as the coach, Mr Sutherland of Tynecastle High, told me to get stripped. I sheepishly got ready and as I replaced the injured Gordon Byrne, both the linesman and Mr Sutherland looked at me quizzically as I showed my 'studs' – or not as the case was – and again bleated out the lame excuse that I had 'blisters'. It was even lamer as it had been raining all day and the pitch was soaking wet.

I trooped on and was not really involved but then the moment came that I was dreading. As we swept forward, George Milligan got to the byline and whipped in a ball to the near post, and, given my instincts, I got there first and promptly had a swing at it. With no balance, I missed it completely and had the biggest fresh air shot ever, but as I turned to see where the ball was, it hit the Glasgow centre-half and rebounded right to my feet. I toe-poked it over the line to give us victory and was immediately swamped by teammates as we made the final.

Mr Sutherland's delight was slightly tempered by the fact that he knew something was not right and to this day he ribs me on what really happened. I have manfully stuck to the blister story until now, so, Mr Sutherland – SORRY! It was a mistake I would never make again and from that day until I retired, I made sure I cleaned and prepared my own boots the day before every match.

That strange ending to the game was a real turning point for me. Because of it, I made the starting line-up alongside Gordon Byrne for the final against Aberdeen Schools at Tynecastle and scored the first goal, which was added to by Gary Mackay and Gordon as we eased to a 3–0 first leg lead. Despite losing an early goal up north, an equaliser by Gary and a double from yours truly saw us leave Aberdeen with the Scottish Schools Wilson Trophy tucked away and a 6–1 aggregate score line.

It was an important victory but one that would yield a bigger prize. Although I was in my third year at Portobello, I was eligible to play down a year and that would prove worthwhile as during the run, David Bowman and Gary Mackay had been picked to play for Scotland Schoolboys in the home international games and finished second to England. My lack of games for Edinburgh and my height were seen as factors for not making that squad, but the manager of Aberdeen Schools, William Harrower, who was to become the new Scotland under-15s manager for the following season was alerted to the fact that I was eligible to play under-15 the next season.

After two successful seasons in the same team as Dave Bowman and Gary Mackay at Salvesen, the club made the decision that all players must play at their eligible age level, and despite being in the same year as all my teammates, I was told that I would have to stay down and play with lads of the same birth year, which meant my first meeting with great friend, and adversary in later years, Paul Kane. Callum Milne was also in a team that included Edinburgh goalie John Wilson, father of Danny, and again we had success winning a hatful of trophies over the two seasons.

But with different training evenings and now travelling from Meadowfield to Broomhouse, which took ninety minutes on the bus on my own and not with Bow, I began to get fed up. I was not enjoying the travel, and the fact I was the only one from that part of town did not help. I eventually had a chat with my dad and decided that I would join the local boys' club team near us and the one that most of my school pals went to, Edina

Hibs. They trained at the Jewel in Magdalene which was just five minutes in the bus or a twenty-minute walk away.

Edina Hibs were based at the notorious Jewel Miners Club in a tough area of the city that bordered Niddrie, Bingham and Magdalene. On one side of the pitches was the old railway line and on the other was the miners club. It was always an intimidating place for opposing teams to visit.

Before our games, we had to carry out and erect the posts and also put up the nets, then remove them all after games for fear of never seeing them again. But for all that it was a tough place to be based, the football was as relentless as ever as we swashbuckled our way, under Bert Melrose and Johnny Walker, to the league title with a very strong side that saw plenty move on to senior football. The main men were John 'Yogi' Hughes (Hibs), Keith Wright (Dundee), David Rennie (Leeds) and probably one of the best talents in the area, Stuart Rae. Stuart signed for Hibs, where they played him, for some reason, at right back, despite him being a strong attacking midfield player who was built well. He left Hibs after two seasons and signed for Manchester City before moving to Leeds then on to Leicester. He then headed back north, and to this day, I still find it incredible that he never went on to greater things, such was his talent. He ended up playing in South Africa and is still there today.

Keith and I scored for fun and in fact it became boring, so boring that I asked to play at right back, a position we did not have a player for. I just wanted to enjoy my football and Bert and Johnny agreed. It didn't dent my goalscoring as I was still bombing forward and getting forty-odd goals to add to Keith's sixty-odd per season. The team continued to dominate the league and we also reached all eight domestic finals and the

Scottish Cup final, only to lose every single one by the odd goal. Three of the games were scheduled in a week when seven of the team were in Germany with the Edinburgh select, and we lost them all to Tynecastle Boys Club who mysteriously had only one player on overseas duty!

The following season we did better domestically in the cups, won the league and went down to Birmingham to represent Scotland in a British five-a-side competition. After winning the Edinburgh and Scottish titles, we lost to Arsenal in the semi-final. At the time, I was playing sweeper in a back three with Yogi and David Rennie. I was enjoying football again, still scoring goals from the back and the team were still very successful. Although I was a defender for the club and a midfield player for my school, I was about to get the call for my country and play up top for Scotland Schoolboys.

I was summoned to see Charlie Tulloch – my English teacher and coach of the third-year boys' team – and immediately thought I was in some kind of trouble as I was not asked to attend the classroom but the staffroom. That normally meant something was seriously wrong.

He asked me to accompany him to the House Office (Duddingston) and the chat there was quite easy-going, about football naturally, but I was still confused as to what was going on.

It was here he showed me the letter from the Scottish Schools Football Association saying I had been selected to represent Scotland at under-15 level for the upcoming season. I honestly don't know who was happiest! My best pal Dave Bowman had realised this honour the year before and now I had an opportunity. An added bonus as that year, unlike Bow's, was the showpiece match against England at Wembley which would be live on TV.

It was a surreal experience as I was told to tell no one for the rest of the week apart from family. Obviously, the news was greeted with great joy at home as it meant I was following in Chris's footsteps: first with Salvesen, then Edinburgh and now Scotland. And he was delighted at the prospect of his wee brother playing in the dark blue. That Friday, much to both my pride and embarrassment, it was announced at assembly in front of the entire school that I had been chosen to play for Scotland. My quiet schoolboy cover had now been blown and I was now a bit of a celebrity whether I liked it or not!

The international side was strong, as you would expect, and had a fair sprinkling of Edinburgh-based players with myself, Andy Bruce, Colin Plenderleith and Stuart Rae involved in a strong Central Belt representation. The majority of the rest were west-based players, with the already hugely talented and most talked about schoolboy talent of his generation, Paul McStay, entering his third and last year of representing Scotland at under-15 level. The team manager was William Harrower from Aberdeen and his assistant was Les Donaldson, largely associated with Linlithgow Rose for many years, and together this group produced an astonishing run of results and performances.

Our first match was down in Wales at Milford Haven, and the line-up in an attacking 4-3-3 formation was:

		Bruce		
McDonald	Coyle		Plenderleith	Connor
	Rae	McStay	Nicholas	
	Robertson	Sludden	Dick	

The pitch had a slight slope and we shot down the hill in the first half. Despite strong pressure, we went behind to a goal from Rees before a quick-fire equaliser from Johnny 'Sluddy' Sludden. Just before half time, a deep cross from Ally Dick found me at the back post and I managed to knock it past the keeper from close range to get my first international goal. We were off and running and a strong second half showing saw us create numerous chances which were finally rewarded twelve minutes from time. Paul McStay released me in the right channel, and I went on to smash a low right foot shot home to make sure the two points were coming home north of the border.

The same team saw off Northern Ireland by 4–1 with me, Ally Dick, Johnny Sludden and Paul McStay on the scoresheet down at Palmerston. That left a showdown against England for the title at Fir Park in Motherwell.

We again played the same side against a strong England side who had a monster of a centre-forward in Paul Rideout who was on Swindon's books at the time but went on to make a real name for himself at Everton. Both Mr Harrower and Les Donaldson told us we would have to use our mobility and pace to outwit the big English side and we came out the traps flying as I released Sluddy down the right and his cross was bulleted home by Ally Dick after only four minutes. Just a few minutes later and I turned in the box and cracked a low shot towards the back post that took a deflection off the English captain, and we were two up. A dream start. More was to follow as I was upended in the box after twelve minutes and we had the chance to go three up. Unfortunately, Ally Dick's penalty crashed back off the bar, and despite laying siege to the English goal, we just could not get the crucial third goal to kill the game as we were thwarted by the keeper, the woodwork and some misses. We could have easily racked up seven or eight before the interval whistle.

Strong words were obviously used at half time in the English dressing room as they emerged with new purpose and new attitude. They battered into every tackle and it became a real roughhouse of a second half. There's no doubt it disrupted our rhythm and style and when Paul Rideout crashed one home with twenty minutes to go, it was game on. Despite some unsavoury challenges all over the pitch, we held on until the final whistle to win the Home International title. It was a massive win for us, a real schoolboy dream. The excitement I felt beating the Auld Enemy was incredible. We had beaten England, and at the time, I couldn't have cared if my career had stopped right then. I was floating about for days with the biggest grin ever on my face, but it felt surreal as I still had to go back to school as normal. It was all a huge adrenalin rush for a few days, then it calmed down pretty quickly. And soon there was more to concentrate on as we were off to France.

We then moved on to the Montaigu Tournament in France, and with that prestigious European prize at stake we soon realised just how tough it was going to be. We were placed with Belgium, Italy, West Germany, and Denmark in Pool A. Pool B looked less difficult with hosts France joining Wales, Northern Ireland, Luxembourg and the Republic of Ireland in a round robin tournament that would see the final played between the top sides in each group.

We started well on the main stadium pitch with a 3–0 victory over Belgium, where I managed a brace, before we played that evening and recorded a 1–0 win over West Germany with a Paul McStay goal.

The rest day was a playing day for Pool B before we resumed and I notched another as we put Italy to the sword by three goals to one, which left us with a final match against Denmark. We needed to win as West Germany had won their other two games and had a better goal difference to boot, so a job still had to be done to make the final. Two first-half goals from yours truly and that was that, as we eased into the final unbeaten, having seen off the favourites. In the final we were up against runaway Pool B winners and hosts France in front of a packed crowd who wanted only one result – and it definitely was not Scotland's name on the trophy!

Stuart Rae scored early, which silenced the home fans, but despite plenty of chances we again could not find the killer goal. In the second half, it was the defence who would provide the key with Andy Bruce and the back four immense as they withstood a barrage of attacks. We held on and our skipper Paul McStay proudly stepped forward to lift the trophy to add to the Home Title. I was given the player of the tournament award and we left France in great spirits for the final trophy of the season and the biggest showdown of them all – England at Wembley for the Dentyne Trophy, live on TV.

We travelled down the day before the big game and got settled in. There was no doubt that everyone was nervous. Mr Harrower, who was out of the Mr Brown mould of the absolute gentleman and fair play regime, reminded us that we must continue to play fair and uphold the laws of the game and represent our country with dignity and pride the following day.

Les Donaldson was the opposite. He had collected a variety of newspaper clippings of interviews with the English team, telling all who would listen that had they entered the European

Tournament then they would have expected to win it and that they had only lost to us in Scotland owing to a poor first ten minutes. They said they would put all this right and put us in our place in the live match at Wembley and that they had by far the best players in all positions all over the park.

Les knew this would have the desired effect and, after a light training session in one of the central London parks, we were off, heading to every Scottish football player's dream, playing England at Wembley. The old Wembley had a magic about it – not for all the right reasons as it was actually a bit run-down and the dressing rooms a bit tatty – but one thing made up for it, which was the sixty-yard walk up a sloping tunnel. You could not see the terracing until you suddenly emerged onto the pitch – you'd be hit by a bull ring of a stadium, intense heat and the 150-yard walk to the halfway line while 72,000 fans screeched their excitement. Now 150 yards might not seem like much but when you're only fourteen or fifteen it's like a mile and it was certainly pretty intimidating. But we were there and we were ready to go.

The president of the England Schools Association said that, 'If we [Scotland] had to win could we make it 5–4 and give the fans and the TV a spectacle worthy of the occasion.' How prophetic those words were.

It was clear from the kick-off that England, as their press releases had said, were up for it. They swarmed at us right from the start and it was no surprise when Paul Rideout gave them the lead after twenty minutes. We had to hang in for a while but eventually settled and Paul McStay levelled with a rasping shot after thirty minutes. All square, and then suddenly we were on top for a bit. I headed one narrowly over and both Sluddy and Ally Dick went close. Then England and Rideout got their second as the ball slipped under Andy Bruce and into the net.

Half time: England 2, Scotland 1.

The first half had flown by and was played, as you might guess, at a frenetic pace that was sure to have an impact in the latter stages of the game. We trooped off after the regulation forty minutes, disappointed to trail and needed a pick-up which was then given by Mr Harrower in his gentlemanly style, all about playing the right way and being positive. Again, Les had different ideas. He believed we had suffered stage fright and told us in no uncertain terms that we had to go out there and get about England and influence the game in our favour as HE was not intent on finishing the international season with our only defeat and certainly not to England at Wembley on live TV!

A fast start to the second half was demanded and that is what he got. Unfortunately for Les, he didn't see it as he was still in the dressing room answering an urgent call of nature, completely unaware of what was happening while he was still in the toilet. Mr D emerged into the sunshine just six minutes into the second half and, in his own words, said, 'What the F**K?', as the massive Wembley scoreboard read: 46 minutes, England 2, Scotland 4! We flew at them and a second from Paul McStay and one from Sluddy was quickly followed by another from Ally Dick as we turned the game on its head and silenced the massive English crowd.

I missed an absolute sitter to make it five as we looked to finish them off and you can imagine my horror ten minutes later when Rideout completed his hat-trick with an astonishing goal from fully thirty yards out that flew into the top corner to pull England within a goal. Then I slipped Sluddy through and he made it 5–3 before another English counter, with just a few minutes to go, made it 5–4, and despite everyone dropping with cramp as the pitch took its toll, we held on to complete a memorable victory and stunning unbeaten season that saw us (somehow) climb the Wembley stairs to claim our third trophy of the season and victory at Wembley in front of a massive TV audience that would – and still do – remember this game for decades to come.

Full time: England 4, Scotland 5.

This time the celebration was even more special. Despite the fact we were physically shattered, we made a good fist of the celebrations with some Coca Cola and then we were into the giant baths at Wembley that looked to us like a swimming pool. Like the previous victory at Fir Park, we were all flying and the train journey the following day was full of chat about specific moments in the game. While I was still raging at missing a sitter once more, you would have struggled to wipe the smile off my face with a blowtorch. When the Edinburgh lads arrived at the station, I walked to get the bus home in my blazer and was stopped by a guy walking past who said, 'Well played, kid! That was some game yesterday – brilliant result!' It was then that the realisation kicked in as to how many people had actually watched the match on TV and once more I floated home in the knowledge it was a job well done. That continued with the family waiting to congratulate me, with Chris at the forefront reminding me that I was still playing catch up with him!

The gauntlet had been thrown.

7

Tears and Trials

Before this year of footballing triumphs, there were tears, major tears, as my world collapsed. The death of my father was heartbreaking for the entire family, and even more so for myself as I absolutely adored my dad. Like most kids, I believed he was indestructible, would live forever and be there to guide me through life.

I had no inkling he was ill. Owing to mine and my sister Heather's age, thirteen and fourteen, the family thought it best not to let us know as they felt it was too much to take in. They were worried about the effect it might have on us. I can imagine that kids of the same age today would probably know a lot more about the illness he succumbed to, but with no internet or documentaries to educate us at that time, the decision was made that we did not need to know about my dad's health.

Dad had gone in for a gall bladder operation a few months previously and doctors found he was riddled with cancer. He required immediate chemotherapy as part of his treatment and all I really knew at the time was that he was not well, would be off work for a while and would not be able to get to any of my games for a few weeks.

This did not stop him sitting in his rocking chair at the front window watching me play with my friends up the park and he would regularly pull me up about missed chances when I was unaware that his hawk-like eyes were taking in everything.

On 18 November 1978, he died. There was no warning. We literally knew nothing about it and when I went to bed that night, I was happy enough. All I was thinking about was that I had the next morning off because I had an important Scottish Cup tie for Edina Hibs in the afternoon against local rivals Musselburgh Windsor at Pinkie Park so a lie-in was welcome.

My father died in the early hours with the rest of my family round him. My lie-in was interrupted when Chris woke me to tell me that the fourth-year Portobello team needed players to play in a cup replay. Despite my protests, Chris said I needed to play and to take a brand-new pair of Adidas World Cup boots with me. I was ushered out the house as quickly as possible but I had forgotten my match kit and went to collect it from where it always was, in the drawer in my parents' room above where my dad would clean and leave our boots, Chris's included.

I picked up my kit and noticed that the cover was over my dad's head. None the wiser, I pulled it back, gave him a quick kiss and proceeded downstairs to the kitchen where I asked why Dad was sleeping with the sheet over his head. My sister mumbled something about the sun being in Dad's eyes in the morning and that he was sleeping as he was not well and, with that, I headed off to Duddingston playing fields and the replay.

I played up front for the fourth-year side and scored a hat-trick in a 7–1 win that, in the end, was quite comfortable. As I made my way out of the changing room, I was surprised to see Harry Wright, Keith's dad, waiting on me. I was delighted for the lift and ready for the game in which I decided I would christen the new boots, having stuck with my tried and trusted for the school game.

It was an eventful game as we were 2–0 down early on, before one each from Keith and yours truly pulled us level at half time. We edged ahead with a Stuart Rae goal before the Windsor scored twice within the space of a minute to take the lead. I then scored a penalty with ten minutes to play, and late on in the game, got the winner, playing a 1–2 in the midfield before driving forward. With the Musselburgh lads dropping off, I got thirty yards out and that strange instinct in my head took over and told me to hit it ... so I did. It went whistling past the keeper and into the top left-hand corner and the win was secured, much to everyone at Edina's delight.

After the game, Harry said that he had spoken to my mum and that she had agreed I could spend the weekend with the Wrights. I was happy with that arrangement as it was a wee change from the mad Robertson household, and even happier when told that we would be going away on Sunday and Monday for a short trip down the coast, which meant a day off school.

By the Monday evening, my school stuff had made its way to Keith's house and I was duly dropped off then picked up by Harry on the Tuesday from school, then taken back to the house. There, a strange sight awaited me, but I didn't think much of it – I was just keen to let my dad and Chris know about my hat-tricks and the events of the weekend.

The sitting room was mobbed with aunties and uncles. I was delighted to see them all but it still did not strike me that something had happened or that there was anything wrong until Chris took me upstairs and told me that Dad had died.

It must have been the hardest thing ever for Chris to say and I still don't know to this day why he was chosen or volunteered to do it. I think I was in shock. I can't really remember as I just shut down and sat there trying to come to terms with the fact that he was dead. Surely it couldn't be true. He was as fit as a fiddle. He cycled to all my games. He was my dad, he was indestructible, he was going to live forever. But he was gone and my world would never be the same again.

Chris was great. He told me Dad said I was going to be someone special, that I was here for a reason after the death of my older brother, and that is why, much to my mum's chagrin, I was named after him – she had refused to let him do it with George and Chris.

Chris explained that I had to use Dad as motivation, to make him proud and that he would be with me every step of the way, watching me and guiding me and that I had to show that he was right about being someone special. I don't think I ever cried. I didn't want to as I honestly did not believe he had gone. But he had and I lost him before I had even got to know him. I was angry with the family for not telling us (Heather had been taken to her friend's house while I was with the Wrights), I could not understand it and it took me years to come to terms with that. But they had taken a step that they thought was right, and I don't blame them for that but I was still angry. I became very quiet and then had an illness where I was taken to the city hospital for five days for tests. Despite my high temperature and listlessness, nothing conclusive was found.

I was in my own little world, still training and playing, but I had no spark. I just wanted to get on with it and show the world I was fine. I wasn't, but as Chris pointed out, I had to concentrate on school and on football as people were starting to take notice. Scouts were beginning to note down the name of the little Edina Hibs player who knew how to score goals despite playing in defence and midfield for most of the games. I was fourteen and despite several of my teammates being scouted and invited to train or trial with senior teams north and south of the border, I had been overlooked despite scoring for fun for all the teams I played for. I was deemed to be too small, sharp but not quick enough.

But all this was to change in one game as I was picked for the League Select against Derby County Youths and, for the first time in a long time, played up front with Keith Wright. I scored six as we demolished them 9–1.

Several scouts were in attendance and the first to arrive on the doorstep was John Ferguson representing Manchester City. Chris was going to be busy over the next few weeks, Rangers player or not!

John Ferguson was keen to get me down to Manchester alongside Stuart Rae, who was seen as the hottest property of our age group. We were driven down for the week in the October holidays. It was a great experience as we trained on a pitch adjacent to the first team at Platt Lane. We watched the first team go through their paces and it was my first real taste of what life could be like as a professional football player. However, despite their attention, I just didn't have the feeling that they were the club I wanted to join – if indeed they wanted me. I went down another couple of times and was well looked after, and the scout John Ferguson was an absolute gentleman, but City was not for me.

Invitations started to come in and I spent a week at Leicester,

Leeds Utd, Blackpool and Crystal Palace in the summer holidays. I was also invited through for trials with Rangers and Celtic as Chris had been tapped by Rangers to see if I would go through, but to be honest, the Old Firm didn't really excite me and I felt if I was going anywhere, it would be to England. At home, I had been alongside Dave Bowman and Gary Mackay and we had been given training facilities at Hibs on a Tuesday and Wednesday where we trained alongside their semi-professionals like Gordon Rae. At the time it was good training, watched regularly by manager Eddie Turnbull, but I didn't see myself staying in Scotland.

The next two invitations to travel were awesome. I loved my time at both clubs. It looked like a straight choice between Arsenal and Nottingham Forest. Arsenal were the first to come calling and I stayed for the ten days with them at their London Colney training ground. It was crazy. I was fifteen and training alongside some of the best players in Britain. Each morning we were split into four groups with equal numbers of first team, second team, youth team and trialists. In the morning, we did four half-hour sessions on various disciplines: running, weights, body circuits and technical skills. It was mind-blowing as in my group I had the likes of David O'Leary, Pat Rice, Steve Gatting and Liam Brady.

After lunch, the afternoon consisted of the alternative of either a four-mile cross country run over the fields surrounding the training ground or the Arsenal run, a 400-metre layout with various zigzag hurdles that lasted twenty minutes. This was run in teams to accumulate as many laps as you could.

It was a surreal experience, the quality of the players was incredible, but not once when this little lad from Scotland messed up did they complain. They encouraged and helped me and went about their work as the perfect role models, showing the standards you were expected to reach if you wanted to pull on the red and white of Arsenal.

As the week moved on, more and more technical sessions were introduced alongside the afternoon running. To finish off, we had a friendly against Spurs to show what we were capable of on the pitch. I played well as striker and scored twice in a 3–0 win and was beaming when Liam Brady wandered over and slapped me on the back and congratulated me on my performance, remarking that he had obviously rubbed off on me.

Their chief scout, Wilf Dixon, was keen for me to stay for another week but I had two days at Spurs and a week at Nottingham Forest booked in. I didn't want to let those teams down but I told Wilf I had loved my time with Arsenal and would like to return. He was happy with that, although he did raise an eyebrow that I was travelling to Spurs next.

The Spurs trial was just basically a game. They had already seen me close up with Arsenal and I scored twice again in a 5–0 win over Crystal Palace, but I had not seen enough to really make a judgement on what they were like as a club so before I could even think I was on my way north to Nottingham.

The team had been watching me for a while and they had just conquered Europe under the maverick Brian Clough. We got fleeting glimpses of the great man in his famous green training top, walking his dog as we trained alongside the first team. He was so impulsive and some of his ways were off the chart. One day we were waiting for the first team, getting cones laid out, only there was no first team to be seen. We waited an hour before Liam O'Kane decided that we would carry on without them and when we returned from the training grounds alongside the river, we were told that Clough had spotted the Notts County players and had promptly organised a practice match on the spot! Truly one of life's mavericks.

Again the treatment I received and the training was first class and there was a strong Scottish presence about the club. I felt comfortable and was enjoying all that was put before me. Nottingham seemed more like Edinburgh than London and was easier to navigate. Then, on the second last day, I got the full wacky-genius treatment of Brian Clough. We were due to play Notts County Youths at the riverside training pitches and I was selected by Liam O'Kane to play in my preferred position of striker when, with five minutes to kick-off, the door burst open and in walked Brian Clough.

'Right then,' he barked. 'Which one of you is the lad Robertson?'

I raised my hand and he looked me up and down.

'Are you Scottish?'

'Yes, Mr Clough, I am,' I replied.

'Right, get the number 9 off.'

'Boss, John is a striker,' Liam said. 'He plays there for his club and for Scotland schools.'

'I don't care,' replied Clough. 'I have a John Robertson in my first team. He is a great player, he is Scottish, he plays number 11 and on the left wing. He has the same name, same country, so this kid plays number 11 and wide left.' Clough then walked out the door.

Liam O'Kane looked at me, smiled, and said, 'You heard him, Robbo. Get number 11 on and play wide left.'

I promptly did what was I told went out and scored five in a

7–2 win. Was there any logic there? I don't know, but that was Brian Clough, European Cup-winning manager, and it worked.

I was sent a personally signed letter from him saying how well I had done, that they wanted me back and that when the time came, Nottingham Forest wanted to offer me professional terms. Over the next few holidays I was regularly at Arsenal and Forest and I really could not make up my mind either way. But the time was coming that I would have to make a decision.

This was particularly tough as obviously I had lost my dad and, while Chris and I spoke about it, I couldn't really make a clear and conscious decision on which club I preferred or where I thought I had the best chance to develop and get through at some stage to the first team. How was I supposed to decide? Arsenal was one of the biggest clubs in England and Forest were champions of Europe! Plenty of sleepless nights were had as I mulled over where I saw my first steps in senior football, and for a fifteen-year-old to be thinking about that and also taking my exams, it was a pretty confusing time.

When back in Scotland I had not been feeling great and had been admitted to hospital for a few days with a temperature and general fatigue and was down, it transpired – not that I knew it at the time – that the death of my dad had caught up with me emotionally. I got very low but Chris was there to cajole me to keep me on at my football.

Then, one day, I told him I didn't think I wanted to go to England and that I wanted to stay in Scotland as I just wasn't ready to move away. We spoke for weeks and Chris was great as he was determined that we made the right decision. He wanted to make sure that I was not just panicking about leaving home and that it would be right for my footballing career. I'd already sat my exams and got five O levels in history, English, arithmetic, technical drawing and art, but as I could not leave school until the following January because of my age, I would have six months more thinking time before I had to make any big decisions.

But I had made up my mind: I was staying in Scotland and that meant I had to make a decision about who I was going to sign for. To me, that decision was easy. I had been training at Easter Road for two years and despite interest from Rangers and Celtic, I would sign for Hibs.

8

Hart to Hearts

With just the extra half-year left that I had to serve at school, Chris and I waited for the summer to end before we decided to let Hibs know that I had made the decision. I informed the coaching staff, including Stan Vincent and Jimmy O'Rourke, that I had spoken with my brother and that I would like to sign S forms with Hibs and could they make the necessary arrangements. By this time, the crop of schoolboys that had been training with them had also made their decisions, with Dave Bowman and Gary Mackay along with Colin Plenderleith joining Hearts and Jimmy Doig, Kevin Hogan and Stuart Rae joining Hibs. Johnny Sludden had gone to Celtic, so Hibs were delighted with my decision.

I was told that I would be invited in to meet with manager Eddie Turnbull, Pat Stanton and chairman Tom Hart the following Tuesday to sign the S form and make it official. I was then contacted by Jim McLean, a journalist with the *Scottish Daily Express*, who wanted to do a story on it as I was the last Scotland schoolboy from the Wembley win to sign for a senior side.

As Chris was training at Rangers, it was agreed that Jim

would pick me up and take me to Easter Road, do the piece and get photographs taken. I was taken into the boardroom, where Tom Hart, Eddie Turnbull and Pat Stanton were waiting. They then went over the terms of the agreement that I would sign, the S form, and said I'd continue to receive my expenses of 50p per night bus fare to and from my house (although I actually walked most of the time!), and that when I left school in December I would join Hibs on a contract of £55 per week with a £500 loss-of-amateur-status signing-on fee. It would be a two-and-a-half-year deal with a review on basic wage each summer. To be honest, it was all pretty straightforward.

However, Chris had said not to sign anything until he'd seen it, just to make sure everything was okay. I informed Tom Hart and the management that everything seemed in order and that once Chris had looked it over I would be happy to sign it and bring it back the following evening. Eddie Turnbull and Pat Stanton nodded their agreement and were happy enough, but Tom Hart asked who Chris was and why did he have to see the contract terms? Pat Stanton informed him that he was my brother and that he was currently playing at Rangers and that, having lost my father, Chris had taken on the role of advisor and would simply look over the deal and advise me to sign it.

Tom Hart, I was told years later, did not really like Rangers or anything to do with them and I can only think that was the reason he came out with a statement that stunned me and set my football career on a totally unexpected road.

'No,' he said. 'I don't want the details going out of this room and I don't want anyone working with Rangers to see it. You have to sign that document now or not at all.'

My reply was that I would not do it as my brother had said

not to until he had seen it. Pat Stanton said to Mr Hart not to worry, to let me take it home and bring it back signed the next evening. And he pointed out it needed my mum's signature anyway.

Tom Hart replied, 'No. Either he signs it now or he never wears a Hibs strip ever again!'

I was stunned, but to be fair both Eddie Turnbull and Pat Stanton tried to reason with him that all was fine and it would make no difference to let Chris see the contract. But Tom Hart was adamant that the contract was signed there and then, or it would be withdrawn.

I was then asked by Pat Stanton to go to the reception where Jim McLean was waiting and have a cup of tea while he and Eddie Turnbull had a chat with the chairman to try and sort it out. Jim naturally asked me how it was going and when I told him he just looked as bemused as I was at the turn of events. After twenty minutes or so, Pat came out and apologised and said that Mr Hart was not for changing his mind. He remained adamant that the contract would remain at Easter Road and once again reiterated that I sign it then and there or never wear a Hibs strip again.

Before I could say anything, Jim McLean stood up and said, 'Right, John, let's get you back to school,' and hustled me out the door, into the taxi and back off to Portobello. I was gobsmacked. My teacher Charlie Tulloch was waiting on the news and when I told him what had happened he was aston-ished, said that maybe I was not meant to sign for Hibs and that if that was the chairman's attitude then 'hell mend them'. Needless to say, when Chris arrived home he felt the same and not happy with proceedings. Despite Pat Stanton talking to

Chris, he just said that I would not be signing, full stop. We decided that we would just let things run and see what came up.

Things took another twist when Chris was released by Rangers and signed by Bobby Moncur at Hearts. All this time, Hearts had never been in the picture. They had assumed I was heading to Arsenal or Forest and had known I was training at Easter Road as it was not far from my family home, but not once did they make a move until the August when Leicester City youth team came north and played a few friendlies. They had been a good side the previous year (I think they may have won the English Youth Cup) and they had arranged a match with Hearts at Saughton.

Through Chris, I was asked by the then Hearts reserve team manager Ian Brown if I would be available to help them out by playing as a trialist. I was happy to play in the game although, when the match came, it was a terrible evening with heavy rain. We walked from Tynecastle round to Saughton which took about fifteen minutes and the Leicester lads got their team bus. I played really well and scored five in a 7–3 win and the Leicester coach was asking who the trialist was, but, unbeknown to me, Hearts manager Bobby Moncur was there with Chairman Archie Martin and obviously liked what he saw. He asked Ian who I was, to which Ian just chuckled and said, 'Why don't you ask your first team centre-forward up the touchline there?' and pointed to where Chris was standing. On seeing his puzzled look, he informed Bobby Moncur that I was Chris's younger brother, that I had turned down Arsenal and Forest and that Hibs had blown their chance of signing me.

After the game, dripping wet and with mud everywhere, I was hustled straight off the pitch, bundled into Archie Martin's pristine white BMW and driven back to Tynecastle with Chris. There, terms were thrashed out to sign an initial S form with Hearts for £50 per week and a £1,000 signing-on fee. In addition, Edina Hibs would receive twenty brand-new training balls as part of the deal.

So that was it. I had joined Hearts, a club that had shown no interest in me whatsoever and, to be honest, were never really on my radar. On leaving school in December, I would join them full time and once more team up with my school buddy Dave Bowman, alongside ex-Salvesen teammates Gary Mackay, Ian Westwater, Stuart Gauld and Colin Plenderleith. I was a Hearts player, signed, sealed and delivered and, as Chris jokingly said on signing the deal, 'You're on your own now – no more advice!' I quizzically asked why and he smiled and said, 'Because I don't want you taking my place in the first team, that's why!' Little did we both know that somewhere pretty soon down the line, that sibling situation was going to play out.

9

Moncur to MacDonald

Before I had joined Hearts there was more unexpected drama. Arsenal were not for giving up on me and tried hard to convince my mum that I would be well looked after in London. They were confident that once I had settled in with the club, all would be fine and that they had an excellent family to look after me while I started out with them. Wilf Dixon made a couple of trips north to speak to Chris as well as my English teacher Charlie Tulloch to whom, I understand, he made a generous offer to try and persuade me to look at Arsenal as the best path. In later years Charlie Tulloch would tease me, saying he could have given up teaching. Chris, on behalf of the family, was told a similar thing by Wilf Dixon which was that a generous fee would be given if I informed Hearts that, despite signing the S form, it only gave Hearts first chance to sign me. I could still simply tell them that I had changed my mind and wanted to head south.

Chris sat me down and explained all this but I had made up my mind. I was staying put and had made a final decision that I would sign full time with Hearts in January. It was just after Christmas 1981 that I had my first training session, having left school when the holidays began. I was nervous as a kitten on my first day but was obviously helped by the number of players in the young ranks I had played with before. Indeed, while I was spending my last few months in school, Dave Bowman had already played several times for the first team and Gary Mackay was tipped to play sooner rather than later.

My first training session was taken by Ian and, due to snow and ice, it was held upstairs in the Brown Gymnasium. Within minutes I was out of action as due to the cold and during the warm-up where we were doing headers and moving on to the next player, I hurt my back. I was in agony. Some start, and I was sent down to see the physio and was informed I had 'tweaked' a muscle in my back and was strapped up with a sticky tape bandage, which I would later discover ripped off your skin when it was removed. As I hobbled off, I walked straight into the first team goalkeeper and dressing room joker John Brough who asked what was wrong. I simply told him about the tweak and he gave me my first Hearts nickname, 'Tweaky', after the little robot on *Buck Rogers*, a popular TV show at the time. In the show, the said robot waddled about in the same manner as I was at that moment. The nickname immediately spread like wildfire. Pop was now Tweaky.

It was only a couple of days before I was back training and I was loving it: training in the morning, ground staff duties in the afternoon. I was designated kit washing duty alongside Gary Sutherland – the worst job allegedly. Now the kit was not like it is today, all the same colour, all numbered, and I soon realised why no one wanted this job. It was a nightmare. Each player in the first team was allocated a maroon match top, white shorts, maroon socks, and a maroon sweat top. That was it.

No numbers. Nothing. We had to simply write their number or initials on them with a black felt pen. If that wasn't bad enough, the players provided their own tracksuit bottoms and their own wet tops, and that was where all the colours of the rainbow came in. Again, we had to get the right kit in the right locker and, added to that, the washing cycle took forty-five minutes. There were at least six separate washes so it was a long shift and we were there at least a couple of hours after the rest of the ground staff had left. I watched as Bow and Gary Mackay got the easy jobs due to their first team involvement and that was another incentive to get playing and one day hopefully get a game for the first team.

Within a few days I was to achieve that in a way as, due to heavy frost and with Hearts having no training ground (we were at Saughton Park most days), and with the indoor hall at the Tartan Club unavailable, Bobby Moncur decided to hold a practice match on the rock-hard pitch at Tynecastle. The pitch was basically unplayable, but he wanted to run his eye over the players as best he could so he called everyone into the home dressing room to announce the teams. These would, as usual, be the maroons, the first team, versus the whites who were the reserves.

He started off saying the maroons would be Brough, Denny, Jefferies, Liddell, Bowman, and so forth, and, as he got to forwards, he said up front were Gibson and Robertson. Then the same process with the whites: Westwater, Gauld, Plenderleith, Mackay, Marr... and, up front, Scott and Robertson. I was delighted as I hadn't played for the reserves due to the weather and now I was getting the chance to play up front with Davie Scott, the current reserve striker.

The manager announced we had five minutes to get into full match kit and I made my way through and got changed but, to my surprise and that of the whole dressing room, Tony Ford the assistant came in about two minutes later and said, 'Robertson, what you doing in white?' I mumbled that I had heard my name and was getting ready to play, with the sudden sick feeling in my stomach that maybe I had misheard him and was not involved at all!

'Yes, you are playing, but the boss wants you in maroon, so get through there. He knows what your big brother can do and wants to see what all the fuss is about with you, so swap with Chris now.'

I couldn't believe it as I walked through to the home dressing room, passing Chris on the way who was jokingly berating the manager about it being a travesty. Chris winked at me and then the first face I saw was Bow, with a big grin on his face. As I sat down, Willie Gibson looked at me and, seeing I was chalk white with fear, calmed me down and just said, 'Look, if I go short, you go long and vice versa. Keep it simple and you'll be fine.'

We started the game and, with conditions being brick hard, it suited me with my low centre of gravity. I got some good early touches and Willie Gibson was brilliant, constantly cajoling me into the right positions and encouraging me. Ten minutes in and a corner was headed toward me. I flicked it on only to see it handled on the line. Penalty! As I made my way out to the edge of the box, Willie informed me that I was taking it and handed me the ball. Strangely I was not nervous as I had taken penalties for school and club regularly and stroked it home past Westy to put us 1–0 up.

Boosted by this, I felt sharp and confident and five minutes later was slipped through, went round big Westy and rolled it into the empty net to double my tally. Only a good save and the post stopped me getting a hat-trick as the first thirty minutes came to a close.

My joy was short-lived as I was told to hand over my top to Chris and watch the second half from the sides so that everyone else got a game. To be honest, I was delighted to get off the pitch as my stomach was still churning. Bobby Moncur strolled over and said well done and mentioned that obviously Chris's goal scoring ability had rubbed off on me – Chris was currently top goalscorer – and that he would have to check carefully in future which initial he put in front of Robertson on the team sheet. My reputation as a goalscorer had been enhanced and Chris was getting tortured by the first team dressing room banter about his wee brother being the one to watch but he would, along with his sidekicks, get his daily revenge on me.

At that time, as well as having kit washing duty, the ground staff and myself were all allocated three players each and our other job was to keep their match and training boots clean. I was given Walter Kidd, John Brough and Chris, and part of my duties was to go and get their lunches each day, which was when they really took the Michael. Chris would inform me he wanted a cheese roll, German biscuit and a can of juice and would despatch me up to Gorgie Road to get it. On my return, Broughy would then give me his requirements of two filled rolls, milk and a cream bun, and off I went again and back down the road. Then Zico would be waiting with his culinary demands! It was then I lost it and shouted, 'What are you three muppets up to? Why can't you just all tell me at the same time and I will get them together?' To which I was politely told to shut up and do as I was told.

This happened for weeks, but as I later found out, it was a test to see if I would crack but also a show of loyalty. I soon found out why as in one of my early reserve games, Frank Liddell, the first team centre-back, had been injured and was playing with us for match practice. During the game we were not quite on the same wavelength. I would come short and he would play it long, then I would go long and he would play it short. After a while he gave me stick and I responded with a shout back bemoaning his passing. He made a gesture with his hand that I thought meant we'd get it sorted, or so I thought, then at half time I found out all about his character. He grabbed me in the tunnel and lifted me by the throat to his eye level and growled you, 'Little f*****g arsehole. Who the f**k do you think you are? If I play the ball long you chase it and if I play it short you come and get it, okay?'

While this may sound harsh, it was how it was, with the senior boys letting the younger lads in the team like me know that standards were required and that you had to earn the respect of the senior pros in the team with your work rate and attitude as well as your skill, and you had to absorb it and learn or you could be swallowed up and end up a shrinking violet.

He then dropped me and walked off. Needless to say, in the second half I did what I was told and made the runs required. This, however, got back to Chris, Broughy and Zico and, unbeknown to me, let's just say that the three of them had a quiet word with Frank (given his size it would have needed all three) that they would not accept this treatment of their ground staff boy. After that, Frank could not have been nicer to me. My 'tormentors' were watching my back!

I made my reserve team debut in a 2–1 victory over Hibs at

Tynecastle in the New Year and scored my first goal the following week in a 2–1 win over Falkirk reserves at Brockville, with Chris scoring the first in a rare brotherly strike partnership. Then in late March, we had a semi-final of the reserve League Cup at Tynecastle against Rangers that drew a sizeable crowd of 2,700. I played well, scored one and set up the others in a 3–1 win over a strong Rangers side and that put us into a two-legged final against Aberdeen.

The first leg we played really well and I scored two second half goals to give us a handy 2–0 lead to take North. Two weeks later the second leg took place, with both teams pulling in first team squad players to bolster their chances. Jim Jefferies was pulled in to partner Frank Liddell and Bobby Masterton was brought into the midfield. Paul O'Brien played upfront with me, but Aberdeen were even stronger. They had Scotland Youth keeper Bryan Gunn in goal, the retiring Stewart Kennedy at the back alongside Willie Garner and Doug Rougvie, John McMaster and John Hewitt providing width, Neale Cooper in midfield and upfront the giant Walker McCall and the legendary Joe Harper (also retiring).

Again, a good crowd saw Bobby Masterton stretch our lead to 3–0 on aggregate early on before a McCall double had Aberdeen right back in the tie. Half time was interrupted by first team manager Bobby Moncur who, after Ian Brown had delivered his demands for the second half, told Jim and Frank that they needed to push up a bit as McCall and Harper were too dangerous to keep sitting so deep which was inviting trouble. Frank told him they were fine, had everything under control and would be able to handle the Dons front men, but their failure to heed the manager's warnings came back to haunt them.

Aberdeen ripped through us, scoring six times in under half an hour, with McCall taking his tally to four and Harper bagging a couple. Despite a late 25-yard strike from yours truly we had been humped 8–4 on aggregate and it was a long journey back from Aberdeen with a losers' medal scant consolation.

*

July 1981 was my first pre-season as a signed player and what a shock to my system it was, as it is to most young players. After three weeks off, we had to report back to the stadium to do our ground staff duties, which was basically the maintenance of the ground with jobs varying from pulling weeds out of the terracing to painting the crush barriers on the terracing, cleaning out all the tiles in the shower areas of all the dressing rooms, painting the corridors, dressing rooms and physio rooms. Most of the time we were unsupervised and you can imagine the high jinks that we got up to during the summer.

It was during one of these mucking about episodes that we made a surprising discovery when, during an impromptu game of head tennis in the corridors, a strong Dave Bowman touch saw the ball shoot upwards and demolish one of the ceiling tiles above us. We quickly hatched a plan to make sure no one would discover the demolished tile by replacing it with one from the boot room where there were already a few missing. Being the smallest, I was sent up the stepladders to replace the tile and, as I popped my head through the void, I noticed a door above me. When I told the rest of the boys – Bow, Gary, Westy – they told me to climb higher and see what was inside. I scrambled up further, pushed open the door to a cupboard and was astonished to see it packed full of ledgers, programmes, pennants and trophies. The lads also had a look after I had come down, but we now had a dilemma to solve – how could we tell Andy Stevenson, the physio who looked after us, how we had discovered the room without getting in trouble for breaking the tile in the first place?

It was decided we would come clean and tell the secretary Les Porteous who asked us to get the stuff down and let him see what it was. The boxes contained old ledgers from seasons dating back decades and the pennants were from Hearts' first European adventures and from North American tours. Alongside them were various trophies and medals won by the club and to this day no one is sure exactly how they had ended up in this unusual cupboard. The main stand had been continually developed to keep up with the latest requirements for press and sponsors and it seemed as though these had been packed up and forgotten about until our discovery. So, instead of getting into trouble, the club were delighted to have recovered such valuable memorabilia.

The serious business was soon on us and the pre-season running and gym work was brutal. The old-fashioned mantra of run them till they're physically sick was in full force (in my case that was easily achievable) and then there were tough gym sessions where everyone had to use the same weights regardless of their physical size. While I struggled, guys like Chris and Walter Kidd could lift them with ease.

Bobby Moncur had been sacked following Hearts relegation and after a couple of weeks the surprise choice to replace him was his English assistant Tony Ford. Tony had assembled a strong-looking squad as Hearts attempted to bounce back straight away. Promotion was paramount in the plans and the squad was added to with the arrival of Willie Pettigrew and Derek Addison from Premier League Dundee Utd. Competition to come back up was going to be tough as Kilmarnock, Dunfermline, St Johnstone, Ayr and Motherwell were all strong in a fourteen-team league that saw everyone play each other three times, with only two promotion places.

For myself, I continued to work away in the reserves and looked on as Dave Bowman continued to cement himself in the first team. Gradually, Gary Mackay was starting to get more game time too and I was doing well, scoring regularly and topping the scoring charts for the second string – or the stiffs as we were often called – with matches taking place on Thursday evenings. You knew who was in the manager's plans as he would leave his entire starting eleven out, and the two sub places for the first team were generally filled by the players that were substituted after an hour or so. Hearts had a poor-ish start and the club took action once more with the appointment as player-manager of another summer arrival, Alex MacDonald, in December 1981. After that, the team immediately started to pick up.

Alex 'Doddie' MacDonald had been struggling with a calf injury and one day, as we were training at Roseburn, I was warned by Bow that as I had been told to train with the first team, I should watch myself if I found out I was not in the manager's team. Doddie was notoriously uncompromising and showed no mercy to anyone in opposition regardless of their age or ability. As it turned out, I was indeed in the opposition when it came to the nine versus nine match to finish off training and I soon realised what the lads meant when I was caught with a late challenge by the gaffer. I dusted myself down and thought that I needed to stand up for myself as it was a man's game. Within a couple of minutes, I had my opportunity for some retribution when I came in on Doddie's blind side and gave him a whack on the back of the ankle as I took the ball away from him. He was not happy with the challenge and as he jogged past me, Bow told me to keep my eyes open and my wits about me as he would no doubt come looking for me. These were wise words as, shortly after, I saw him moving in from the side to do me. I stopped, turned quickly and sped off. He stretched to try and get me then yelped out in pain as his calf tore again. If looks could kill, I would have been dead on the spot! He glared at me as he hobbled off the pitch.

Later on that week the reserves were down to play Falkirk away and as we sat in the dressing room Ian announced that the manager was in attendance and that it was an opportunity to impress him. He then continued to name the team and I was horrified to find that not only had I failed to get starting position (despite being top scorer), I had not even made the bench as one of the two subs. As the lads started to get changed, I quietly asked Ian why I was not involved. He just shrugged his shoulders and said the manager had told him who was playing. Disappointed, I made my way to the stand and had to sit and watch the game with the manager yards away and he completely blanked me the whole night.

The following week we had Falkirk at home and once more I was nowhere to be seen as the team won. The next week was the same again, and without a word being said, I wondered if my brush with the manager at training was now going against me. Maybe I was on my way out because of his injury? I spoke to Chris and asked him what he thought I should do, and he said, 'wait and see'.

The next reserve game was against Hibs away and I decided that if I was not selected, I'd go and see the manager and ask what the problem was. I again found myself not selected but this time was on the bench and, despite being behind for most of the game, I was not asked to strip off and go on and play. I was disappointed, and decided the following day I would knock on the manager's door and see what was going on. Now that was not the easiest thing to do for a rookie player and, to be honest, I was totally bricking it.

The manager asked what I wanted and I blurted out that I couldn't understand why I had not been involved in the last four reserve fixtures and that, being top scorer in reserves, was my omission down to the incident in training a few weeks back? He glared at me, and I thought, 'Oh, here we go!'

'No,' he said, 'it has nothing to do with that.' Turned out the reason he had made Ian not pick me was that he rated me highly, he liked how I handled myself and thought that I had a good future in front of me if I knuckled down, worked hard and continued to listen and learn. He went on to say that the reason I had not played was that he wanted to see all the other players in action as he wanted to give them the opportunity of some game time. He wanted to be sure that they were not good enough – because l was seen as a good prospect, he didn't need to see me anymore as my immediate future was secure.

Hugely relieved, I went back to training and told Chris who advised me to get my head down and work hard. A couple of weeks later we played Morton in a reserve League Cup tie on a horrible night in Greenock and I struggled in the first half up front with Derek O'Connor. At the break, we were 2–1 down. Ian was not happy and gave us all a bit of stick for dropping our standards and he had a pop at me for not working hard enough to close down the full backs. Because I was so frustrated, I chipped back that I wasn't in the team to chase full backs, I was in the team to score goals. He exploded!

We trotted off into the wet night, me with a flea in my ear and a warning that if I didn't up my work rate I would be sitting watching the second half from the bench. I responded by smashing in a twelve-minute hat-trick and setting up Derek O'Connor for a goal before giving Ian a wink next time we made eye contact and asking him if that was okay.

A couple of weeks after that, we had a match on the Monday evening against East Fife away and I bagged another hat-trick in a 3–0 win. The following morning, I was awakened by the constant ringing of the phone. I just ignored it as I knew I was in at 3 p.m. later that day for a league match against Queen of the South. We had to report then to put the kit out and put the nets up. But the phone kept ringing so eventually I answered it and it was Chris asking how the match the night before had gone. I responded that despite scoring three I had not played as well as I had been but had at least taken my chances.

'Well,' he said, 'you must have done something right because the club have phoned me to tell you that you are in the first team squad for tonight's game, but they couldn't get hold of you this morning.'

To say I was nervous as I sat on the number 44 bus was an understatement and it seemed to take a lot longer than the normal forty minutes to reach Gorgie, but I was there in plenty of time and was first in the dressing room. I sat patiently as the players started to arrive and they poked plenty of fun at me because I was as white as a sheet. Chris tried to calm me down, pointing out that in all reality I would be fourteenth man as that was the norm for younger lads in the first team set up. The gaffer then arrived and named the team with Robertson, Pettigrew and McCoy up front and then named the subs Peter Marinello and John Robertson! Chris kicked me in delight and I took my place, stunned, excited, nervous, every emotion in the book. I had made the bench and the bonus was that Chris was there, too.

The warm-up whizzed by and then I was sat in the dugout. After only sixty seconds, we scored, Chris heading home for the opener, but before we could celebrate, Rowan Alexander and Queens raced to the other end of the park and equalised. As we sat for the start of the second half, Alex MacDonald turned and said, 'I tell you what, wee man (he was just about taller than me). If we go three ahead, I'll throw you on to play with your brother, all right?'

I just nodded. I was still nervous but within minutes those nerves got worse as Willie Pettigrew made it 3–1 and within two more minutes Gerry McCoy added another for 4–1. I said nothing, just sat there thinking, this is it! But nothing happened. Sixty minutes came and went, then seventy minutes and a few minutes later Chris smacked one off the post and the gaffer turned round and said, 'What a shame. If he had scored you would have been on as we would have been three ahead.'

Peter Marinello looked at him and said, 'But, Gaffer, we *are* three ahead – it's 4–1!'

Doddie looked at me. 'Why the hell did you not say anything? Do you not want on?'

Within seconds I was stripped and standing on the track about to replace Gerry McCoy. With twelve minutes to go I was about to make my debut. I could hear the murmurings of the crowd as I stood there and was wondering what they'd make of this wee guy standing waiting to come on with shorts miles too big for him. But it really was happening. I was on! The nerves went instantly. I had a few good touches and then nearly scored after playing a one-two with Willie Pettigrew and smacking a sixteen-yard drive over the bar. I then had a late shot saved by the Queen's keeper before the ref brought my debut to a close.

That was it for the rest of the season as I was then back in the reserves scoring goals. The first team were knocked out the cup at home to Forfar and there was plenty scarf throwing from the fans to show what they thought of the performance. But after that match, Alex MacDonald told the fans that he would be making major changes to the squad and that, while still fighting for promotion, all of the first team were playing for their future. I was nowhere to be seen until the last match when title winners Motherwell arrived at Tynecastle. We needed to beat them and hope that Kilmarnock did not win heavily, but, in the end, we lost 1–0 and Killie won 6–0 to ensure they went up, leaving Motherwell and Hearts in Division 1 for another season.

10

George and Bert

Alex MacDonald made two major signings in the close season, both big names and both hugely influential ex-Rangers players. Willie Johnston and player-assistant manager Sandy Jardine were the new arrivals and Doddie had now decided that the way forward was a mix of the old guard – himself, Sandy Jardine, Stuart McLaren, Roddy MacDonald, Willie Pettigrew, Paddy Byrne and Willie Johnston – and younger players including Gauld, Mackay, Bowman, McCoy and Murray as well as players around the twenty-three years of age mark in Henry Smith, Walter Kidd and Peter Shields. The rebuilding had begun.

The club set off to the north east of England for three pre-season matches against North Shields, Whitley Bay and Blyth Spartans. I was in the travelling party but my main brief was simple – I was the hamper carrier. I was still seen as potentially breaking through and the manager thought that the experience of being in the first team training environment would be a good one. The fact that I was cleaning all the match boots and helping with the laundry was immaterial. I was not expected to play any part as the first team players needed to get match fit.

We drew the first match at North Shields 1–1 before dispatching Whitley Bay 4–2. The last match was at Blyth Spartans and, with us leading 2–0 and just a couple of minutes left, I was told to go on as a sub. It was a token gesture for my week's hard work but it paid off as I managed to deflect the gaffer's late drive past the Blyth keeper. I had scored my first goal for the first team.

As I made my way back, Sandy Jardine grabbed my hand and said, 'Well done. If you continue to work hard and listen, this could be the first of many.' I don't think either of us were expecting just how true that statement would turn out!

It was during that summer that the younger players were introduced to two guys who were going to have a massive impact on their development on the fitness side of the game, George McNeill and Bert Logan. Pilmar Smith, one of the directors, was a bookmaker to trade and had a keen interest in professional sprinting. The Powderhall Sprint was a huge event then, as was the Stawell Gift sprint in Australia, and they had a talented school of sprinters that trained out of Meadowbank under the supervision of George and Bert, who both still ran occasionally.

The gaffer and Sandy wanted the players to be super-fit and, for the younger players they saw as potentially breaking through, they wanted an extensive programme in place to bring us on as quickly as possible. We were taken down to Meadowbank and put through a series of drills and exercises to see what stage of development we were at, ahead of the new regime we were going to start. The sprinting and various runs and stretches seemed fine and then they took us to the gym to test our strength on what they called a Toga circuit. This consisted of seven exercises: raised feet press-ups, jump-ups on a bench, squat thrusts, burpees, arm dips, abdominals and pull-ups. The aim was to do six repetitions of each exercise three times round, and as fast as possible.

For Dave Bowman and Ian Westwater it was a breeze. Both had the physiques of grown men. Stuart Gauld was rangy but strong, so he was fine. However, Colin Plenderleith, Gary Mackay and myself had no power in our arms or upper body. In fact, Gary, on his first round of maximums (as many as you can do of each exercise in one go) could only just make one pull-up. I fared little better, managing three while the rest were double figures. I remember wondering what on earth was going to happen and was worried about the pain we were going to have to through to get stronger, but this was nothing compared to our last test of the day: speed balls! They're commonplace in the boxer's gym, suspended from a hinge, and we watched in amazement as George and Bert battered these things, barely missing for a two-minute spell.

When it was our turn, what seemed like an easy exercise turned into mayhem. Anyone who has tried this exercise will tell you it's all about timing, as every time you hit the ball, it has to bounce three times before you hit it again, but those three bounces happen in a millisecond. None of us got any more than thirty hits in the allocated time and we looked on in bemusement as Bert announced that our target over the next month would be at least a hundred hits and, in time, a minimum of two hundred hits a minute. As we retreated for a shower, the common opinion was that Bert was a lunatic if he thought we would ever be able to do that. And what was this to do with football anyway? How would it make us better players?

Our training also included a trip to the sand dunes at Gullane, a place much loved by our player/management duo. Gullane was a strength-sapping endurance test up various dunes until you reached 'Murder Hill', a sand dune around a crop of rocks at the west end of the beach. The last runs of the day on the highest hill left most of the team looking for a hole in the sand to bury their heads so they could reacquaint themselves with their breakfast. It was agony at the time, but within half an hour you felt great.

George and Bert started working with us and explained their theory that core and upper body strength was key. 'Try running fast with your hands in your pocket,' said Bert. And he was right – you can't. Let your arms hang loosely and you will walk slightly faster. Get your arms pumping fast and your legs will automatically go faster to keep up. So strong thighs, strong core and strong arms were vital.

I loved these sessions. I'd struggled with the cross country running and anything over a hundred yards was no advantage to my short stride pattern, so a chance to improve strength and pace was a godsend. And once we worked out the timings of the speed ball, vast improvements were made quickly. Most of the players were getting to around the two hundred hits per minute mark and with the Toga circuits kicking in we were soon improving rapidly on our physical development programme.

Gary Mackay had now joined Bow as a first team regular and they were the catalyst for the rest of the younger squad. Bow was like his dad, Andy, well-built, powerful and streets ahead of us physically while Gary was skilful but was now adding strength and fitness to his game to go with his guile. The rest of us were improving but had a long way to go. Management had made it clear to everyone we were going to be the fittest side in the League and that this would be a strong principle for the club going forward.

Pre-seasons were brutal, with the morning starting off with a twenty-minute fartlek, a session that increased five minutes each day up to forty-five minutes. The gaffer and Sandy would lead and when they blew the whistle you started jogging. Then they blew it again and you ran at their pace (a good clip). When they blew the whistle again you went back to a jog, with no walking at all. Sometimes you would do a short burst of ten seconds, sometimes the run would last over a minute. Then a fifteen minute rest and stretch was followed by 6 x 400 metre runs in seventy seconds, with ninety seconds' break in between. Another fifteen minute rest was followed by increased lap running alternating between jogging and running, picking up the pace until it was really tough. It was not for the fainthearted – or for someone with my short legs!

In the afternoon it was back to Tynecastle for gym sessions in the Brown Gymnasium. This was the Toga sets of seven, three times round and then followed by 6 x 3 minutes on the speed ball at 200 hits a minute with abdominals and press-ups in between. Tough stuff, but you felt the benefit. I never heard any player disrespect these sessions because once you got the technique right it was massively beneficial. It allowed everyone the opportunity to do well because we were not lifting weights – George and Bert did not believe in them – but instead working with our own body weight, like we did on the football field.

Over the years, George and Bert became great friends with the players and were in full-time with us. There is no doubt they were the first of the new breed of the fitness and conditioning coaches you see today. They had given Hearts an edge, they had given me an edge and I wanted to make full use of it. John Colquhoun, Craig Levein and Sandy Clark often joked later that I had to perform well in September because if I failed to score in two games in a row I would be heading down to Meadowbank to join the sprinting school to top up my fitness as they built up for the New Year sprint.

The conversation with the gaffer and Sandy would be the same:

'Come in, Robbo. Sit down. How you feeling?'

'Fine boss, thanks.'

Sandy would then say, 'I was thinking you look a wee bit flat at the moment, not quite as sharp as you were earlier in season! How's your weight?'

'Weight's fine, boss. Same as it was last month when I was scoring and I still feel sharp!'

'Well, we just think you have gone off the boil so we have arranged with George and Bert for some extra sessions for you with their sprinters.'

'Okay, boss, cheers. Thanks very much, looking forward to it already.'

Every year was the same so, suddenly, every Tuesday, Wednesday and Thursday evening I was off to Meadowbank to do sessions as well as my normal football sessions with the team. To be honest, I enjoyed them, particularly Wednesday and Thursday evenings as speed ball circuits and flying 50s were the norm and that was ideal for me. Tuesday was a different kettle of fish as in the morning I had to do a full session under the watchful eye and timings of George and Bert and there was no hiding place, then an afternoon session of circuits. When I reached the sprint session at night I was knackered. It was tough, but over the years I did enjoy it and they were instrumental in my development into being a far fitter player. These guys took me from a wee lump of lard (Bert's comment on day one) to someone who could handle the fitness side of things at Hearts and last, in the end, to the age of thirty-five before retiring. I owe both of them massive amounts of credit and thanks because I would not have been able to achieve half the things I have if it was not for their dedication, hard work and the sheer torture they put me through. The biggest compliment I can say is that there is not one player during their time there that did not improve their physical condition and well-being. Years after they left, their ideas were still the foundation for the Hearts' fitness regime.

*

Hearts had a mixed start to the season and it soon became clear that this would still be a tough league to get out of, but with Willie Pettigrew spearheading the attack and Derek O'Connor chipping in, confidence was high that we could get back to the Premier League. Whilst I was improving as a player, it looked like I was still a long way off from joining Bow and Gary in the first team on a regular basis, despite the fact I was still scoring regularly at reserve level. That was to change just one week after my eighteenth birthday.

As usual, I made my way to do my duties at Tynecastle for the match, this time against Alloa Athletic. I laid out the kit as directed by physio-kit man Andy Stevenson, and, once completed, we were told to go and get our lunch and be back for 2.10 p.m. We made our way up to Gorgie Road for lunch at the Gorgie Fish Bar. Colin Plenderleith, myself and a couple of others duly tucked into our preference, mine being a fish supper. We went back to the stadium for 2.10 p.m. as instructed and I was told to report to the manager's office. Once inside they asked how I was, as I had picked up a knock in training the day earlier. I said I was fine, it was sore but it was just a bit of bruising. Sandy, who had a ball under his foot, said,

'Kick that as hard as you can.'

I did and a pain shot through my ankle.

'How was that?' he asked.

'Fine, a bit sore but okay, boss.'

'Right, get yourself along to the dressing room and stay there.'

When I walked in, Chris (who had not featured all season) asked what was going on.

'Don't know, just been told to report here,' I said.

Five minutes later, the team was named with the addition of Robertson on the bench. I got up to go when the gaffer said, 'Sorry, the Robertson on the bench is John.'

I was again shocked but delighted and got stripped, but during the warm-up felt queasy as my heavy lunch kicked in.

It was 0–0 at half time and, to my surprise, I was told to get stripped. I was on in place of Willie Pettigrew who had been having nasal problems. The rest was a blur. I had a good shot saved before an own goal put us in front. I then hit the post after racing through before Roddy Macdonald put us 2–0 up. Then Paddy Byrne drove into the area and from the corner of the six-yard line had only the goalkeeper to beat. Much to my delight, instead of shooting as the keeper expected, he unselfishly rolled the ball square for me in the middle to tap the ball home and score my first ever competitive goal for the club. We won 3–0.

I couldn't believe it – I had scored and Bow was as excited as I was as we made our way off the pitch. To cap it off, Chris was standing at the top of the tunnel beaming away, waiting to congratulate me. I still remember that as much as anything that day, and just to bring things back to reality – I don't know if it was nerves or shock – I quickly exited to the toilets and brought up my lunch. Alf Tupper, I was not!

This boost saw me train fully with the first team and even harder with George and Bert. The gulf in fitness was big but the difference in game knowledge was huge and football can be a tough place as, no matter what your age, experienced players give you short shrift. You had to survive or you'd sink without trace. After getting a taste, I was prepared to do anything to make it and so my long relationship with George and Bert began in earnest. I knew that without their detailed plan for my fitness, there was no way I would have been able to handle the physical side of the game. I have no doubt their input was as important for my career as the advice and direction given to me by players and managers alike.

11

Going Up in the World

The rest of the season was a dream for me and one I could scarcely have thought I was heading for until my introduction in October. I was now involved fully in the first team at training and games. A few weeks later I came off the bench and scored a vital late equaliser against Partick Thistle before I was given my first League start in a match at home to Airdrie. Although this ended in a disappointing 4–2 defeat, I was now beginning to find my feet and getting to the pace of the game slightly better. With Willie Pettigrew still struggling with injury I was kept in the side and was involved in the second leg of the League Cup semi-final at Tynecastle against Rangers. Although we went down 2–1 (4–1 on aggregate) on the night, it was a great experience to play against a Premier League side and the following Saturday I was on target in a 3–0 victory over Clydebank at Kilbowie Park. I then got a brace the following week against Falkirk in a 3–1 victory, although this was slightly disappointing as I missed a penalty for a first half hat-trick. It was now mid-November and I was soon back on the bench, then back in the reserves as Willie Pettigrew returned. He battered in seven goals in four games to signal his return to fitness so I was not required again until February.

Alex MacDonald took me out of the first team reckoning to develop in the second string. I was champing at the bit but the form of Willie Pettigrew and Derek O'Connor meant I had to bide my time. I was determined to show I was capable and, with my physical strength and speed improving, I was determined to be ready when called on.

My opportunity came when injury ruled out Derek O'Connor and I was selected to play at Hampden against Queen's Park. It turned into a special day as my best pal Dave Bowman was made captain to mark his hundredth appearance for the club at only eighteen years and eleven months old! And I got back on the score sheet, bundling in a right foot shot that had been parried by the Queen's keeper to give us an early advantage. I then headed one home with eight minutes to go before completing my first senior hat-trick two minutes later, shooting home left-footed to claim the match ball and give the Parsons Green boys a day to remember. A brilliant day which was enhanced further when Pilmar Smith handed Bow a bonus for the team of £100 cash and told us to go and have a good evening. We didn't need a second invitation!

We came down with a bump when we were dispatched 4–1 by Celtic at Parkhead in the quarter-finals of the Scottish Cup. It was a controversial match as we were well in it before Willie Johnston was sent off for an off-the-ball incident with Dave Provan. That led to some ill-feeling and we had no chance after that.

We hosted the next game, which was a vital match against fellow promotion rivals Partick Thistle at home. It was a tight affair with Henry Smith having two wonder saves from Donald Park before I gave us the lead, chesting down a poor headed clearance twenty yards out before smashing a right footer into the top corner to give us a half-time advantage. An hour in and I raced through, rounded McNab and slotted home before Mo Johnston twice hit the woodwork for the visitors. But we made the game safe when Willie Pettigrew scored with a sharp finish and then, late on, I nicked another to complete a second hat-trick of the season and give us a morale boosting 4–0 victory.

Goals quickly followed in wins over Clyde, Airdrie and Queen's Park, before another double against Clydebank was added to my total, although they did grab a precious point with a wonder strike from star man Gerry McCabe. It was now getting to the vital stage of the season as we were vying with Clydebank, Partick and St Johnstone for the title and promotion places and we were going through a sticky patch with losses away to Raith and St Johnstone which added to the late draw with Clydebank. This was compounded when Gary Mackay missed a late penalty as we drew away at Alloa and things were now really tight at the top, with Saints just ahead of us and Partick and Clydebank just adrift in third and fourth places.

All this meant that the home game against Dunfermline became vital and I struck twice in the first half before the Pars pulled one back after an hour. Then I smacked one in to complete my third hat-trick of a red-hot spell and when the Pars went down to ten men, the points looked assured. Incredibly though, we slipped up again as they struck twice in the last ten minutes. Another point had gone and, for the first time after a game, I saw the gaffer's annoyance as he ripped into us, questioning our bottle and whether we had the mentality or desire to go up.

There were two games to go, and we had to travel to Boghead where we had a poor record. We knew that victory would guarantee at least second place and, with the manager's warning ringing in our ears, we were in no mood to let this opportunity slip. I scored twice in the opening twenty minutes and a Derek O'Connor header and a Gary Mackay piledriver saw us take the victory and, along with it, promotion back to the Premier League. The pitch invasion by our delighted and relieved support said it all as they celebrated a massive win for the club.

Our dropped points were to prove crucial in the race to finish top of the League. We trailed St Johnstone by a solitary point and needed them to drop a point at home, but a single goal victory over Clyde meant our two-goal win over Hamilton was meaningless as the title went to Perth. This match, however, was to have bizarre consequences for me as I had been selected to play for Scotland in the European Under-18 Championships held in England, which started the night before that match with a 3–0 victory over Russia. I was driven south by Jack Steedman, an SFA official and owner of Clydebank, to meet up with the squad, and we got to the squad base just outside Birmingham in the early hours of Sunday morning. Later that day I was put on the bench for the match against England for a 1 p.m. kick-off as Andy Roxburgh felt the lack of sleep would work against me. England raced into a two-goal lead and when they doubled that advantage before half time I was told to warm up and get ready to start the following half. I immediately scored to get us in the game before heading home after an hour to half the deficit. Another header hit the bar as we hemmed England in. Two more shots were saved before I hit the post late on and England held out to win 4–2. Despite this, we were still in a good position, knowing that a draw against Spain would be enough to get us out of a tough group and into the semi-finals.

However, the drama was just about to start. I was summoned to see Andy Roxburgh for a meeting the day before the Spanish match. I was told that I had been banned from the tournament as England had complained I was ineligible. Andy explained that in the competition rules it stated that once a tournament had started no player could play in another competition and that, as I had played against Hamilton, I was therefore breaking the rules. They also wanted the match awarded 3–0. This was important as it gave England a better goal difference and reduced ours to zero which meant we now had to beat Spain, whereas a draw would see them through on goals scored.

Andy explained that Scotland had lodged an appeal as I had not left the squad or the tournament but came after the first match and no advantage had been gained. This was thrown out, England were awarded a 3–0 victory and I was now banned from the tournament. I watched from the stands as we missed a host of chances and the game finished 1–1, allowing Spain to progress.

Back at home the Scottish papers blazed out: HEARTS ACE KICKED OUT OF EUROS! and HEARTS STRIKER BANNED FROM TOURNAMENT and, with no mobile phones, my family were wondering what I had done to be expelled. It also immediately put me into the world of quiz trivia: Who are the only two Hearts players to be banned from a major tournament? (Willie Johnston having been banned from the World Cup in 1978). I spoke to Chris and he was relieved it was only a clerical thing but it brought an eventful end to an eventful season.

12

Doddie and Sandy

Alex MacDonald and Sandy Jardine had a huge influence over everything at Hearts from the moment they got together at Tynecastle. Alex was a fierce competitor in everything he did and while Sandy looked and acted with grace and had an aura of class about him, they had both been hugely successful with Rangers and were winners. This was the main attribute they wanted to bring to the dressing room and they would lead by example. Both were extremely fit, brought through the harsh and brutal fitness regime that Jock Wallace had instilled at Ibrox, but both were hugely talented players and, despite their years, could still hold their own in the team and at training. They had installed George and Bert but they also demanded everything from the players in the technical training sessions which had to be done at match pace and had to be competitive. NO coasting. NO taking it easy. You would work hard and give everything to the cause or you were cast aside. It was simple but clinical and we knew there would be no passengers.

As we started our first season back in the top flight, they discarded Willie Pettigrew and brought in a new partner for me, someone who would look after me on and off the pitch – Jimmy Bone. Jimmy was immediately drafted in to sort out the youngsters as a member of Doddie and Sandy's head tennis team, a game that we had been introduced to every second morning and occasional afternoon. Sounds quite straightforward: three-a-side played over a six-foot net, one touch each, you can only score on your service and first to twenty-one wins. They tortured any three of the young players' combinations as they were masters of the game. We played in the Brown Gymnasium, high up in the stand at Tynecastle with the sloping room that made the degree of difficulty even greater as the emphasis was on touch and technique, using all parts of the body to try and win points. We couldn't get near them and it was a tactical masterclass on how to play the game, with them spinning the ball off the walls and pipes in the room. Alex had this way of heading a ball down so that it hit the wall and floor at the same time and didn't bounce, making it impossible to play it back.

And to add insult to injury they demanded that every game was played for a signed pound note and religiously took it from us after every game. NO passengers. NO easing up. EVERYTHING competitive. It took months for us to give them a decent game and even when we occasionally got close we still couldn't beat them. But we kept at it and gradually got closer and closer until one day we got to match point and managed to set up Dave Bowman with a clear header at the net, but as he went to head it, Jimmy Bone challenged him at the net and sent him flying through the air. We immediately claimed the point, only to be called down by the gaffer saying it was perfectly legal and that they had won the point. Despite our protests, we were not given it and, to make matters worse, Bow stood up with a hole just below his eye socket, revealing he had suffered a fractured cheekbone. To our dismay, Sandy took him downstairs and the gaffer demanded Gary Mackay and I carry on to finish the game 2 versus 2!

That was the attitude they brought to training. Not so brutal that they wanted players injured, just a desire to win and treat every session as vital. Practice games were split up to young versus old, east versus west, as they got every single per cent out of the players in everything: games, running, gym sessions, technical sessions and head tennis. Everything mattered. They wanted a winning mentality and they got it, year in, year out.

They spoke to us all the time. Bow, Gary, Stuart, Gauld and myself had come through the youth ranks and on day one of training for the new season, they brought us in and told us that despite the other three being nineteen and myself eighteen, we were no longer regarded as youngsters and would be treated as men, just like the rest of the squad. And we would have to be ready to play against the country's best.

They had already brought me in and explained that while I had a year of my contract left, they wanted to extend it by two more years and that I would go from £70 a week to £120, the same as Bow and Gary. The first team were on £150 plus £25 appearance and £150 a win at this stage but the youngsters received £50 appearance and the bonus if we made the thirteen. I was wondering about asking for a signing on fee, but by the time they had got to me about playing against Miller and McLeish, Hegarty and Narey, Aitken and O'Leary and McClelland and Paterson, that they were not sure I could make it at the top level and that I was lucky that they were taking a chance on me after all, I just wanted to get the deal signed and get out of there.

I walked out thinking how lucky I was only to be told the following day by Jimmy Bone that I was done up like a kipper and that I should have demanded the same as first team and a signing on fee. I didn't care. I was happy to have another three years to develop further. He just shook his head and said he would be finding me an agent in future and that I would have to learn quickly about football. Sandy and Doddie may have done a number on me but I was looking forward to the season and was confident I could continue to improve.

I got on well with the gaffer, despite thinking he didn't like me after our training ground confrontation. We had similar physiques, were the same height and bizarrely had the same size of feet, with his right foot being a size 5½ and his left foot a 5. I was the opposite, so every time we got a new pair of boots we did a quick swap so we each got exactly the right sizes. The main difference at that time was our weight as I was seven pounds heavier than him and he reckoned I should be the same weight. It was a constant talking point over the ten years he was in charge and used as an excuse all the time to send me to sprint school in the winter months. Over the years, Doddie and Sandy were fantastic, always encouraging us, always there for advice, always wanting the best for us and urging us to follow their lead. And given their ability and fitness, they led by example, with Sandy completing over a thousand matches and playing to the age of forty – only constant calf injuries stopping the gaffer from playing on even further than he did. They brought a new mentality to the way we trained, ate and played and they expected the players to mingle and socialise with each other as often as possible.

They turned us from being a joke club into one of the most respected teams in the League. Opponents would know they had been in a game when they played against us and it was a period when Hearts reclaimed their pride. Those two were completely responsible for it as we embarked on a decade-long adventure.

13

Yo-Yo to Europe

Hearts were favourites to go back down as we had become the yo-yo team but the gaffer and Sandy were determined that this would not be the case. After a three-game trip to the Highlands, two high profile matches against Leeds United and Leicester City at Tynecastle were staged. The first against Leeds was a typical pre-season game, lots of possession but not much else as a goalless draw against the Yorkshire side ensued. But the Saturday game against Leicester, on a baking hot day, saw them go ahead early before I scored with a header then a crisp shot to give us the lead, only for their top striker Gary Lineker to score two late goals to win the match. But we were in fine fettle and ready to prove the bookies wrong.

Fate saw us travel to our rivals from Perth as they raised their Championship flag but an early goal from my new strike partner Jimmy Bone saw us return with both points. We had recruited well, with Jimmy Bone, Donald Park, Peter Shields, George Cowie and Gregor Stevens drafted in to supplement the younger players of Bow, Gary, Stuart, Gauld and myself, and we had experience in the shape of Stewart McLaren, Willie Johnston and Derek O'Connor. We were given the unkind tag of *Dad's Army*, despite the young guns we had been playing regularly.

We started the season in a League Cup section that saw us pitted with Rangers but the gaffer had decided that this tournament was not a priority for us and that a campaign to re-establish Hearts in the Premier League was our aim. He would be resting players at various stages, the League Cup section being one of them. The following weekend saw the match that we had all looked for when the fixtures came out, Hibs at home. We all got a first taste of this special derby atmosphere as the press built it up through the week. Hibs had dominated the fixture from the late 1960s and all through the 70s, with the famous New Year's Day victory at Tynecastle (7–0) in 1973 – Hearts only crumb of comfort being a 4–1 victory. Hibs were the top dogs in the capital and they were determined to put us in our place. Just under 20,000 fans were in Tynecastle as the two old foes produced a classic match. The gaffer and Sandy sat us down on the Thursday and detailed exactly what was required and how we would go about ensuring a victory both from a team and an individual perspective and that if we followed this plan it would bring us the victory that the supporters craved. He left us in no doubt that this fixture was all about the fans and what it meant to them.

We started the game well. Dave Bowman saw a long-range strike parried over and then a deflected free kick from Bow again saw Rough save well. I had a strike deflected past the post before Hibs took the lead with a rapier-like counterattack that saw Ralph Callaghan put them ahead. It was a blow given our whirlwind start, and Hibs took full control of the contest. We were fortunate to be only a goal behind at the break and the Hibs fans were in full voice, including my eldest brother George, as we left the field at half time. Once more the gaffer and Sandy calmed us down and told us what was required, how we had to go about it and that it would pay dividends if we stuck to the plan.

The gaffer then made a big decision. Gary Mackay, who had been charging about getting caught up in the adrenalin of the derby fixture in the first half, was replaced by the gaffer himself. Like all of us, he had been caught up in the derby hysteria and was playing the match like a fan rather than a player. It was tough on Kay as he had been looking forward to the game. As a fan and a pupil of Tynecastle School, which was just over the wall, this was his game, but the gaffer and Sandy called the substitution. There could be no passengers and no compromise. Winning was paramount.

The second half was incredible. We equalised with what is, without doubt, the best goal I have ever scored in my career. Henry launched a long kick out and, with the wind behind, it came down just short of the Hibs box and over my right shoulder. Instinct took over and although, in real time, what was about to happen took a couple of seconds, to me it was all in slow motion as I controlled the ball with my right foot before it bounced, slipped inside and nutmegged Arthur Duncan, before sending a left-footed curling chip toward the top right-hand corner of Alan Rough's net. The ball seemed to take forever as it curled, clipped the underside of the bar and the post and then went into the net. I was woken from my slow-motion slumber by a blast of noise from the Hearts fans as I took off in the general direction of a joyous Shed. It's hard to describe how I felt at that moment as everything was so high paced. I was swamped by the team and, football being the sport it is, I was immediately back in the zone. With the derby flying along, the concentration had to switch back on immediately, such were the demands of the match.

Our joy was short-lived as Hibs raced up the park just eight minutes later to take the lead, with Willie Irvine hammering them ahead. In a breathless spell, I equalised again as the gaffer sent through a ball that was just too far for me to get onto, but I had a feeling Benny Brazil, the Hibs defender, was going to attempt a back pass and decided to gamble on that. He did and miss-hit it, giving me the opportunity to get there fractionally ahead of Alan Rough and toe poke it under him. I watched as the ball rolled along the line pursued by Jackie McNamara (Snr) before going in at the back post. The score was 2–2, game on.

Just seven minutes later and Tynecastle erupted once more as I swivelled thirty yards out and hit a cross-field pass to Donald Park who knocked it past Duncan first time and then whipped in a great cross for Jimmy Bone to rise and bullet it past Rough. Now we had the lead with just thirteen minutes to go. The rest of the game was frantic as a stunned Hibs side tried to muster a response, but we had them. Our fitness regime kicked in and we continued to cause more problems. We finished off the contest with the experience of Jardine, Roddy MacDonald, McLaren, the gaffer, Parky and Boney proving invaluable. And when Bob Valentine blew the whistle it was utter bedlam as the Hearts fans went wild with delight. The prize scalp had been taken and victory was ours.

Many things have been written about the derby, but no one in the crowd would have imagined this result. Hearts' new mentality and preparation would pave the way for over three decades of dominance over our city rivals. And for us, this was the start of a run of sixteen matches and four years with no defeats to Hibs.

The following Wednesday saw Rangers arrive in Edinburgh for a League Cup section match but with them also due on the Saturday on League business, Alex MacDonald rang the changes as five players were taken out the starting line-up, including Boney and myself. The League was the priority, staying up was first on the agenda and while Rangers won the match with ease (3–0) it was all change on the Saturday with all five players returning to the team.

We raced into a three-goal lead through the gaffer, Boney and me, and a late Mitchell goal did not take any shine from the victory as we won our third straight League game. Jimmy Bone and I continued that run, both scoring as a last-minute winner saw us defeat Dundee away and then big Roddy MacDonald scored in a 1–0 victory in Paisley. After five games, Hearts were top of the League and even then relegation was no longer on our minds. A highlight of our first season back has to be a late fightback against Rangers when Derek O'Connor pulled a goal back in the eighty-eighth minute and then, with the last kick of the game, I hit an over-the-shoulder volley to snatch a point and send Tynecastle wild.

Aberdeen and two Peter Weir goals brought our run to a halt, but the seeds had been sown. We were not a joke side anymore and we would compete with anyone. We knew we were the fittest team in the League and had good players who could play well, with a nice mixture of experience and youth.

We battled on through the season and became tough and resilient. Three more draws were achieved against Hibs, and we drew sixteen games overall. A fourth-round defeat to a strong Dundee Utd side cleared our minds for the run-in that would see a Willie Johnston free kick equaliser clinch a point and a move to European Football. It was a tremendous achievement for us at the time and marked a terrific return to the top flight.

To finish the season, Hearts held a benefit match for the gaffer against Rangers (who else), and 18,000 were at Tynecastle to honour it as Rangers defeated a Hearts side that fielded Kevin Keegan by 3–2. Just a few days later, I was honoured by the SPFA, picking up the Young Player of the Year award on the back of scoring twenty-one goals in my first top-flight season. The gaffer and Sandy sat me down and, while congratulating me on my season, said the hard work was just beginning and that a good summer with George and Bert was vital ahead of another season. And, to top it all, would I consider another year's extension? I'm sure they both smiled when I said my new agent would be in touch soon. Advice was plentiful, but good advice was vital. I would talk to Chris, Boney and my new agent before signing anything else.

14

Agent Orange

Jimmy Bone introduced me to Bill McMurdo at Ibrox (where else) after a League Cup tie and told me that I needed someone to look after me going forward. Bill, as well as others, represented George Best, and he was just the man for the job. Chris was in agreement as he realised that I was now starting to get noticed and that while we all trusted the gaffer and Sandy, they had a job to do and a budget to work to at the club to keep the wages in place.

We arranged a meeting and Bill explained how he worked. I liked him and despite his quirky way and trademark cowboy boots, we hit it off. I can honestly say it was one of the best decisions I ever made and over the years Bill became a real friend rather than an agent.

Bill, as everyone knew, had a tremendous affection for Rangers and never hid it, but what a tremendous job he did and he was honest with his dealings. The first question he always asked was straight to the point, 'Do you want to stay at Hearts?' His reasoning was simple. If I was happy, he would go straight into negotiations with club Chairman Wallace Mercer. Or if I said I wanted to look at other options he would do exactly that.

I was happy at Hearts so told him to crack on. The process was always simple: what would be the minimum you would be happy to sign for in terms of wages and/or signing on fee. Once this was established he would go and talk to Wallace and I can honestly say that he always delivered – and always negotiated more than a fee I would have settled on.

Meetings with Bill were in either Edinburgh or his house in Uddingston, nicknamed Little Ibrox, with his red, white and blue railings. Bill was a real tea jenny and would drink pot after pot as we talked all things football and he would tell me about his other clients and daft stories about them, as well as tales of George Best and how different he was in real life to his public persona. People saw this wild playboy, but Bill told me he was actually quite shy in company.

Bill invited me through to Little Ibrox one day for a meeting about a potential boot deal and to introduce me to a few people. After an hour with Bill, talking over the deal about the boots, he asked me to join him in the lounge. We walked through and there chatting away to Helma (Bill's wife) was none other than George Best himself. I was star struck and just sat there not really knowing what to do. George chatted away in that soft Belfast accent and I could see that everything Bill had said was true. He was shy in general company but was an absolute gentleman and, like most footballers, only wanted to chat about the game.

After about half an hour the lounge door opened and in walked what I can only describe, even to this day, as the most stunning woman I have ever seen. She had blonde hair and was dressed in casual jogging bottoms and a little blue T-shirt – although I cannot for the love of me understand how I still remember this! George stood up and introduced his current girlfriend Mary Stavin, ex-Miss Sweden and Miss World! And there I was, a wee eighteen-year-old from Edinburgh, sitting in Bill McMurdo's house with one of football's greatest-ever players and a former Miss World drinking tea! I can't really remember what we spoke about for the half-hour or so (I was distracted for some reason). I left shortly after thinking that football wasn't too bad a business to be involved in. Surprisingly, and again I can't think why, I left that afternoon completely forgetting to take my three pairs of sample Puma boots to try out at training.

Bill was great to me over the years and became a bit of a father figure in a small way. I could talk to him about things that I might not want to chat to Chris or George about and, of course, he was responsible for one of the biggest signings in Scottish football at the time – Mo Johnston.

Mo had used Bill in his transfer from Partick Thistle to Watford and then again for Celtic and on to Nantes before the biggest move that rocked Scottish football to its core: Mo Johnston went to Rangers. Bill had brokered the deal to take Mo back to Celtic but, by all accounts, Celtic wanted to rush it through as they had wanted to counteract all the high-profile Rangers signings Graeme Souness had been bringing in over the years. A press conference was arranged to announce the re-signing of Mo for Celtic, where he had been adored by fans during his previous spell. But, despite showing him off to the press, the deal had not been signed and after the brief appearance in front of the cameras there was still no contract in place.

Bill then received a call from Souness asking if a deal could still be done and simply trumped the Celtic offer. After speaking to Rangers and listening to what Souness had to say, Mo decided that he would sign for Rangers. Mayhem ensued, with Celtic raging at Bill and Mo – and Rangers fans raging at Souness. Bill, Mo and Scottish football watched with bated breath to see what would happen next.

Bill was unfazed over it then and still is to this day. It was simply business and, had Celtic concluded the deal, he would have happily got on with it. Mo moved to Edinburgh (a wise choice) and we actually became great pals and frequently socialised at his flat. Again, despite his reputation, he liked to stay in rather than go out in Edinburgh.

One of the lasting stories of the Mo-to-Rangers move was hilarious but summed up the early mood of the Rangers fans. When I was speaking to my pal and big bluenose Dougie Bell one Saturday evening, I hadn't caught the scores, and asked him in the pub how Rangers had got on that day at home to Aberdeen. He said it had finished 0–0 and that it was a poor game. About an hour later someone had mentioned that it was good day for us as we had won and that Aberdeen had lost, so we were above the Dons in the League, with Mo scoring the winner.

I looked at Dougie and said, 'Some Rangers fan you are, when you don't even know Rangers won and Mo scored his first ever goal for them.'

Dougie looked at me and with a deadpan face, said, 'His goals don't count,' and went back to his pint! Mo won them over with a last-minute winner against Celtic but it still remains one of the most sensational moves that Scottish Football had ever seen.

Bill was good with all his contract work and never once touted me to another club. That was how he worked, and although he got a fair bit of stick over the years, I cannot think of any player who was disappointed with his services. Managers and club chairmen would be out slaughtering him in the media for taking a player elsewhere but then were on the phone minutes later with 'can you get this guy' or 'find someone else', saying that they had to give him some stick in the press to appease their fans about a player leaving the club. To Bill it was simply business – nothing more, nothing less.

Bill was a really funny guy and laughed about his nickname, Agent Orange, due to his Rangers affections, but I can honestly say that he never did Rangers any favours in his dealings with them. He always did what was right for his player. He got pelters from the clubs but that to me is the sign of an agent doing his job and getting the best possible package for his guy. We weren't on fortunes in those days but Bill made sure we got what we could from the negotiations and was worth his weight in gold. Unlike today, footballers were not that comfortable and clubs still held the power as this was pre-Bosman. So even if you were out of contract, the club holding your registration could demand whatever they wanted for you as long as they matched the wages from the previous year. And unlike today, you simply could not move to another club. Jean-Marc Bosman challenged the law. When he won, the world of football was changed forever. The players now had the power and agents then became crucial, putting Agent Orange right in the thick of it as, after all, business is business.

15

The Great Waldo

My first months at Hearts were hectic playing-wise, but off the park the club was in turmoil financially. It had to find around £120,000 or the bank was going to close the club down, so a public battle for control of the club took place between two Edinburgh businessmen, Kenny Waugh, a well-known bookmaker, and Wallace Mercer, described then as a commercial property entrepreneur. They both entered negotiations to buy Chairman Archie Martin's share of the club. Mr Martin was a great guy, very friendly, he knew everyone's names and wanted the best for the club. But he had realised that the game was moving forward and Hearts needed fresh blood and investment to get it back to where it should be as a force in Scottish football following relegation, promotion and then relegation again.

Wallace Mercer arrived in his Jaguar XJS with the soon to become famous XX1 registration plate and, with smiles and handshakes, took control of Hearts. Life was never dull under Wallace and despite his lack of knowledge on the game itself, he had the club buzzing as he set about trying to pull us back up to where everyone felt we belonged in the Premier League.

He knew that playing in front of 3,500 to 4,000 fans in the First Division was not helping the revenue and so, with Tom Ford being replaced by player-manager Alex MacDonald, he set out his master plan to get Hearts back on top. He had full faith in the gaffer and as the signings arrived, it was clear he would try everything to get the club up. Bonuses increased slightly and appearance money as well as he tried to incentivise the players, and despite us failing the first season, he let the gaffer go ahead and sign experienced players for a second campaign in the First Division in the year that we eventually got promoted behind St Johnstone.

Wallace loved the spotlight and was brilliant with the press. He held court, telling everyone about his plans for the club, frequently succeeding in getting the club in the press, raising the profile and expectations among the fans as we headed into the new season. He brought in new shirt sponsors very early on and opened a new sponsors' lounge to attract businesses to eat at the club.

He famously went to Miller Homes, our sponsor at the time, to create a competition. A house was put up for sale that could be won simply by buying a match day programme and entering a grand draw. The winner was announced at a big pre-Christmas game against Rangers. He was always thinking up new ways of getting money into the club or getting lines in papers and on TV, anything to get that elusive piece of silverware.

When Wallace realised the benefits of cup runs and the bonuses around actually winning one, he came up with one of the most lucrative bonus schemes of its time to make sure the club would finish in the European places. The accumulator bonus was his big plan and it worked quite simply by rewarding players with an extra bonus if we were successful over each set of four games. We were not on massive money at Hearts at the time, with most lads getting between £300 and £400 a week, supplemented by a £100 appearance fee per game plus a win bonus of £200 per match.

Wallace decided that the more we won, the more crowds would come and the more revenue he would generate on the road to the ultimate goal of achieving European qualification. We played thirty-six games and he split these into nine blocks of four matches. The bonus would be simple: our normal appearance and win bonus would apply to the four games but on top of that was the accumulator bonus meaning that if we won all four games in that block (a total of eight points at that time) we would receive an extra £1,200 on top of our normal bonuses. Seven points would see us get £1,000, six points £800 and five points £500. Four points or less and we would receive nothing other than the normal bonuses. After each block of four games, the points total started again.

This was attractive to the players as we knew we could really earn some great money if we won matches. We never actually won all four in a section, but we did pick up a few three wins and a draw. Overall it was a great incentive for the players. And, of course, if we were making bonuses then we were also were racking up the points.

I only ever fell out with Wallace twice, once over the Hands off Hibs campaign and then over the sacking of Alex MacDonald. We'll come to those two incidents later. For now, what I can say is that Wallace Mercer was an astute businessman who loved the cut and thrust of life and was pretty much a constant presence during my Hearts career. And whatever anyone thought of him, one thing I learned was that you could never, ever ignore him.

16

Heart Surgery to Heart Broken

We had strengthened again that season with Brian Whittaker coming in at left back and Kenny Black arriving from Rangers to bolster our midfield, alongside Neil Berry from Bolton. After two draws and a penalty shoot-out victory over Cowdenbeath, we had paid a nominal fee for their impressive young defender Craig Levein, who initially played a couple of matches in midfield before cementing his place next to Sandy Jardine in central defence. It was, of course, the start of his journey to becoming one of Hearts' best-ever defenders.

Our first season back had brought us European football and we got a plum draw when paired with French giants Paris St Germain who played at the Parc des Princes in the capital. We were drawn away from home in the first leg of our first European campaign of the 1980s and arrived in fairly good spirits. Sandy Jardine had seen them play in a French League game and declared that while they were a really good technical side, they had their flaws, and that if we performed well, we could get something to keep the game alive for the return at Tynecastle.

We arrived in Paris on the Tuesday afternoon and were given

the afternoon off as we were training that evening. Donald Park and I made our way to the Palace of Versailles, a short walk from the hotel, before returning for an afternoon sleep as we prepared for match prep at the magnificent stadium that evening. The weather was warm and the stadium tremendous and we were buzzing as we worked on possession with some crossing, and finished with a competitive eight versus eight game. We had our set plays but deliberately went through a routine of bogus ones as everyone knew the home side would be having the session filmed or watched. The gaffer named the team when we got back to the hotel, and we watched footage of PSG in action. There was no doubt they had some great players in their side, notably their little midfield playmaker Safet Sušić, and Dominique Rocheteau leading the line.

We had gone with a solid looking 4-4-2 with Jimmy Bone and I up top. Henry was in goal, Kidd, Jardine, Levein and Whittaker at the back, with Mackay, Bowman, MacDonald and Black sitting in front of them. Having two strong banks of four was a system that had served us well. However, we had failed to realise that no system was of any use when you were playing against the football genius that was Safet Sušić. He tore us apart and whipped in a great free kick after twenty-two minutes to open the scoring before he set up Rocheteau for a second just before half time. He slotted home another after the hour and Richard Niederbacher completed our misery with fifteen minutes to go. In the end we were lucky to escape with just a four-goal beating.

We had a couple of chances, with Gary Mackay sliding the ball wide at 2–0 and Kenny Black rattling one just wide late on. When we trooped off, we were still roared on by the brilliant travelling support who, while disappointed with the result, were not going to allow our performance to ruin their short trip to Paris. We were feeling bruised and battered but they went on to party long into the night.

The return leg saw us fare much better as 11,000 turned up on a wet September evening. Sušić continued where he left off, setting up Niederbacher to score early before we equalised, Jimmy Bone nodding a cross into my path for me to rifle home. Sušić then set up another for Jeannol, and Rocheteau almost broke the bar with another rocket while the giant and lightning-quick Toko was tearing up the right flank and causing all sorts of problems late on. Much to our and our supporters' surprise, I latched onto a long through ball and lobbed the outrushing Baratelli to grab an unlikely equaliser and give us a morale boosting draw. It was a relief to get something out of that game against that quality of opposition.

Sušić was incredible, and one particular moment encapsulated him late on in the first leg, he was given a hospital pass by one of his teammates which saw Watty Kidd and Dave Bowman both come charging in on his blind side. This was their opportunity to exact some revenge for the chasing he was giving us. As they both dived in, he somehow sensed them coming and simply let the ball run through his legs and jumped, letting Bow and Watty clatter each other as he danced round the other side and sped off with the ball, leaving our two would-be enforcers requiring treatment for doing each other.

It was a lesson learned for the younger players in the team. We had a strong core of younger players all between eighteen and twenty years old; George Cowie at twenty-three and Kidd, Whittaker, Smith and Iain Jardine all mid-to-late twenties. Sandy

Jardine was still immense and the gaffer used himself sparingly and we still had the considerable experience of Bone, Johnston and Park to rely on. The arrival of another strike partner for me in the shape of Sandy Clark brought more experience but there was no doubt the gaffer and Sandy were quickly shedding Hearts of their *Dad's Army* tag. However, more surgery was needed as we had finished a disappointing seventh in the League, a place above our city rivals, but we realised we needed to improve. We left for the summer to ready ourselves once more and try to do better in the League and the cups with no knowledge about what was to be the most dramatic season in the club's history for nearly twenty years.

The arrivals continued with Andy Watson, Colin McAdam and Billy MacKay – all good, experienced bodies – and the dramatic signing of the dynamic and exciting Celtic winger John Colquhoun, who had played several times for the Hoops but had not managed to dislodge Davie Provan. The £50,000 fee was to turn out to be another masterful stroke from our management duo. It was one of the best signings the club had made and showed how street savvy they were, especially alongside the bargain £40,000 paid for big Craig Levein. We now had a core of early-twenties players alongside the experienced figures already at the club – a strong team as we tried to force ourselves back into European qualification contention.

We had travelled to Germany for a five-game tour and training camp to get to know our new teammates. It was an eventful trip, based at a tennis centre that had four cracking pitches for us to train on. Alex and Sandy topped up our heavy running from back home with shorter, sharper runs and lots of technical training, in between five games in ten days, so it was a tough introduction for the new guys. It did, however, finish with their inaugural sing-song in the cellar of the hotel after consuming some of the local wine the gaffer had acquired on his vineyard visit.

The games were tough as the standard of regional German sides was high, and it started with a match abandoned after eighty minutes due to torrential rain and an electrical storm while we were leading 2–0. So we were in good spirits as we geared up for the rest of the week, battling out a tough 0–0 draw against SV Wiesbaden before comfortable wins over Ingelheim (5–1) and Bad Kreuznach (4–1). This led us to our last match against a formidable regional team, champions and unbeaten on their home patch for five seasons, SC Birkenfeld.

The reason for their home dominance soon became clear: the pitch was large and sloping, a mixture of stone and red ash. Our players and management were a bit bemused that no one had told us – the only bonus was that the rain had softened the playing surface a little. However, it was not one for the sort of sliding tackles that Messrs Kidd, Cowie and Black favoured, that was for sure.

It soon became clear that the local referee was intent on keeping the hosts' unblemished home record intact as they smashed into tackles all over the pitch and were allowed to play on while our attempts to match them were punished by free kicks and yellow cards. They took the lead after twenty minutes and then continued, with the aid of the referee, to keep control of the match until half time, roared on by a very partisan home support that were enjoying the battle of Birkenfeld being played out in front of them.

The gaffer was going nuts at the officials at half time and was threatening to stop the game but he soon calmed down before proceeding to make a couple of changes to replace the lads on a yellow card. He told us to go out there and play them at their own game, to get physical but to play smart by putting the ball in behind them to turn their big defenders. This was not a game or a surface to play silky soccer.

The second half was mayhem as both teams scrapped it out. We eventually got level with just under ten minutes to go when Gary Mackay and I played a one-two and he drilled it home. Then, with a couple of minutes left, Kenny Black dinked a ball over the top and I ran on to clip it over the keeper and give us the lead. Despite a long period of injury time, we managed to see out the game for a brutal victory that will live long in the memory of pre-season 'friendlies'.

Our first match in 1985/86 was a home game against Celtic and a crowd of 22,000 attended in brilliant sunshine. They were not let down as both teams started at a high tempo, determined to get off to a flier and it was the old former-player curse that struck Celtic as John 'JC' Colquhoun raced through to poke the ball home and give us the lead midway through the first half. We had held onto this slender lead into the final minutes when I managed to turn the ball back to Sandy Clark who looked to have sealed the game when his ten-yard shot was struck, but somehow Packie Bonner in the Celtic goal managed to get a toe to the ball and it rolled inches wide of the post. That save was rewarded when, deep into injury time, Paul McStay picked up a headed clearance twelve yards out and under pressure from our defence tried to smash it home, only to completely miss-hit his shot. It somehow deceived three on-rushing defenders and goalkeeper Henry then bobbled in off the left-hand post to snatch Celtic a point. And what a vital point that was.

The feeling when you lose a late goal is unbearable, especially given the effort put into winning any game. You are always upset and it takes hours, sometimes days, to get over it as you feel sick to the pit of your stomach. If we felt bad about that, the following week was worse as we scored first through John Colquhoun and last through me but shipped in three in either half in between. We lost 6–2, although it has to be pointed out that we lost Henry Smith to an unexpected injury in the dressing room before the game when he slipped and hurt his back. With no substitute goalkeepers at that time, Sandy Jardine had to fill Henry's number 1 top and be custodian for the day, but to no avail, as we were well beaten. We readdressed the balance with a hard-fought victory over Montrose away, where Zico, Gary Mackay and I all scored in a 3–1 League Cup victory, before heading to Ibrox the following Saturday where I cracked one home just before half time to give us the lead. Then two goals in four minutes halfway through the second half saw Rangers edge ahead, and despite our constant pressure, Bobby Williamson grabbed his second and Rangers third at the death to send us home pointless.

We saw off Stirling Albion after extra time away from home, with Paul Cherry grabbing the winner before the first Edinburgh derby of the season saw JC score again as we got off to a flier in front of 17,500. Gordon Durie equalised ten minutes from half time, but our derby dominance continued when Sandy Clark banged the winner home with less than ten minutes to go and the fans trooped out of the stadium happy that we had secured victory.

Our early inconsistency continued with Wednesday and Saturday trips to Aberdeen where we first lost 1–0 to an Eric Black goal in the quarter-finals of the League Cup before being thumped 3–0 at the same venue with Black again among the scorers. We immediately bounced back with a 2–0 home victory over Dundee Utd, with big Roddy MacDonald heading home in the opening minute before I finished off the game with a neat lob late in the game. Our away form continued to be poor and we followed that win with league defeats away to both Motherwell and Clydebank to leave us on just five points from eight matches and just above Clydebank in the table. The gaffer held a sit-in after the game and made it clear that despite some of the performances being good, we were not being clinical enough at either end of the park and that changes would be made unless form improved. No names were mentioned, but the gaffer had this unique way of talking that everyone in the dressing room assumed he was talking and looking directly at them.

We fell behind early in our next home game but equalised just before the hour with an Ian Jardine header, but, despite our best attempts, we could not force the winner. However, few in the crowd realised what the significance of that equaliser would be and that it would start us off on an incredible sequence of League and cup results. We had played the first round of nine matches and were sitting ninth in the table. The following week we travelled to Celtic Park where we had not won since the 1960s. The pressure was on.

It turned out to be another memorable game for me with two major incidents that would ultimately capture the headlines. The first was when I swivelled on the six-yard line, chesting down a Sandy Clark knock down from a JC cross and lashed home to give us the lead just after the half-hour mark. We were then indebted to a fabulous rear-guard action as Smith, Kidd, Whittaker, Jardine and Levein, ably backed up by our midfield, kept the swarming Celtic attack at bay.

Then with only minutes to go, we had the chance to double our advantage as Craig Levein launched a ball over the top and I got in behind the defence, pursued by Roy Aitken. As we tussled at the edge of box, I felt a searing pain in my neck from a flailing elbow and just collapsed. The next thing I knew was that Alan Rae was talking to me – unbeknown to me he had rushed on while the game was still going on as the referee Jimmy Duncan had waved play on. I couldn't feel anything so Alan got the stretcher ordered and I was out the game with a neck brace on. Alan was worried I had damaged my neck or my spine in the incident.

To make matters worse, while Jimmy Duncan was lecturing Alan about coming onto the field of play, the stretcher bearers – who looked like they had an average age of eighty – proceeded to drop me and I fell back onto the pitch. Back in the dressing room, Alan tried to organise an ambulance as I had no feeling in my feet or my legs but a Celtic director had invited a doctor to the game and he offered his services. Within minutes he was sure that I had not broken anything but said that an X-ray was still required, just to make sure, as he felt the collision may have given me a pinched nerve in my neck. I was listening to the radio as the ambulance men had the game on, and we all chuckled as Derek Johnstone had announced that they had heard from the Royal Infirmary that I had a broken neck! The fact we were heading to Glasgow's Victoria hospital made me feel much better, along with the fast-returning feeling in my feet and legs. Indeed, the doc had been spot on – I had a trapped nerve in the neck but would be fine in a couple of days. That, and the fact that the lads had seen the game out and we had won our first game at Celtic Park in two decades, helped me feel right as rain.

My Lazarus-like recovery continued as I scored twice early in the second half against St Mirren. The following weekend, as we continued our climb, a Craig Levein header at home to Aberdeen saw a third win and a move into the top half of the table for the first time that season. A late Richard Gough goal snatched Dundee Utd a point at Tannadice before we secured another point and another derby game undefeated with a bruising goalless draw at Easter Road. We then thumped Rangers 3–0, Motherwell 3–0 and Clydebank 4–1 in three successive home games as we closed in on a top three spot. Two draws followed with Dundee and Celtic before we blasted ourselves to the top of the table with four consecutive victories over Christmas and New Year as a Kenny Black goal saw off St Mirren before JC produced a masterclass on a frozen Ibrox pitch and scored both in a 2–0 win. Hibs were then battered 3–1 on New Year's Day at Tynecastle with Clark, Jardine and me on target in front of 26,000 fans. We rounded off that incredible run by coming from behind at half time at Motherwell to win by 3–1 with Black, Ian Jardine and me on target. We were now top of the table and Alex MacDonald left us under no illusion that he wanted us to stay there as our unbeaten run now stood at fifteen, with eleven of them wins.

Although we were top, we had played two or three games more than Celtic, Aberdeen, Dundee Utd and Rangers due to some postponements and the fact that Scotland World Cup play-off fixtures had forced the Old Firm, Aberdeen and Dundee Utd to cancel games because their players had been called up. Surprisingly, no Hearts player had been requested which suited the gaffer right down to the ground. We had the points on the board so the rest had to win their games. That was his message.

A late Eamonn Bannon goal gave United a point at Tynecastle but we got back to our winning ways with a late JC goal at Pittodrie as we stayed top of the table. This win boosted the spirits as we prepared for the Scottish Cup third round at home to Rangers. This was another blood and thunder game played on the rock solid Tynecastle pitch and, unlike today when there's absolutely no chance the game would go ahead, once more the referee, Mr Muirhead, deemed the pitch flat and playable, albeit with sand spread on it and both sets of teams wearing pimple-soled footwear. So, it was game on.

The first talking point was the substitution of both Craig Paterson and Sandy Clark after a sickening clash of heads, leaving both needing stitches. Rangers brought on Dave MacKinnon but we were a change for a change as the fearsome ex-Ranger Colin McAdam replaced Sandy through the middle. McCoist put Rangers ahead with the last kick of the first half before two goals in six minutes from Colin McAdam and Gary Mackay had us in front early in the second half. Then the emerging young star Ian Durrant hammered home to level once more as both teams slugged it out for a winner, with a replay looking favourite. Luck, however, swung our way. With five minutes left, I followed a lob over the defence from Gary. With big Colin chasing in, Hugh Burns seemed to have the situation under control as his keeper Nicky Walker came to collect. But Colin's presence had the desired effect as they looked for him rather than the ball. The defender and the keeper ended up colliding and the ball dropped away from them and into my path. The place erupted as I knocked it home and sent us into round four.

Another disappointing display at our bogey ground, Kilbowie, saw Sandy (with stitches) grab a last-minute equaliser. We then came from a goal down to dispatch Dundee 3–1 at home, with another to my tally, before I scored just before half time to cancel out a Mo Johnston goal, which kept the unbeaten run and the gap between ourselves and Celtic the same. We came back with a valuable point and the continued belief that we could win our first title since the 1950s.

A much-delayed fourth round Scottish Cup tie eventually went ahead and we found ourselves one down in twenty-five seconds, but I cracked one home two minutes later and Gary Mackay clinched a hard-earned quarter-final place halfway through the second half. That set up a quarter-final the following Saturday at home to St Mirren, where we raced into a 4–0 lead after an hour as Saints were put to the sword. It has to be pointed out that they lost keeper Campbell Money early to injury but we took full advantage. Four straight league victories followed when I netted five of the goals as we beat Motherwell 2–0, Hibs away 2–1, St Mirren 3–1 before another double in a 3–1 win over Rangers saw us arrive for a semi-final showdown at Hampden with Dundee Utd. We were still top of the table but facing back-to-back matches in cup and league against a United side still looking at the double themselves.

The match at Hampden was a drab semi-final with one piece of quality, but, my goodness, it was worthy of winning any game. Sandy Clark knocked down for JC to smash the most gloriously struck volley high past Billy Thomson. We were in the final and still unbeaten, now in twenty-eight games. The following Saturday it became twenty-nine as we swept United away 3–0 at Tannadice. I smashed in one of my best goals with a left-footed half-volley that screamed into the top corner and, although Sandy and I added to that in the second half, only a Henry Smith wonder-save from a free kick kept us ahead going into the last twenty minutes.

We were further buoyed by the announcement that Aberdeen had scored a last minute winner to defeat Celtic which saw us move to the brink of clinching the title. This was soon tempered when we were informed in the dressing room that, in fact, it was the other way around and it was Celtic who had snatched the points up north.

Our destiny was now in our own hands as we faced Aberdeen at home with just three matches to go. It was filmed live on the Sunday and not many chances were created before the Dons were handed a controversial penalty by referee Bob Valentine after seventy-two minutes when a cross from the right was chested away by Ian Jardine off the arm of Peter Weir. To the astonishment of the home fans, he pointed to the spot. Despite our protests, the aforementioned Weir slammed it home and suddenly we needed to score. Wee JC got on the end of a headed clearance to slam home and rescue the point that kept us in control. Celtic still had to win all four of their games.

In the midweek before the Clydebank game, Scotland had a friendly and I had been called into the squad after Celtic pulled out Paul McStay. Gary Mackay was drafted in too, and we headed to Eindhoven to face Holland where we were told by Alex Ferguson that we would both be on the bench but would not play. He did not want either of us injured ahead of the last two League games as he did not want to incur the wrath of our gaffer if anything happened. So we both watched as Scotland battled to a 0–0 draw before returning for the visit of Clydebank on the Saturday. Despite battering them, all we had to show was a brilliant Gary Mackay goal, but another two points were secured which meant that we headed into our last game at Dundee needing a draw at worst to win the title and that would not be required if Celtic failed to beat Motherwell on the Tuesday at Fir Park.

A few Hearts fans sneaked along to watch but Celtic won their tenth straight match with a late goal to win 2–1. That meant they trailed us by two points and four goals going into the last game of the season where they would travel to Paisley while we headed to Dens Park, Dundee.

Doddie and Sandy kept the week's training sessions exactly as they had been the whole season so as not to disrupt anything that the players had been used to, and by the Friday we were all set, having gone through the match prep and what we were required to do. The press had their day, but everyone kept it calm and said what was required, that we were expecting a tough game and that we needed to be at our best to get the result and bring the title back to Gorgie for the first time since the 1960s.

On the Friday afternoon we heard that the referee had been changed and that David Syme had pulled out through injury, to be replaced by the only official available, Bill Crombie from Edinburgh. We weren't sure if that was good or not as he would obviously be keen to show no favouritism toward us. Indeed, rumours abound to this day that when it was announced he would get the game, he told Jambo workmates that unless someone punched the ball off the line there would be no penalties awarded, a comment that no one has been able to collaborate since and one that was to raise its head in the game.

We stayed in our homes the night before and boarded the bus the following day en route for the Swallow Hotel for pre-match. The first inklings that something was wrong was at the bridge where we picked up our Glasgow and Fife contingent. There was no Craig Levein and we were told that he had gone down with a sickness bug and was in no fit state to play. Roddy MacDonald would take his place and although this was a massive blow, we knew that big Roddy was more than able to take his place in the side.

Maroon and white scarves were everywhere as we made our way to the hotel. A huge support mobilised north to shout us on and there were, no doubt, a few nerves as we ate the pre-match meal and made our way to Dens for our day of destiny.

The Hearts supporters were already in place as we prepared to play the most important ninety minutes of our careers so far. As we were roared off from the warm-up, the hairs were already standing up on the back of the necks. The fans were ready and so were we.

We shot down the slope and started really well, and then came the moment that had Hearts fans wondering for years what might have been. Colin Hendry tried to be cute and turn past big Sandy, who robbed him and then bustled past him on the byline. He got in front and big Colin tried to lunge in and knock ball out for a corner but Sandy poked it away from him, and while Colin got a bit of the ball, he also got a big bit of Sandy first. It looked a clear penalty and we were up and appealing within moments. Bill Crombie brought his whistle to his lips but decided it wasn't and waved play on. He was surrounded by us as we felt it was a foul. But he was adamant, and for years the debate has raged about the alleged comment that no penalties would be awarded. In fairness, we spent the majority of the first half pouring down the slope and Gary Mackay and JC had decent long-range efforts well saved. Big Sandy nodded one just over the top and we were disappointed that it was still goalless at the break.

The gaffer and Sandy were in deep conversation at half time and one or two of the lads had gone to the toilet and been physically sick before we sat down. The gaffer said:

'Look, guys, Celtic are 4–0 up in Paisley so we are getting no help from St Mirren. It's down to us. We have had no help all season and we will have to do it here in Dundee.'

People have asked to this day if he should have told us and if it affected us and, to be honest, I don't believe it did. We had so much belief in each other that we knew we could win the game and the title.

The second half was tighter and we had two real opportunities to get the all-important opening goal. First JC raced through and arrowed in from a tight angle. I was screaming for one across the face of the goal but, in fairness, it would have been an incredibly difficult ball to play and he did the right thing when he smashed one toward goal. It took a good save from the keeper to deny him. With fifteen minutes to go, I then had an opportunity as Roddy MacDonald met a goal kick from their keeper just inside our half, I gambled on it going in behind them and took off and the ball arrived as anticipated. I tried to get it down some thirty yards from goal, chased by McCormack and Glennie and by the time I got another ten yards closer I had a decision to make – either cut across McCormack or attempt a dipping volley. I decided on the latter and caught it sweetly (too sweetly) as it dipped a yard over the bar with the keeper beaten.

As we waited for the game to restart, Dundee made a change with Albert Kidd coming on and within seven minutes he was to write his name into Celtic and Hearts folklore. With eight minutes remaining, Vince Mennie hit a shot from eighteen yards that looked to be going a couple of feet wide but Big Henry could take no chances and he parried it wide for a corner. The ball was played in and, as a posse of players went for it, the red hair of John Brown got a flick and the ball broke to the back of the six-yard line where Kidd was lurking. As he prepared to hit it, Walter Kidd and Sandy Jardine threw themselves in front to block it and, had Kidd caught it sweetly, they would have done. But he slightly miss-hit it and caught it on the outside of the boot, it arced over the defenders, over Henry and into the postage stamp. Dundee were ahead.

We could see that the clock at the bottom of Dens showed we still had time and we charged up the slope looking for the equaliser. The outstanding Roddy MacDonald bulleted a ten-yard header that was tipped over as we searched to grab the goal that would win the title. With just two minutes to go, Kenny Black saw a good tackle ricochet away to Kidd and he skipped forward, played a one-two, and smacked it past Big Henry for 2–0. The game was over. The title was gone.

Bewildered. Sick. Devastated. We had all these feelings and more. We were in a daze and I still can't remember to this day how we got back to the dressing room. The silence was

The Robertsons in 1968. I am the camera-shy child in the front row!

Mum, Dad and me in the Canongate.

The Squad: Parsons Green Primary, 1975.

COURTESY OF JAN ROBERTSON

Wedding bells for
Mum and Dad.

COURTESY OF JAN ROBERTSON

Mum's 'little gifts from God' . . .
Heather and me.

Winners again! Salvesen Boys Club, 1976.
Can you spot future Hearts teammates and fellow Scottish
internationalists Dave Bowman and Gary Mackay?

Nottingham Forest Football Club

Founded 1865

European Cup Winners 1978/79·
Champions 1977/78
Runners Up 1966/67, 1978/79

Football League Division 1
Champions 1977/78
Runners Up 1966/67, 1978/79

Football League Cup Winners
1977/78, 1978/79

F.A. Cup Winners 1898, 1959

Anglo-Scottish Competition
Winners 1976/77

City Ground
Nottingham NG2 5FJ
Telephone 868236
Information Desk 860232
Pools Office 864808

Telegrams
Forestball Nottingham

Manager:
Brian Clough

Secretary/Treasurer:
Ken Smales

President:
G.N. Watson, J.P.

Chairman:
S.M. Dryden, J.P.

Vice-Chairman:
G.E. Macpherson, J.P

Committee:
H.W. Alcock, F.C.A.
B.J. Appleby, Q.C.
G.T. Thorpe
F. Reacher
F.T.C. Pell, F.C.A.
D.C. Pavis
Dr I. Loch

Ref:- BC/GDP   21st August, 1979

Mr. Robertson,
36 Meadowfield Drive,
Edinburgh,
Scotland.

Dear Mr. Robertson,

Following the report on your son John by our Scottish scout Mr. Gibson, and our Youth and Schoolboy Organiser Mr. Newton, I would like to confirm the club's interest in John.

In this respect, may I invite him to come and spend a week training and coaching with us at the first available opportunity, which I understand could be at the October break.

If agreeable, permission should be obtained from his Manager/Secretary of Edina Hibs and nearer the date Mr. Gibson will be in touch as regards John's travelling arrangements etc.

Looking forward to seeing your son here at Nottingham.

Yours sincerely,

B. Clough,
Manager.

ARSENAL FOOTBALL CLUB LTD.

ARSENAL STADIUM
HIGHBURY
LONDON N5 1BU

23rd November, 1979.

Dear John,

We are holding a get-together early in the New Year, which will take place from Wednesday 2nd January, 1980, to 5 January 1980.

Would you please let us know whether you will be able to attend as soon as possible, so that we can make the necessary arrangements.

I hope that you are keeping well, and we look forward to seeing you very soon.

Kind regards,
Yours sincerely,

W. DIXON.

Leeds United
Association Football Club Limited

3rd July 1979.

Dear John,

Our Associated Schoolboy Outing will be held from MONDAY 16TH AUGUST to THURSDAY 19TH AUGUST 1979.

We hope that you will be able to join us. If you accept will you please write to us as soon as you can so that all necessary arrangements can be made. Should you later find that other complications occur please let us know at once.

Best wishes.

Yours sincerely,

E. SLATER
ASSISTANT MANAGER
LFC SCOTLAND

John Robertson
36 Meadowbank Drive

It's 1979 and interest is hotting up.

My first photo call, July 1981.

Alex 'The Gaffer' MacDonald.

If the cap fits . . . brothers with our schoolboy caps.

My debut joy: Scotland versus Romania, 1990.

Spot on. Scoring against Switzerland, 1990.

Instantly recognisable: with the legend that is Kevin Keegan.

Pre-season hell: attacking the dunes at Gullane.

And so it begins! Goal no. 1 against Hibs in September 1983.

Off to celebrate with the Shed.

Tannadice Screamer: the first against Dundee United, 1986.

Breaching the green wall with goal no. 27.

The game's not over till
the fat striker scores!

Heartache: defeat in the League Cup
final against Rangers.

Record Breaker: scoring my way into the history books, 10 May 1997.
Hearts 3 Rangers 1.

'That's for you, Dad.'
Celebrating my record-breaking goal with Neil McCann.

deafening, apart from the sound of someone being sick in the toilet. No words were needed. There were tears in abundance and not one player was immune as the gaffer somehow tried to lift us as he knew we had given everything and had fallen at the final hurdle.

It took forever to shower and change and troop onto the bus. The hurt, the frustration, the anger of losing the title was there in all of us. No one needed to speak. We knew how we were all feeling. We had lost the title with just eight minutes remaining and we had been kicked in the guts. There was a sense of injustice, with the penalty decision still in the mind. Look, we could have got the penalty scored and then still lost the game. I might have missed. We will never know. But I remain convinced that had we scored first we would have gone on and brought the title home.

The history books will tell you that Celtic won the title on goal difference and their players have the medals, not us. When you analyse their closing run they won nine and drew two (Hearts and Rangers) in their last eleven games to snatch the title away, and our mood was not lifted when the press revealed that had Derek McWilliams not been injured in training on the Friday, then Albert Kidd would not have been in the thirteen. Indeed, he pleaded with Archie Knox, the Dundee manager, to be put on the bench as he was convinced he could help his boyhood heroes Celtic win the title. Knox was convinced and history proved them both right.

One of the strange stories afterwards was the conspiracy theory that Craig Levein was not ill and that he had bottled it for that game. Had that been the case, do you honestly think that our managerial duo would have entertained him playing for our side ever again, never mind in the Cup Final the following week against Aberdeen? Either way, several players went down with the sickness bug over the next couple of days. And it is one of these stories that has always popped up but it simply was not true.

On the following Tuesday we assembled once again, ready to work towards winning the Scottish Cup at Hampden. Training was sharp and focused, and the gaffer and Sandy had told us to forget our League disappointment and concentrate on creating history by bringing the Cup back to Gorgie. The intensity was as high as ever and we were confident as we made our way to Hampden for the big showdown. As we made our way up the Hampden stairs, we were met by some Aberdeen players and management. They immediately praised our League campaign and said how gutted they were for us that we had lost the title to Celtic and that they had not wanted the Glasgow club to win the race. We were later to find out that this was part of Alex Ferguson's masterplan for the final as he knew the gaffer and Sandy would be telling us to forget what happened at Dens, concentrate on winning the Cup and get all the negative feelings and thoughts out our heads to be ready for the final.

Alex had arranged for the bus driver to get Aberdeen there thirty minutes earlier than normal and when we arrived, he wanted his Aberdeen players to stroll out to reception exactly as we came in the front door. They were to subtly congratulate us on the title charge but remind us that we had indeed lost it on goal difference. He hoped it would bring back the bad memories of the previous week; a small insight into why he became the greatest manager Britain has ever produced. It didn't worry me. I was focused on the game and winning the cup and knowing the team as I did, there were only maybe one or two that it might have affected at worst. The rest were strong-minded and experienced enough to know that we were there with one reason in mind: TO WIN THE CUP.

The game started terribly and we were one down early on from a John Hewitt goal. Roared on by an expectant support, we rallied and Gary Mackay shaved the post. I had a great chance when the ball broke fifteen yards out. I lifted it over Jim Leighton but was a couple of feet too high as it landed on the roof of the net. But we had finished the half clearly on top and that was pointed out by the gaffer as he urged us to start strong, get the next goal and use that momentum to win the match.

However, like the first half, Aberdeen came out and grabbed a second with Hewitt again scoring. We were on the ropes but we never lacked character and we kept battling away as I cracked one a foot wide and Sandy headed a difficult chance over the top before Neil Berry smacked the bar with Leighton beaten all ends up. Then we got hit by a sucker punch as Billy Stark added a third for the Dons and with that goal came the final realisation that the Cup had gone the same way as the title. Our dream and the fans' dream of that long-awaited silverware had been dashed once more.

After a remarkable season that had seen us go thirty-one games without defeat, we had lost to Dundee and Aberdeen in the space of seven days. It was cruel and heart-breaking, but football is a cruel mistress and she had decided that we were not to be the triumphant heroes that year.

The bus journey home was, once again, quiet and no one said anything. It is one of the most horrible journeys in sport when you have lost a cup final and you return to your city, despondent and very, very down. That was the scenario and as we reached the outskirts of the city. A few fans were waiting to cheer us home and we started to understand that the fans were hurting as much as we were. Along Gorgie Road there were even more fans, a few hundred at least, and then double that at Haymarket. As we turned toward the Caledonian Hotel there were at least a couple of thousand fans there roaring us off the bus to show appreciation of our efforts. There were plenty of tears from both groups as we eventually made our way into the hotel and, as the night wore on, both the fans and the players, aided by copious amounts of alcohol, realised that while it was an unbelievable season and we had deserved to win something, the stark reality was that we hadn't. We had missed a glorious opportunity.

Little did we know that it was going to become even harder to achieve in the future and that the Scottish League's landscape was about to change. Graeme Souness's arrival in Glasgow, backed by David Murray's millions, was about to blow Scottish football's wage salaries sky high as he raided England for their top players, aided by the European Football ban, and set Rangers on their way to a decade of dominance. They would also drag Celtic kicking and screaming with them, and even to this day the changes would give all other teams north of the border the impossible task of trying to keep up.

As a steady stream of high profile English players like Butcher, Roberts, Woods, Steven, Stephens, Walters and Hateley started to arrive at Ibrox, it dawned on most of our squad that our title tilt in 1985/86 may have been our best chance to win the title since the 1960s and it was going to be a long time before such a chance was going to present itself again. The Glasgow sides had squared up, flexed their financial muscles and a new era had begun.

One small footnote at the end of the season is that, despite the fact that we had come so close to winning the League and being beaten in the cup final, and had achieved a thirty-one game unbeaten run, not one Hearts player was picked to represent Scotland that season. Very strange.

17

Tynecastle to Tyneside

There was always going to be a hangover from losing out in such cruel circumstances and there was still a feeling of what might have been when we returned for what we knew would be another tough pre-season with the manager and Sandy. Naturally we had a good chat about what had happened, and we still felt we should be challenging for all three trophies. There was a mood of determination to go and win the first major trophy since the 1960s.

Doddie had made a couple of signings in the break, bringing in Wayne Foster on the recommendation of Neil Berry who had played with him at Bolton. We also signed another forward in Allan Moore from Dumbarton. Both had pace to burn (Sandy loved guys with pace), and we had an exciting young talent coming through in the reserves in Scott Crabbe, another striker, so competition for the front places was going to be severe. Having knocked in twenty-five the previous year, I was confident that these lads would have to battle past me. And in Crabbo I had a youngster willing and ready to learn from me – although at twenty-two I wasn't exactly senior!

After the usual annual trips to the Queen's Park, Braid Hills and, of course, the Gullane sand dunes, mixed in with Doddie and Sandy's relentlessly tough running and circuits under the watchful eye of Bert Logan and George McNeill, we were off on an 'overseas' pre-season trip to the Isle of Man where we were in a group consisting of Stoke City, Wigan Athletic and Bohemians, with the winners progressing to the final.

We played well against Stoke in the first match but lacked the cutting edge in front of goal. We were punished for our misses when Shaw scored just before half time to give them the lead, and despite the second half being more of the same with us pushing for an equaliser, it remained elusive and we lost the match.

The training intensity did not drop as we were put through gruelling fitness work the following day. The gaffer made a lot of changes for the next match to make sure everyone was getting game time and there was a sense of déjà vu as the English side scored against the run of play five minutes from the interval. Again we pushed hard to get back on level terms, this time getting a little reward when JC netted a late equaliser, but the draw ultimately put us out of the chance of progressing as Stoke were disposing of Bohemians to set up a decider against Wigan for the group.

That meant a game for us the following evening against Bohemians, and this time we got our reward with a comfortable 3–0 win with JC, Andy Watson and Willie Irvine on target.

Stoke beat Wigan to progress and we ended up second, but with another tough session on the Friday, we were afforded a night out. This was well received but saw an odd end to my evening.

We were in a pub having a few beers and had been given an

11 p.m. curfew as we were travelling the following afternoon. It was about a five-minute walk back to the hotel and, as we were leaving, I opted to nip in quickly to the toilet near the door. As I came out and was running to catch up with the rest of lads so as not to be late – Sandy and Doddie were sticklers for time and a fine was a guarantee if late – I ran straight into some guys on the corner. I apologised but then one guy pulled out a small knife and demanded my money. To be honest I was more surprised than anything else and the fact was I only had about a fiver in my pocket. I hastily handed it over and bolted off toward the hotel, more concerned about the wrath of the managers than what had happened.

I just made it and was told to go with the rest of the team into the bar where the manager had ordered up drinks for everyone. Despite it being a curfew, the gaffer liked everyone back in and socialising together and over the next hour I told them what had happened and it was brushed off as a bit of a laugh. However, unbeknown to me, the hotel manager who had joined us at Doddie's request was mortified and the following morning I was asked to go downstairs to meet a police officer and the head of tourism.

The police officer asked if I recognised the guys or could give a description but that wasn't really much good as it was really over so quickly. No real harm had been done so I was happy to let it go. Then, after he left, the head of tourism guy apologised profusely, to which I said not to worry as I couldn't see it being much of an issue from my side. I wasn't going to be making it public so it shouldn't harm the good reputation of the island. He thanked me for this and handed me an envelope and said it was a small gift from the tourist board.

I said it wasn't needed but he said he wanted me to have it, so I headed back to the room and threw it in my bag. I later discovered it contained a £20 note and an apology on behalf of the tourist board. I'd been mugged but ended up making a profit and I took some stick for that on the way home, I can assure you.

A 2–1 win over Watford completed our build up with early goals from JC and Sandy Clark before Luther Blissett pulled one back for the visitors. So that was us ready to right the wrongs of the previous season and win that elusive silverware.

We started at Paisley, scene of the Saints collapse against Celtic, and the Hearts fans let them know what they thought of the home side's efforts on the last day of the season. This time, the home side were surprisingly resolute as the game battled to a no scoring draw.

Wins over Hamilton and Falkirk saw us close to the top before a quite horrendous performance against Montrose at home saw us emptied out of the League Cup at the first time of asking. The wrath of the management awaited and it didn't lift as we suffered a defeat at Tannadice the following Saturday, losing by a solitary goal.

Thankfully our saviours and neighbours were next to visit us at Tynecastle and goals from Sandy Clark, Ian Jardine and me had us three up and cruising. A late Joe McBride goal for Hibs wasn't enough and another victory was achieved. This sparked us off to five consecutive wins against Hibs, Clydebank, Aberdeen, Motherwell and then Dukla Prague, who we beat in a topsy-turvy first leg at Tynecastle. I found myself on the bench for that game before coming on and netting a late winner to give us a slender advantage.

We had also thrown in a friendly against Manchester United when, on a truly horrible night, nearly 12,000 fans turned up to see a strong United side including Sivebæk, Albiston, Whiteside, McGrath, Hogg, Strachan, Duxbury, Stapleton and Olsen all in starting line-up. Goals from Ian Jardine and Andy Watson had us two goals to the good before a quick-fire double from Jesper Olsen and Terry Gibson saw honours even at the finish. However, we then had a poor run of only one win in the next eight League games and it was clear that we would not be challenging for the title. Once more, the Scottish Cup looked like a fair chance to go all the way and in one-off games we showed we were more than a match for anyone.

It was a busy period and in the October, between the St Mirren and Hamilton games (0–0 and 3–1), I married Tracey.

We had been seeing each other for three years and had got engaged the previous summer. The marriage took place in Slateford on Tuesday 14 October and after taking the following day off, it was back to training on the Thursday – which is what you have to expect in the footballing world.

We were drawn at home to Kilmarnock next and it was to prove a marathon of a tie to get through. It was also part of the reason the SFA finally found the sense to finish matches at the end of a replay.

The first game was a dour match of few chances, played on a brick hard pitch and with players wearing pimpled trainer-type footwear. Neither keeper had much to do in a match that had 0–0 written all over it and was no surprise that we headed to Ayrshire for a replay the following Tuesday evening in a quick change around.

Killie got the lead through a Bryson penalty right on half

time but a Wayne Foster rocket had us level with twenty minutes to go and I had a late chance to win it but didn't quite connect properly and it drifted wide. So it went to extra time with neither side netting again. The match finished level and so a third game was needed the following Monday with a match against Rangers preceding it on the Saturday.

A packed Tynecastle saw us level briefly through a penalty from me but we were 5–1 down before I netted a second spot kick with just five minutes left as fatigue set in. Rangers had started to rebuild their battered reputation from the previous few years, with Chris Woods, Terry Butcher, Roberts and West the early recruits from England that Souness brought in from Liverpool, and a solid array of Scots lads in Robertson, Munro, Fleck, McCoist, Durrant and Cooper. It was not what we needed as we headed back to Ayrshire for a second replay with Killie.

Doddie changed it slightly by going for a 4-3-3 formation with Jimmy Sandison coming in to play centrally, Roddy MacDonald and George Cowie sitting in central midfield alongside Gary Mackay and Kenny Black, and JC and me playing slightly wider, leaving Sandy through the middle.

After weathering an early storm, we took the lead with a neat move involving Blackie and me, and we got it to Sandy who rolled it into the path of 'Cup Tie' (Gary Mackay) and he smashed it home. Then with Kenny Black heading home a JC cross in the first minute of the second half and looking well set for the fourth round, Martin scored a controversial goal for the home side after he headed the ball out of Henry's grasp in the air. Then it was backs-to-the-wall stuff before super-sub Fozzy headed a late third to send us through to a nail-biting tie with Celtic at Tynecastle. Finally, the Hearts fans in the crowd of over 14,000 could go home happy after the second replay, but it had been a marathon to get there.

A crowd just shy of 29,000 were present for the fourth-round tie on a weekend that also saw Scotland take on Ireland just over the road at Murrayfield the same afternoon. Edinburgh was bedecked in green for a sporting weekend to remember.

Alan McInally rattled the bar for Celtic early on before big Roddy MacDonald bulleted a header off Bonner's post. It was a first half of blood and thunder football that finished goalless. I had a decent effort that went inches over before Anton Rogan headed past his own keeper, but the crossbar saved his blushes. As we pushed for the winner, we were roared on by the Shed as they sensed we had the beating of Celtic.

With just seven minutes to go, we got an opportunity as Walter Kidd was crudely chopped down by Celtic great Roy Aitken (no surprise there!) and we got a free kick about twenty-five yards out and at an angle. This is where a little bit of inside information came into play. Henry Smith had been selected for international duty and was third choice keeper for Scotland versus the Republic of Ireland, but the Scottish scouts had noted that Packie Bonner had a tendency to wander further away from the ball and trusted his wall to take care of the near post area. So anyone who fancied their chances might just be able to go for the wall side of the goal.

Sandy Jardine and I were discussing it and I had told him I wanted to shoot but he was in favour of chipping the ball into the middle for Sandy Clark, Roddy MacDonald and Neil Berry to attack; and that he felt Bonner wasn't far enough across to take on the shot. As he said that, and was about to clip the free kick into the middle, I saw Packie take one more step to his right and in a flash decided to overrule him and hit it near post with pace and curl. I struck it well. It clipped Paul McStay on the shoulder which took a little pace off the ball but it then arced past Bonner and into the net. Cue bedlam as I took off to celebrate with the fans, hotly pursued by the rest of the team.

Andy Watson was thrown on for JC to tighten up the midfield as Celtic threw the kitchen sink at us but we held out and the fans were ecstatic to hear the final whistle. We were through, and those in green trooped out to be told over the Tannoy that Ireland had also suffered defeat, the main protagonist being another JR as John Rutherford had scored the vital points to record a famous Scottish victory in the rugby. The following morning, I was asked to meet up with him in the Black Bull pub in the Grassmarket as the *Daily Record* wanted a back page photo with the headline: 'JRs Shoot Down the Greens'.

Another home tie awaited us in the quarter-final in the shape of Motherwell and, with both halves of the Old Firm out, we really felt that we had a great chance of going all the way again. A crowd of 23,000 were in attendance at Tynecastle and all looked good as I headed us in front right on half time, getting on the end of a knockdown from big Roddy. But a mix up between Roddy and Henry let in Paul Smith and he squared for Andy Walker to roll home, which gave the visitors great inspiration as they swarmed forward. We nearly snatched it when Fozzy came off the bench and bulleted a header off the underside of the bar but honours even meant a trip on the Tuesday to Lanarkshire.

We played well in the replay but just couldn't conjure up that little bit of quality in front of goal and the longer the game went on, the more it looked as if it would drift into extra time. However, we got a piece of luck when Blackie overhit a deep cross and Gardiner in the home goal thought it was going out. Instead, it dipped at the last minute and came back off his far post to a lurking JC who gleefully stooped to head home. This sent us to Hampden and a date with St Mirren. It was the sort of narrow margin in football that keeps us right on the edge of our seats, never knowing if it will be a night of triumph or despair.

It was then that fate and Albert Kidd's head reared up again and cost me the opportunity to play in the semi-final. Kidd had joined the Bairns after leaving Dundee after the final game of the previous season. The match itself was pretty nondescript and we looked tired after the midweek replay. It was heading for a goalless draw despite our best efforts to breach a packed home defence. I hit the post just before the break, before a decision that to this day still baffles.

We cleared a long ball out of defence and I came short to get it. As it bounced up, I initially knocked it back towards the midfield and it then became a race for the ball between myself and Albert Kidd. I got there first, knocked it to the side and went after it, and then held him off before knocking it forward and taking off. As I did so, I felt a crude attempt at a tackle from him but kept going. I hit it down the line where another Falkirk defender came across and put it out for a throw.

I took my position for the throw-in and then saw there was a stoppage as Kidd required treatment. I assumed he had hurt himself trying to tackle me and thought no more about it. In fact, I saw that referee O'Donnell had his yellow card out waiting for him to get up from his treatment.

He had a word with Kidd who appeared to be holding his chin and then yellow carded him. Then, to my astonishment, he signalled for me to go and see him. As I did, he said that I had retaliated from Kidd's tackle and he pulled out a red card. I could not believe it and asked again, what had I done? He repeated that I had retaliated after the tackle and, despite my protests, would hear no more. He was immediately surrounded by Hearts players and, to be fair, a couple of the Falkirk lads too. But there was no changing his mind. I was off and sat in the changing room, bewildered, reeling. Worse was to follow as, despite Doddie asking to speak to the referee, the ref would not entertain him and stood by his original decision. It was even more mystifying as all it said in the report was I was sent off for retaliation. No one could understand that as I had won the ball, ridden the tackle and was well away from Kidd when he went down.

Then the bombshell arrived. Due to the topping up system, my previous two seasons' red and yellow cards came into play and with that came a three game suspension. It meant missing two games in the League against Clydebank and then Hibs at home in the derby, and if that wasn't bad enough, the third game was the semi-final against St Mirren.

There was no right of appeal. A Central Belt police officer even contacted the club to say he was on duty at the game and that he could confirm that nothing untoward had taken place, but the SFA were having none of it and I was banned. As footballers, we know that sometimes we need to deal with difficult situations, and that we have to take the consequences for our actions, which is all fine. However, when something feels like a complete injustice it can be hard to take. This was one such occasion. I felt I was harshly treated. I was angry and upset but could do nothing but accept the ban.

We drew at Clydebank and then big Roddy and Sandy Clark scored in a 2–1 win over Hibs to maintain our unbeaten run against them since coming back up.

In the next match against St Mirren, Neil Berry and Brian Whittaker were also missing, through injury, and it was Ian Ferguson who gave the Paisley men the lead after thirty-three minutes. In truth, we didn't look like we could get an equaliser but with fifteen minutes to go, Gary Mackay scored a cracking individual goal and we were level. It started to look like we could grab a winner when Saints broke up the park and Frank McGarvey nipped in and forced the ball home. And with that, St Mirren were in the final and we were left bitterly disappointed once again. It was no consolation that they then went on to beat Dundee Utd and lift the Scottish Cup. As Ian Ferguson cracked in an extra time winner in the final against a lacklustre United side, I couldn't help thinking it was another chance missed.

We finished in fifth place in the League that year after winning twenty-one and losing only nine of the forty-four games in the extended Premier League, but it was the fourteen draws that cost us the opportunity of putting pressure on those above. On a personal note, I finished with twenty goals for the season which was a little bit disappointing. It was the minimum that the manager wanted and expected.

If that was a sore semi-final loss to take, the following season saw even worse as we somehow snatched defeat from the jaws of victory in a game that ultimately would be my last for Hearts for some time.

We finished off the season with a nine-day tour of America with games against San Diego, San Jose and California Kickers, before a pitched battle against Seattle Storm that was stopped several times due to fighting. The home team wanted to take advantage of a very biased local referee with some strong challenges. At first we resisted the temptation to react, before Doddie had enough and told us to 'look after ourselves' as it was clear the referee wasn't going to.

The match finished 1–1 with all twenty-two men staying on the pitch, which was incredible given what was going on in the last twenty minutes.

Dave McPherson and Hugh Burns were added to the squad for the new season as the gaffer raided his old side. We paid big money for Dave, and later in the season Mike Galloway would join from Halifax and winger Mark Gavin from Leeds Utd as we set about trying to close the gap at the top from the season before.

Germany was the chosen country for our pre-season trip and ten days were spent in roasting hot conditions as we set about getting match fit. Five games were played as we readied ourselves for the campaign ahead, the second last one being a throwback to school days for the west of Scotland lads and a new experience for the east lads as it was played on a blaise (red ash) pitch. To say the gaffer was furious when we rocked up was an understatement but we battled to a 1–1 draw with no injuries but plenty of 'scrapes'.

Our first game of the new season was at home and saw us off to a flier, with JC netting inside thirty seconds against Falkirk. And when Sandy scored just nine minutes later, it looked as though we could score a barrowload, but missed chances and some incredible goalkeeping from Gordon Marshall kept us at bay before I netted on seventy minutes. We then switched off as two goals in as many minutes from Burgess and Baptie got

Falkirk right back into it before I scored again with ten minutes to go to secure the points.

We travelled to Celtic on the Wednesday evening and looked like we were going to come away with a well-earned point when referee Kevin O'Donnell (the ref who sent me off at Falkirk) ignored a clear foul by Mark McGhee on big Dave and allowed him to go on and slot past Big Henry. Doddie was furious but once more the referee was oblivious as he made for the dressing-room at the end of the game, hotly pursued by our gaffer.

A 1–1 draw at Paisley, in which I scored a penalty, saw the first tranche of games completed before we faced Killie at home in the League Cup first round.

The penalty goal was significant as during pre-season Ian Jardine had asked me why I didn't take them? As striker, he felt I should be taking more responsibility rather than let Gary Mackay take them. He pointed out that by taking them it could easily add another half-dozen goals onto my total, reminding me that if I had genuine Scotland ambitions then I needed to up my tally. Given that I was up against an impressive array of strikers in the national set up, he had a point.

We battered Kilmarnock 6–1 which, given the marathon cup ties the previous year, was impressive to everyone but yours truly! While everyone was celebrating, the gaffer stopped and asked why I was rather quiet? The answer was simple, I said – I hadn't scored. We had scored six and I hadn't got one of them. I was raging with myself – how could we possibly score six and I hadn't got one? Jesus, even Big Chuck got one!

The gaffer just burst out laughing and patted me on the head and muttered, 'Well, you'll just have to make up for it another time,' then wandered off. I was left brooding in the corner, analysing the chances I had missed and still boiling mad with myself.

I suppose that's what made me the striker I was. I hated not scoring. My life and my career were about scoring goals. And here I was, none from six. I vowed that wouldn't happen again.

Another penalty against Dundee Utd in a 4–1 win set me off on a six-game scoring streak that saw me score the only goal against Hibs, after a cut back from JC fell to me, and a double against Clyde got us into the quarter-finals of the League Cup and a trip to Ibrox to play Rangers.

Rangers had continued to build but hadn't strengthened as much as people had thought they might, given their title win the previous year. But they were still a formidable side and had now signed Ian Ferguson from cup winners St Mirren, as well as Avi Cohen, the Israeli international.

They were sensational in the opening forty-five minutes and blew us away, racing into a three-goal lead with two from Durrant and one from McCoist. Frankly, we could have been further behind had it not been for the defence and Big H.

I got one back early in the second half and we had a few chances to get right back in it as both Kenny Black and myself hit the woodwork. We also forced Chris Woods into a few fine saves before McCoist got his second at the death and it finished 4–1.

Once more, a competition that we felt we had a genuine chance of winning had gone, and our record in the League Cup was poor considering we had reached the semi-finals back-to-back in 1982 and '83.

But then nine wins and one draw from ten games saw us go top of the League. This run, along with our unbeaten streak of wins against them since being promoted, was brought to an end by Hibs. Eddie May scored early before I replied, only for Paul Kane to head what would be the winner just before half time. Despite our best efforts shooting down the slope, we just couldn't get the all-important equaliser.

We bounced back, winning five and drawing three of our next eight matches before we returned to Ibrox, where, despite battling back twice from behind, a late Durrant goal gave Rangers a rather fortunate victory – to say the least.

Off the pitch, I had happy news as my first boy Marc was born late on the Thursday evening before I scored in a 2–2 draw at Parkhead. We led 2–0, only for Celtic to snatch an undeserved point with two late goals from Andy Walker and Paul McStay.

Back on the pitch, we had beaten Falkirk the previous Saturday and that win sparked another long unbeaten run, but this was to cost us as the draw with Celtic was the first of five draws in a row, before we thumped Dunfermline 4–0 at East End Park. My double there was my first since the Celtic game and we then won two and drew three of the next five before losing 2–0 at Brockville to Falkirk. Seven more wins and two more draws would follow this as we maintained our challenge at the top of the table. We produced yet another good unbeaten run, but we simply could not close the gap to Celtic who celebrated the title in their centenary year.

Victory over the champions with goals from Mike Galloway and Gary Mackay came too late and we had goalless draws with Aberdeen and Dundee Utd then a 1–0 loss to St Mirren as we closed the season as runners-up to Celtic for the second time in three seasons. This time, however, the Hoops had won by a convincing ten points.

In forty-four League games we had lost just five, but once more the sixteen draws had killed us. There was some consolation in the fact that we had finished ahead of Rangers, Aberdeen and Dundee Utd and secured European football once more. For me, having taken Ian Jardine's advice on the penalty situation, I had recorded a personal best of thirty-one goals despite not playing the last five games of the season, something we'll get to shortly.

Our Scottish Cup campaign sent us to the tricky Brockville Park and a meeting with Falkirk, who treated these games as a derby of sorts with Edinburgh being the closest city to them. They always seemed to produce a raised performance when we visited and this game would be no exception.

Nearly 16,000 packed into Brockville and it was a great atmosphere for a real cup tie. We went behind when Stuart Romaines headed the home side in front but with JC, Fozzy and myself being a real handful, I got us an equaliser right on half time before firing us ahead early in the second half. Fozzy slotted in for a third that would see us through to round four after a rousing and bruising cup match.

Round four saw goals from Sandy and Gary Mackay see us win comfortably against Morton at Tynecastle and it was a similar story in round five as we disposed of Dunfermline at home where, despite my best efforts, I could not get past Segers in the Pars goal. Then, when I finally did, on three occasions the woodwork thwarted me. However, JC, Fozzy and Mackay goals saw us progress in front of another great crowd of 22,000 and we headed to Hampden for a date with champions Celtic in a game that was to prove every bit as painful as losing the League title to them two seasons earlier.

The game saw 67,000 in Hampden and the first half was a

dour affair with Mike Galloway and Andy Walker having tame efforts on goal before the first controversial moment arrived. I was tripped by Anton Rogan just inside the box, but to my, and the Hearts fans', chagrin, it was denied by Kenny Hope who claimed it was an accidental coming together.

Celtic started the second half better, Big H had a couple of good saves and Blackie hooked one off the line before we took the lead on the hour. Celtic cleared a corner out to about twenty-five yards and as they rushed out, Brian Whittaker lobbed the ball back into the penalty area which allowed big Slim (Dave McPherson) to go and challenge for the ball in the air. As Slim went for it, Packie Bonner seemed to be more concerned with him than the ball and it sailed over him. He and Dave then ended up in the net as they clattered into each other. Everyone looked at referee Hope, he looked at his linesman and as the flag stayed down, he signalled a goal. Cue bedlam from the Celtic players and their keeper. It may well have been a foul, but the ref had given the goal.

Celtic were raging and they threw everything at us in the last half-hour, with Big H producing save after save and the defenders block after block. It looked like we were going to hold on and reach the final and a date with Dundee Utd. Then in the eighty-ninth minute Celtic got a corner and threw everyone forward. It was lofted in by Tommy Burns and Big H, who had caught everything, came for it and caught it cleanly above the heads of Roy Aitken, big Dave and Brian Whittaker. However, on his way down, the ball hit the top of Dave's head, spun out and dropped to the floor at the feet of Mark McGhee. He turned and slashed it goal-wards. Had he caught it properly, I'm sure one of our defenders would have blocked it as they dived in to defend. However, it went through one set of legs, just past another and somehow it found the bottom corner despite our efforts. Celtic were level.

We couldn't believe it. A final ripped from our grasp and a replay the following Wednesday evening was now on the cards – or so we thought. Then, just past the ninety-minute mark, Celtic forced a throw-in and it led to a deep cross thrown to the back post. Big H again rose and caught the ball, then was clattered into by Mark McGhee. It was a clear foul on him and as the ball dropped, it was lashed into the net by Andy Walker.

This time it was us who were going berserk as, incredibly, referee Hope once again awarded the goal. Whether he felt he had got our one wrong was neither here nor there. In our eyes this was a clear foul but the goal stood and we were out. Having been two minutes from another final, yet another chance of silverware had escaped our grasp.

Unbeknown to me, that was the last time I would pull on a maroon jersey for some time. Come January I had been scoring freely and Bill McMurdo had begun talking to Doddie and Sandy about a new deal. While Doddie was keen, Sandy, it seemed, was a bit cooler in the initial stages but not to the extent that I didn't feel a deal wouldn't be agreed. As was the norm at the time, it was taken over by Wallace Mercer as this was the game the great Waldo liked to play, the cut and thrust of getting the best possible deal possible whilst playing up to the media and the fans. Previously it had been the usual routine – he would make an offer that was on the low side and we would come in with a counter at a higher level. Then the joust between him and Bill would take place as Doddie, Sandy and I waited to see which one of them got the better of the other before the deal was signed.

On the pitch I was getting frustrated as, despite the fact I was scoring regularly and was currently sitting on twenty-nine goals, I kept being substituted off in games. I found this strange. I was playing well, obviously scoring but Sandy kept dropping small remarks about my fitness or sharpness which I didn't take too much notice of. We were winning, challenging at the top and going deep in the Cup, but as February turned to March, Bill told me that Wallace was being very elusive and that he couldn't tie him down to a meeting to discuss a new deal.

I wasn't that bothered as I had seen this before, and I had already told Bill that I was happy to stay at Hearts. This was still the first question he always asked, so he was preparing to negotiate with Hearts and Hearts alone.

Eventually I went to see Doddie and Sandy and asked what was going on. They said it was in the hands of the chairman, so Bill and I headed for the meeting at Wallace's office. Earlier in the season, Gary Mackay had made his international debut, coming on and scoring against Bulgaria with a goal that famously sent the Republic of Ireland to their first ever finals and made Gary an instant hero on the Emerald Isle. It was the first cap earned by a Hearts player since Donald Ford, and there was more good news as John Colquhoun and Henry Smith joined him in the February.

The fact that Gary was to get only get three caps, JC two and Henry only one is shocking for such talented players and bore similarities to the Terrible Trio of Jimmy Wardhaugh, Willie Bauld and Alfie Conn Snr, who also only gathered the same total – an absolute travesty in my humble opinion.

This international status earned all three of my colleagues new, improved contracts as the club rewarded them for their calls ups, and with big Dave joining in the summer, it was no surprise that the basic wage for these players had risen over the rest of the squad. They were all earning between £100 and £150 a week more than the rest of us.

At this stage my basic salary was around £450 a week and I was hoping that, thanks to scoring over twenty-five goals at that stage, I could be up there with these guys as I felt I was an important part of the team. I may not have been deemed good enough for Scotland, but I was still a valuable asset to the club going forward.

Wallace was at his imperious best, telling his receptionist to get us a cup of tea in reception while he finished off some business and we laughed as we waited fifteen or twenty minutes for him to finally grant us an audience in his office. When we finally sat down, he produced a leather folder and said that in it was the best contract any Hearts player had ever been offered, and that he was looking forward to me continuing to play for Hearts. Bill calmly asked if he would like to tell us the offer or would he like to speak privately to him while I left, as I generally never got involved with these meetings. Wallace, however, said he was happy for me to stay.

Wallace did his usual great speech but twenty minutes later he was still no closer to revealing what he was offering. Then, eventually, he asked, 'What are you guys after to get this done?'

Bill and I looked at each other and said we were waiting on the offer Hearts were proposing (the one in the leather folder) but he said before that he wanted to know the ballpark figure we wanted before revealing his offer.

We had already decided that our high ball was going to be £750 a week with £15,000 signing-on fee; but I would settle at around £600 and an £8,000 to £10,000 signing-on fee plus the usual appearance and team bonuses, a bonus if I scored more than thirty competitive goals and another if I was 'lucky enough' to get picked for the international team.

Wallace looked at us and blew his top. 'I have international players in this team who are not on that so there is no way we can look at that type of salary here!'

Bill remained calm and said, 'No problem, let's hear what you are proposing and we can discuss it from there.'

To our astonishment, Wallace said, 'No, these discussions are over. We will not be offering anything and if a club meets our valuation then John goes.'

Bill said once more, 'Don't be silly, Wallace. John wants to stay so let's hear your offer and see what we can do to come to an acceptable agreement as we have not heard your offer yet.'

Wallace said no and then said, 'Sorry, Bill, we won't be doing a deal so we will await offers for John. Despite not being able to do a deal, I want to let you know that both of you are welcome at Tynecastle anytime in the future as we appreciate your efforts and John has done everything we could have asked of him.'

At that, he stood up and said he was going to organise a taxi for us back to our cars at the stadium.

I was stunned. Bill just said, 'No problem, Wallace, that would be great.'

Wallace left the room and Bill walked over to the desk, picked up the leather folder and opened it. It was empty, nothing in it at all. There was no offer, never mind the best contract ever being offered to any Hearts player.

Before I left, Wallace thanked us for our time and said that it was important that I continued to finish the season strongly.

In the taxi, Bill said he assumed they must have had an offer for me and had decided to sell. As this was pre-Bosman, I could only leave the club if a fee was agreed, and if it wasn't, then Hearts retained my registration and I couldn't go anywhere. I could sign for a team without a fee being agreed but that would mean a tribunal and buying teams didn't fancy that as they often got a raw outcome.

The following day we saw the other side of Wallace in the press as he claimed we had asked for £1,000 a week and £100,000 signing-on fee, that it was preposterous and that Bill McMurdo was no longer welcome at Tynecastle. At the same time he was phoning Bill saying, 'Look, you know I have to play the game to the fans. We are going to lose John, and I have to make it his or your fault.'

My response was to score my thirtieth goal of the campaign but I was still starting and then being subbed. After our Scottish cup semi-final defeat, I was pulled into the office and told by Sandy Jardine that the club had received an enquiry and they were now allowing me to talk to other teams. As a result, I would not be in the squad for the following two matches at home to Dunfermline and Celtic.

Doddie wasn't there – he told me later that he hadn't wanted to be – but it was clear that Hearts were selling me – but to who?

That answer came soon. Bill got the call that the club had agreed terms with Newcastle for £625,000. We met with the manager Willie McFaul, the chairman and another director of Newcastle at his farmhouse in the Borders, and talked over the move. The terms were never going to be a problem as they offered three times my current Hearts salary and double the signing-on fee. We shook hands on a three-year deal and that was that – it was Tynecastle to Tyneside.

We then drove to the hotel that Newcastle had arranged for us for the evening. While we were having a bite to eat, a staff member approached the table with a phone call. When Bill came back, he said, 'Sorry, but that was Ajax on the phone wanting to buy John, but I told them the deal had been agreed and they were too late.'

I have always thought back to what might have happened if that call had come ten minutes earlier.

18

Black, White and Gold

The move to Newcastle was immediate, there were no transfer windows in those days, but I had signed after the cut-off date of 31 March and that meant I could not play in the remaining games unless the opposition gave their permission. With Newcastle safe in the top six, their remaining five games were all against teams at the foot of the table so there was little chance of getting my debut before the end of the season, although I did play in a couple of friendly matches and a couple of testimonials. One of these games was at Leeds to honour Don Revie, and Paul Gascoigne and I were dispatched to take part in the select side that included the likes of Chris Woods, Phil Neal, Graeme Souness, Kevin Keegan, Peter Shilton, Billy Bremner, Jack Charlton and Norman Hunter. It was a terrific night in aid of Motor Neurone Disease, which Don Revie was suffering from.

It was my first glimpse of Gazza and he did not disappoint, with some outrageous skills and even showboating, despite Keegan and Souness taking it deadly seriously. Gazza was still wanting to entertain and scored an outrageous backheel goal during the game.

Afterwards at a reception, Graeme Souness revealed that Rangers had submitted a £500,000 offer for me, but Wallace had turned it down and told them they would not get me for a million pounds because he would not sell me to another Scottish club, something the great Waldo had kept to himself.

There was one bonus to finish, though, as despite not making my debut, there was a club end-of-season tour to the Caribbean where we were to play Bermudan Trinidadian and Jamaican national teams. I turned up at the airport in a collar and tie, as requested by captain Kenny Wharton, only to see the rest of the squad in club tracksuits. Yep, they got the new guy like a kipper!

Manager Willie McFaul just smiled and, once I'd changed, asked if Hearts always travelled in collar and tie. I said yes, that was the way, to which he replied, 'Blimey, you will be telling me next you weren't allowed to drink on the plane either,' as he laughed and opened a can of beer!

The trip was great for me as I got to really know the players and, with a couple I already knew from watching TV – Gazza, David McCreery, Glenn Roeder – it was good to get to grips with the rest of the squad. I obviously knew Darren Jackson from Edinburgh and quickly got to know his best mate down there, Michael O'Neill, who was breaking through into the team. So, all in all, it was a great trip to finish off a season where I had notched thirty-one goals and I was feeling good about the season ahead.

It may have been a sign of things to come, but as I left Edinburgh at 6.30 a.m. to head down to prepare for pre-season, I was involved in a car accident. I was waiting at traffic lights on the one-way system in operation at the time as they were making an overtaking lane on the Soutra Hill south of Edinburgh and, as it changed to green, I set off. After a few hundred yards, I came round the corner only to see a car flying towards me, having obviously jumped the lights at the other end thinking no one would be on the road at that time of the morning. As his side of the road was dug up, I had to swerve off and as I went round the corner on the embankment there were three large diggers parked up and I couldn't stop before banging into the first one.

I wasn't going that fast but the force smacked the front of my Vauxhall Cavalier in and I bounced off it. I got out and looked around but the other car had kept going and wasn't for stopping as it made off into the distance. At first I thought I would be fine as the car didn't look as bad as I thought. I got it into reverse and then first gear but when I tried to put it into second, there was a loud crunching noise and the car started to shudder. I had no option but to walk to the base of Soutra Hill and knock on the door of a farmhouse. The farmer was kind enough to let me phone the club and the manager came and got me. His panic was tempered when he saw I was all right and no damage done.

Pre-season at Newcastle wasn't as hard as the torturous regime of Doddie and Sandy but there was still plenty of running and lots of heavy weight circuits, which was new to me but something of a staple in the English game. Despite not being a lover of pre-season, I got through it and was ready for the ball work and the matches.

United had added to the squad and my record signing tag didn't last long as John Hendrie from Leeds was signed along-side two of the crazy gang, Dave Beasant and Andy Thorn from Wimbledon, who had shocked everyone by beating Liverpool in the FA Cup Final that year at Wembley with a Lawrie Sanchez winner. With a strong base of players like Glenn Roeder, John

Anderson, Kenny Wharton, Dave McCreery and Liam O'Brien, the team was packed with experience, and with youngsters like Jackson, O'Neill, Ian Bogie and Kevin Scott breaking through, it looked like we had a well-balanced squad going forward.

We had lost the mercurial Gazza to a British record fee at the time of £2.2 million, a pittance when you consider his talent, but it wowed everyone in 1988. It also meant that the onus was on another character to step forward in the shape of Brazilian cult hero Mirandinha who had arrived on Tyneside the year before and had scored twelve goals. The Toon Army had taken him to their hearts and adored him.

Pre-season saw us off to Sweden and I scored a couple in the first game, an 8–0 victory over an amateur side, and with another against a lower league side a few days later, I felt my sharpness and link up play was coming along nicely. I was left out of the third game before scoring again in the last match before we headed back to England and a trip to Peterborough where I started up front with Mirandinha for the first time. It went well, with me setting up three of his four goals as well as getting one myself late on in a 6–0 win. Then, despite going down 2–0 at Dundee, I felt sharp and ready to go.

Our first match was a new tournament and was for the top eight teams in the League from the previous year. We were drawn at home to Wimbledon, a real grudge game as we had signed Dave and Andy from them, but despite having lost other players due to their success, they were still a formidable and very physical side. What followed was the most bruising ninety minutes I have ever been involved in and it finished 0–0 at full time. The Newcastle fans loved it as we gave as good as we got, something they like to see alongside good football.

I assumed we were going straight to penalties as I thought there was no extra time but that wasn't the case. I managed to wriggle away from Eric Young, squared it to Michael O'Neill and he did the rest. That goal was enough to take us through to the semi-finals and Manchester Utd at Old Trafford later that month, although we lost there 1–0 after extra time.

Everton away was the first game of the season and I was amazed as 6,000 Newcastle fans made the trip, every single one wearing the famous black and white stripes. We got off to the worst possible start as debutant Tony Cottee, a £1.5 million signing from West Ham, scored inside the first minute and, despite forcing good saves from Neville Southall twice, I watched as Graeme Sharp scored just before the interval to put them two up.

We rallied in the second half and Mira and Michael went close before Cottee put us to the sword and completed his hat-trick – it ended with a 4–0 thumping from the Blues.

It was a solemn trip home and a sharp introduction to how tough the season was going to be. Our next game was against Tottenham, with new signing Gazza arriving with full pomp, and the Toon Army made it clear they wanted a victory over their former talisman.

Willie McFaul and his assistant John Pickford had hammered into us all week that, despite the talent at their disposal, Spurs were looked upon as Southern softies at the time and we had to be right at it from the off. And we were told we could forget about Gazza and his antics as he would get caught up with the crowd and would not be as effective as normal.

Darren Jackson and I started up front with Mira injured, and John Hendrie and Michael O'Neill were to come in from wide areas. We flew out the traps, with Darren opening the scoring after I had whipped in a free kick. Andy Thorn headed another and we were two up inside the first fifteen minutes, swarming all over them. We had another three or four chances to extend our lead before the break but couldn't add to our tally.

Again the gaffer told us at half time to keep at them, another goal from us and they would be gone. He had been spot on about Gazza: from the first few minutes when he went to take a corner and was met with a hail of Mars bars, Marathons and so on thrown from the Toon fans. He tried to make light of it by eating one and sticking another down his sock, but he'd had no impact on the game.

We started the second half on the front foot and had Spurs on the rack, but in a rare break they pulled a goal back through Terry Fenwick. It rocked us, but roared on by the home fans in the 33,500 crowd, we went for the killer goal, only to be pegged back level by a late solo goal from Chris Waddle. The match finished in a draw and a stolen point for the visitors.

I had moved into a house in Morpeth where Darren Jackson also lived and Dave McCreery in nearby Hepscott, so I was settling in well enough. Despite the first few games not quite going to plan results-wise, I had played okay in those matches. But we lost the next two League games 2–0 away to Derby and at home to Norwich before a fighting 2–2 draw at Charlton. Then we got hammered 3–0 away at Sheffield United in the first leg of the League Cup and found ourselves second to bottom of the League.

I had been unlucky not to get my first goal after hitting the woodwork twice against Norwich and had a few chances against Sheffield Utd, but I was now goalless in seven games.

It was a huge disappointment but no real surprise when I was on the bench for a game that I had dreamed about all my life. It was the day before my twenty-fourth birthday and the game was Liverpool at Anfield.

Having been a Reds fan all my life and worshipped the likes of Keegan, Toshack, Heighway, Souness, Dalglish and the rest, here I was dropped and watching from the sidelines. We found ourselves a goal down after just twenty-eight seconds to a team that had a reputation for hammering the opposition at their fortress-like home, but fortunately on this occasion John Hendrie had us level after seven minutes. With us shooting towards the Kop second half, I felt fate was going to play its hand and that I would get on and score the winner at the Kop end.

As the game entered the last ten minutes my chance arrived. I was summoned to get stripped and be ready to go on. As we waited for the ball to go out, we broke forward and John Hendrie was brought to the ground for a penalty to us.

The manager looked at me and asked, 'Are you the penalty taker?'

'Yes,' I said, 'and don't worry, get me on and I will take it and score.'

He looked at me, paused and looked at the bench.

I said, 'Don't worry, Gaffer, put me on and I'll score.'

Again, he looked and then said, 'No, I can't put you under that pressure,' so we waited and Mira chipped it down the middle and we were ahead. Then I was on and late in the game I hit the post on the break. It stayed out but we won and had beaten the current champions. They would win it again that season, but our 2–1 victory that day moved us up a couple of positions before being brought back to earth with a chastening 3–0 home defeat to Coventry City. Once more I started on the bench, then came on and injured myself in a tackle with David Speedie that saw him helped off, much to the delight of the St James' Park faithful who he'd taunted all afternoon.

My injury wasn't serious but I felt I had maybe strained something in my lower stomach muscle area and high up on my groin. I was fine to train but could feel a little bit of discomfort and was on the bench again for the matches at West Ham (0–2) and the 2–0 win over Sheffield Utd that saw us go out of the Cup 3–2 on aggregate. I then came on and set up the third goal and nearly scored a couple as we beat Middlesbrough 3–0 in the north-east derby, and I came on against Forest in a 0–1 defeat at home. Despite starting the next two games, at QPR 0–3 and Arsenal 0–1, I was dropped completely for the match at Millwall and sat in the stands as we lost 4–0 to a rampant home side that included Sheringham and Cascarino up front.

The Forest game had seen the end of Willie McFaul and I felt I had l let him down as I hadn't scored. That, after all, is what I was brought in to do. Willie was replaced by Jim Smith – the Bald Eagle as he was known – and it was pretty clear he wanted changes. Everyone was for sale; he wanted to rebuild his squad. He had spoken to me and said the board were allowing him to spend whatever he brought in from selling players, and that while he was keen to keep me, he needed money.

My injury had been diagnosed as a hernia. It didn't need operating on right away, however, and could be managed until the end of the season.

The word was put out that Newcastle would be accepting offers and within a couple of weeks Sheffield Wednesday and

Coventry had put in offers of £500,000, alongside Rangers, but the club had dismissed these as Dundee Utd and Hibs had offered £600,000. I told the manager that I couldn't see myself going to Hibs and that if I was returning to Scotland it would have to be Rangers or United. He said the board were looking at United's bid as it was close to their valuation. I asked if Hearts had been in touch, but he said no, although he was expecting a raft of clubs at our reserve game against Liverpool on the Tuesday evening.

I played and scored twice, alongside a young schoolboy player Lee Clark who also scored twice in a 4–4 draw, and the following day the manager called me in to say there had been plenty interest in me, that Hearts had matched the £600,000 offer but Dundee Utd had now upped theirs to £700,000 meaning that was still the board's preferred route.

I said that if the teams interested were wanting to sign me then I would prefer to go back to Hearts, but he told me that would not be happening unless they matched United's offer. It was now a waiting game, with my future hanging in the balance.

Hearts were doing great in the UEFA Cup and were travelling to Velež Mostar the following week with a healthy 3–0 lead. So it looked like there was going to be a wait if it was going to be them and, in fairness, Jim McLean was pushing for an answer as United were keen to get me.

I then got a call from Bill McMurdo who said Wallace had been on the phone and was trying to broker a deal to take me back. The night Hearts were playing the second leg, I was informed by Jim Smith that the club had agreed terms with Hearts at £750,000 and that I was free to travel to discuss terms. I drove north and met with Bill and Wallace at the Sheraton, where he told me he had brokered a deal for a local businessman, Ramez Daher, to pay part of my wages. The deal was only marginally better than the money I had previously been on at Hearts but getting a sponsor to help was a real coup for Wallace. By this stage I just wanted to get back and return to a place I knew well and had been successful. Mentally I was feeling pretty down with things not working out how I'd hoped. It had been a great experience at Newcastle and I loved my time down there but I knew I now had to draw a line under it and rebuild my career.

The deal was wrapped up pretty quickly and announced just after Hearts had qualified with a draw in Mostar to reach the quarter-finals of the UEFA cup. There was no time to rest on my laurels as I returned to Newcastle to pick up my boots and say my goodbyes. I was told by Doddie and Sandy, who had travelled to see me at the Liverpool game, that I was starting against Rangers at home on Saturday.

The game was a blur, to be honest, as 27,000 packed in. The reception was tremendous and to cap it all off, goals from Mike Galloway and my replacement on the day, Iain Ferguson, gave us a 2–0 win. I was back; we had won, but that pain in my stomach was still there and would definitely need sorting. I got my first two goals since returning against Celtic away but we went down 4–2. Never great to lose but I was back where I wanted to be and back on the scoresheet.

The hernia was playing up and holding me back so I was nothing more than a bit-part player for the next spell. Fergie had been playing well in any case and he topped off a good season with a rocket of a free kick against Bayern Munich that gave us a famous win. We were unfortunate to go out as JC twice hit the post and I had a header cleared off the line late in the game.

In the end, we failed to get the away goal that would have taken us through to play Napoli and the mighty Diego Maradona.

There was one bright spot as I got the winner in my first game back against Hibs in the derby at Tynecastle, and it was significant as it set us up on a record-breaking run of results that would see us go an incredible twenty-two matches before tasting defeat to our bitter rivals. It was a strange goal as I thought I was on the end of a great cross from Tosh McKinlay, who had joined at the start of the season. But I completely missed my header – I lost the ball in the sun, honest – but it rebounded off Alan Sneddon and I smashed it in for the victory.

A few weeks earlier I became the recipient of an unwanted record as I became the first player in Scotland to be punished in trial by TV. We had played Celtic in the Cup and I was on the bench to witness an extraordinary first half that saw us a goal down to a Mark McGhee finish. He should already have seen red for a challenge that saw Craig Levein having to be subbed off. Then after thirty-five minutes, McGhee stumbled in the box with no contact, only for referee David Syme to award a penalty. Dave MacPherson was yellow-carded and Alan McLaren red-carded. Roy Aitken scored and we were two down and a man down.

Mayhem broke out two minutes later as Tosh McKinlay went over the top on a challenge with Chris Morris and, in the melee that followed, punched Mick McCarthy who had to be held back by Watty Kidd.

Tosh asked the ref to deal with Mick first – he knew what was coming. He bolted up the tunnel as quickly as he could and locked himself in the dressing room and pushed the physio table up against the door. An astonished Alan McLaren asked what he was doing. Tosher told him what happened and said he expected Mick McCarthy to burst the door down, to which Al said, 'You're on your own!' and headed for the bath. Legend has it that only the locked door and some robust intervention from the stewards stopped Mick getting into the dressing room.

With twenty minutes to go and still 2–0 down, Doddie told me to go on and make something happen. We needed a spark to get us going and nick a goal back. So on I went and, within a minute, I was involved with a challenge on Tommy Burns. I won the ball off him and we ended up tussling. I passed the ball, Tommy grabbed me and wheeled me round and for some crazy reason, as I broke away, I lashed out, catching him straight on the chin!

I don't know who was more surprised, him or me, but the game raged on and referee Syme hadn't seen it so no action was taken. Within a minute, a clearly upset Roy Aitken took Tommy's retribution into his own hands as he brought me down for a free kick which Eamonn Bannon smashed in. We were back in the game. We poured everything forward and had a couple of chances to snatch a draw but we went out 2–1.

The following day I was in Uddingston picking up boots and clothing from my sponsors Puma at Bill's house, and I asked if he had Tommy Burns' number. I felt terrible as I hadn't seen him after the game to apologise. I phoned Tommy to say sorry. He was very good about it and said he had done a similar thing against Gordon Strachan and that he was delighted I had been man enough to apologise. And that, we thought, was that.

Scotsport, however, decided differently and they showed it three or four times in the match coverage then again in the analysis, this time with a big circle round it and a close-up. The outraged presenters were demanding that I face punishment. The SFA agreed and I was given a two-game ban for aggressive behaviour, making me the first to be punished in this way.

To say I was delighted when the season ended is an understatement. I had come back from a move to England and finished the season with only four goals. Surely this was as bad as it could get?

People have often asked if I enjoyed my short spell in England, and the honest answer is that I did. I loved my time down there. It was so refreshing, even for a short time, to come up against different opposition and see different stadiums. One thing that was great was that you only played the opposition home and away once each season, something that I had never experienced in Scotland.

Yes, as I had watched from the stands, Newcastle's last four or five games were meaningless in that they were not challenging for the title and were nowhere near the relegation zone, but they played a few younger lads and the crowds turned up in force. They never accepted that the Toon played any meaningless games and their thirst for victory was and remains the same. They want to win every match home and away, they absolutely adore their team and being a one club city, it's surely just waiting for the day that they bring home a major prize. They have been starved of silverware for so long that when that day happens it's going to be the biggest party the city has ever seen.

The Newcastle fans were great with me. They know their football and could see I was trying my best and giving them everything I had. It just wasn't happening in front of goal and my confidence dropped. I sometimes wonder how different things might have been had I got a few goals and some form going, but in the end, I started seven and was a sub coming on in seven more. It just didn't work out.

The defenders were bigger, stronger and quicker at Newcastle. While I had the extra bonus of playing up front with a bigger striker in Jimmy Bone and Sandy Clark with Hearts, at Newcastle it was Mira, John Hendrie and me, with Darren Jackson being the biggest at around five-foot-eleven – until Jim Smith brought in Rob McDonald just before I left. But in all honesty, who knows if that would have helped. I had tried it but it hadn't worked out. I have absolutely no regrets apart from letting the fans down as they deserved better.

That summer, I was sent for a hernia operation that would see me miss most of the pre-season work which normally any player under the Doddie/Sandy regime might have been happy about, but I enjoyed the punishing schedule even though I was not the greatest at the long running. When you completed the final day on the Gullane sands, you certainly felt ready for anything.

I had to do my own gentle build up as I recovered from the operation, and although I was at all the sessions and monitored by physio Alan Rae as he built up my rehab programme, the six weeks of no activity and then the pre-season work on my own meant I did not start a competitive match until mid-September at Motherwell. In my absence, Doddie had signed Husref Musemić from the then Yugoslavia as a striker to lead the line, joining Wayne Foster and the emerging talents of Scott Crabbe and Ian Ferguson. There was plenty of competition for places up front. And with these guys in pole position, I had a point to prove after my injury-riddled but nevertheless poor previous season.

So I travelled and watched as the lads did their pre-season

up north with all the strikers getting amongst the goals as they rattled in twelve past Nairn, Inverness Caledonian and Peterhead, which made my impatience to be back all the greater.

Celtic were first up at Tynecastle and I was in the stand as we went down 3–1, with Tommy Coyne being the main man for the visitors, but we bounced back with a couple of wins in both the League – a win over Hibs with big Husref scoring the only goal – and the League Cup, led superbly up front by my apprentice and now blossoming striker Crabbo.

Crabbo was steeped in HMFC, a supporter who was now living the dream and we worked well in training as we were of similar physique and style of play. He was an eager pupil and wanted to learn everything, and he did just that over the months to come. We would sit and talk about various ways to play and worked together in training on different aspects like holding the ball up, little round-the-corner plays, stepovers and spins for return passes as well as the art of putting the ball in the back of the net – and he did not lack talent in that direction. His technique was second to none and he scored some spectacular goals, added to which he was deadly from set pieces. I was always on at him about the bread-and-butter goals inside the six-yard box, but he could find the net, that was for sure. I used to say to him I would teach him ninety per cent of what I knew but he would pester me for the extra ten per cent. Even when he left Hearts he would ask whenever we bumped into each other. I would just smile and simply say, 'No, I can't. If I do that, you'll take my place, so the ten per cent has to remain a secret.'

In all honesty, I did teach him everything I knew but I had to make him think there was more to learn so that he thought I would always have an edge on him. The reality was he had nothing more to learn other than experience from playing more matches and he would get that in time in his career. To this day he thinks I only gave him ninety per cent, but I had to keep these young guns thinking. I was only coming up for twenty-five myself but had enough experience to see the talent he had and felt we were going to be productive as a pair.

The two wins over Montrose and Falkirk (who had three sent off in the match) set us up for a quarter-final tie with Celtic with over 25,000 packed in for a midweek game. Crabbo put us in front with a brilliant free kick in twenty minutes and despite an equaliser by new Celtic poster boy Dariusz Dziekanowski, we held the upper hand in the game. I replaced Crabbo late on and after the game went into extra time, Andy Walker scored before I managed to get the equaliser with the last kick of the game to send the match into penalties. Unfortunately I was one of three players to miss and we went out 3–1.

Crabbo continued to lead the line with Husref as I built up my fitness and sharpness. Then one day, when we were sitting in the dressing room awaiting Doddie, he started his mischief and winding me up about the apprentice being nine goals (11–2) ahead of the master. This was much to the delight of the dressing room as it drew howls of laughter and a few asked, 'Well, Robbo, what you saying to that then?' I was sat next to new signing and former Newcastle teammate Dave McCreery (who Doddie had asked me about when he found out he was available) and he just smiled at me and in his devilish Northern Irish accent, whispered, 'I think you need to take this on.'

So I jumped up and quite confidently asked Crabbo would he care to have a wager as to who would finish up top scorer at the end of the season, which the dressing room loved. He had no way of backing out and he confidently took the bet but was left with the decision of how much it would be. I knew he still wasn't on great money and it was more the challenge that I was after, so the bet was struck between us and we faced up to St Mirren with him starting and myself again on the bench. His lead soon became ten as he netted another brilliant free kick to put us ahead on twenty-four minutes, and by the time he trotted off after fifty-five minutes, we still had that lead. He shook my hand as he was replaced, then grinned and said, 'Double figure behind!' before winking. I burst out laughing, but there was serious business to be done.

Within two minutes I had scored from a Fozzy header that rebounded off Campbell Money and I made the game safe with another strike with nineteen minutes to go before setting up JC with five minutes left. I should have had a hat-trick but blazed one over from close range at the death. Still, the match had been won, the deficit reduced to eight and the game was afoot.

We both netted in an inspired JC hat-trick 6–3 win over Dundee as Doddie stuck with the smallish front line of JC, Crabbo, Fozzy and me, and what we lacked in height we made up for in movement, touch and pace. But I suddenly found myself ten behind again within a few weeks before a double against Dunfermline and then a double against Hibs on New Year's Day saw the start of the year in with a bang at Tynecastle. Another brace of quick-fire doubles against Motherwell in the League and Falkirk in the cup and the gap was closing rapidly, and by the time we beat Well 4–0 in the Scottish Cup, I was ahead. I was soon collecting my reward as another double in the derby win at Easter Road saw me stretch away and see a concession that the game was up. I finished on twenty-two,

Crabbo on seventeen, and my reward for finishing was doubly rewarding as it gave me the Golden Boot for being Scotland's top League scorer for the season. But even more importantly, and financially pleasing, was that, in front of the whole dressing room, I got the reward for my victory. My prize? A signed £5 note from my apprentice and a kiss on the cheek!

With our wins over Falkirk and Motherwell, we advanced to the quarter-finals of the Scottish Cup but went down to Aberdeen. There was nothing in the game before three late goals saw the Dons go through on a rather flattering 4–1 score line, and it was the Dons who would pip us for runners-up on goal difference as we both finished on forty-four points, seven behind Graeme Souness's big-spending Rangers team.

As I had been scoring for fun in the second half of the season, there had been a swell of support for me to be given an opportunity at international level. In March, Craig Levein and Dave MacPherson had been involved in the national team, with Craig in particular showing his class by man-marking Claudio Caniggia out of the game and putting himself on the radar of big clubs. He had everything you wanted in a defender, strong, quick, aggressive in the air and was good on the ball. There were very few better than him. He was cruelly robbed of many years with the two cruciate knee injuries he had and goodness knows where he would have ended up otherwise as he was simply sensational.

Scotland had qualified for the World Cup in Italy and it was everything I had dreamed of, playing for my country and in a World Cup too. I thought that, at worst, I must be in with a chance of a cap in the final preparation games for the finals, and if I could score and impress, then I might make the final squad itself.

I had played in two B internationals against Yugoslavia (fifteen minutes) and then got ninety minutes against East Germany. I had done quite well in both and, added to my domestic form, it looked like a cap may be in the offing.

Scotland were due to play Egypt, Poland and Malta before heading for Italy and a group comprising of Costa Rica, Sweden and Brazil. I thought that surely I had done enough to finally warrant an opportunity. At this stage I had over a hundred and twenty goals for Hearts and been very consistent at domestic level, and although competition was fierce with likes of Dalglish, Jordan, Sharp, Speedie, McAvennie, McClair, McInally, Johnston, McCoist, Nicholas and one or two others, I felt I had at least earned an opportunity. It was increasingly frustrating being constantly overlooked by the national team and if I was ever going to be considered, I thought now was the time.

Alas, it was not to be. I played no part in any of the three games as Andy Roxburgh decided on taking Ally McCoist, Mo Johnston, Alan McInally, Brian McClair and finally Robert Fleck and with them the dreams of the nation. Craig Levein and Dave McPherson both made the squad and deservedly so. While I was delighted for them, I was hugely disappointed and frustrated that I was not on the radar of the international team. There was nothing more I could have done to get their attention. It really hurt.

That frustration was even worse when it was pointed out that of all the teams competing in Italia '90, Scotland were the only team that had not brought their top domestic goalscorer!

19

Summer Carnage to Sackings and Cappings

I could not have foreseen that, having won the Golden Boot and missed out on selection for Italia '90, the summer of 1990 was going to be remembered in Edinburgh for something far more damaging than Scotland crashing out the section. After losing to Costa Rica and beating Sweden, we needed a draw against Brazil in the final group game. Despite a brave performance, a late mistake by Jim Leighton saw Scotland exit and face the wrath of the nation for another missed opportunity to progress from the group stages for the first time.

While the Tartan Army were bemoaning another perceived failure and, frustrated, making their way back to Scotland, all hell had broken loose in Edinburgh when it had been revealed that Wallace Mercer had embarked on the process of buying up Hibs shares and that he was attempting to merge Hearts and Hibs into one club. It was his attempt to get an Edinburgh team with the combined support to financially challenge the Old Firm.

That decision brought carnage to the city as the Hibs fans went ballistic and immediately started organising the Hands Off Hibs campaign, headed by the likes of Kenny Waugh and Douglas Crombe. As the summer weather heated up in the capital, so too did the temperature of the Hibs fans as frustration and anger at what they perceived as a hostile takeover from the chairman of their city rivals made their blood boil.

Events sprung up everywhere as news spread rapidly that Wallace Mercer was fast approaching the seventy-five per cent of shares that he required at the time to take control of Hibs. They had a large meeting in Holyrood Park as Hibs fans rallied to the cause and a huge turnout at Easter Road headlined by a then relatively unknown duo called The Proclaimers, as the Easter Road faithful fought for their club's survival.

One such event had been organised by the Hands Off Hibs committee and it was scheduled to take place in the Usher Hall in early June. It was a 3,000 sell-out and was called the Hands Off Hibs Rally, in which a raft of speakers were being lined up to voice their protests at what was happening. A couple of days before, I got a phone call from ex-Hibs captain George Stewart, who was the coach when I trained at Easter Road, asking if I would be prepared to attend the event in a show of solidarity against the takeover.

To be honest, it left me in a real quandary as I had had my own brother George hurling abuse down the phone at me about Hearts killing his club. I could not understand why Wallace had taken this course of action and I couldn't see how one Edinburgh club could work. There had always been Hearts and Hibs, they needed each other and there was nothing greater than beating your rivals in the derby match to the joy of our support. But I also knew that if I went up against my own chairman then it could have serious repercussions for my future at Hearts. Wallace was not a man to be messed with and could be extremely ruthless.

I spoke to my agent, Bill McMurdo, as being a Rangers man he was obviously neutral in the whole scheme of things. I told him I felt that I should attend and show support for the Hibs players and that I genuinely believed the city needed both teams. His advice was to think carefully as he knew Wallace would react to me showing face at a Hibs rally and that it could spell the end for me at Hearts.

I then spoke to Chris and although he was not worried about me showing support to the cause, he acknowledged that the reaction of the chairman could be severe. He asked if I was prepared for the anger it might bring and the possible consequences, so I was still pretty undecided on the best course of action to take.

On the afternoon of the rally I got another call from Jackie McNamara Snr and he asked if I felt I could do it. He said they realised that what they were asking was a huge commitment and that no one would hold it against me if I said no. He finished with a statement that swung it when he said, 'Wee man, what if it was the other way around and Hearts were being bought by Hibs? Would you want support from us?'

It was a powerful argument and I knew then that it was the right thing to do. I felt strongly that Edinburgh needed both clubs, that the rivalry was huge for the city and that to lose either would be wrong, and so I decided that I would attend as a show of support but wouldn't actually speak at the event.

I was picked up by George Stewart and Jackie and, when we arrived, there were a lot of astonished looking Hibs fans, with quite a few saying, 'What the fuck is he doing here?' and, 'Fuck Hearts and Wallace Mercer.' They got short shrift from George and Jackie who reminded them why I was there and that it was a brave thing for me to do. I must admit, at that stage, I was wondering if indeed it was the right thing to have done as emotions were high in the hall. The noise got louder and more vociferous as the night went on, with more and more passionate speeches on how and why Hibs had to be saved.

The plan seemed simple and straightforward. I was to be walked on stage with a few of the ex-Hibs players and be announced as a supporter of the Hands Off Hibs campaign. To this day, I still don't know what happened. As I went on, there was a stunned silence and then the place erupted, a microphone was thrust into my hand and I was 'invited' to say a few words. At that point, I wasn't left with much option.

I was gobsmacked and had nothing prepared but I managed to mumble some words that I felt told the truth of the situation, along the lines that Edinburgh needed both clubs, that it was a rivalry that had spanned over a hundred years and was there any better feeling than beating your city rivals in any game that they played? And was there a better feeling than turning up at work on a Monday after a derby victory for your club? But, most importantly, I was there to support the Hibs players as a takeover of any sort would mean players losing their jobs.

It felt like I was there on stage for an hour when, in reality, it was probably no more than five minutes. And the most stunned person in the room was probably my brother George as he'd had no idea I was even there!

Obviously, despite all the high-profile names that spoke that night, the press jumped on my appearance and what appeared to be a stance against my own chairman. This now took over as the main story of the summer and the headline banners screamed out that I had defied Wallace and was against his plans.

Although we were not due back for pre-season for another week or so, I got a call from the gaffer saying that while he felt I was right and honourable in my actions, he had received a call from the chairman who had told him to tell me I was required to attend a meeting at Tynecastle on the Thursday morning with the manager, Pilmar Smith and Wallace Mercer at 2 p.m.

I got there at about half-past one and Pilmar and Doddie were already there. Both were very supportive about what I had done but were concerned about what the chairman was going to do. He had given them no indication of what action he was going to take but both were in agreement about one thing... he was not happy.

Just after 2 p.m., Wallace arrived and summoned Pilmar and Doddie into the boardroom and I was asked to wait in the players' lounge. As I sat and had a cup of tea, I could just about hear raised voices through two sets of walls, and although I couldn't hear what they were saying, it was pretty plain that it was heated. To be honest, I felt the worst was going to happen and my mind went through various scenarios. Heavy fine? Suspended? Sacked? The last one I thought was the least likely as I was still a valuable commodity but maybe transfer-listed looked the likely outcome.

After about thirty minutes, Wallace appeared and asked me to follow him. To my surprise, he headed down the tunnel and onto the pitch in blazing sunshine and strolled towards the centre circle.

He then looked at me and boomed out, 'Right, what in

hell's name have you got to say for yourself?' I spoke out in a confident tone that I felt he was wrong and that to buy Hibs and put them out of business was the wrong thing to do. I said that I did not see any way that his plan of having only one club in Edinburgh and merging both supports could possibly work and that I was showing support for the Hibs players rather than standing directly against him. In my head, I thought that he was going to do what he was going to do and that was not going to change regardless of what I said.

After I finished, he looked skyward and then looked me straight in the eyes and exploded, 'Who the hell did you think you were standing up against me?' He said how dare I oppose what he felt was his business and that it was nothing to do with me and that I was paid to score goals and not get involved in matters that did not concern me. The rant lasted fully ten minutes and I thought I was definitely not going to be pulling on the maroon of Hearts ever again after that.

Eventually the tirade stopped. I was resigned to the fact that I would be transfer-listed and sold as he had made it clear how angry he was but he simply strolled off the pitch and told me to go and see the manager. As I knocked on Doddie's door, I thought the worst was yet to come.

The gaffer smiled and asked how I'd got on. I told him I had been verbally slaughtered and told that it was nobody's business but his and that I was to come speak to you about my punishment. He then told me that he and Pilmar had spoken up for me and eventually had calmed him down from the opening gambit of, 'Sell him. I never want to see him again,' to transfer-listed to fined and run the bollocks off him at pre-season, and that was the final decision. I was to be heavily fined and warned that if

I ever spoke out against him again, I would be sent packing. I was thankful to the gaffer and Pilmar. If they had not put up a staunch fight for me then that could well have been the end of my Tynecastle career.

As I left the office, the gaffer warned me that from then on I could not take on the chairman in any way as he would not be able to save me again. I told him not to worry, I had only one intention and that was to get my head down and work hard, to keep scoring goals and to get the club some silverware. And I promised that I would not criticise the chairman ever again.

That promise lasted just three months!

Scotland had returned from the World Cup with one win and two defeats and again there was much wailing in the press that once more we had not got out the group stages. It ended with a lot of players deciding to retire from international football to concentrate on their club careers. I still cannot get my head round that even today, probably due to my frustrations at being constantly overlooked despite having a goal tally comparable, if not better, than a lot of the guys who had been picked ahead of me over the years.

I had played for Scotland at all levels on a regular basis from a schoolboy right through the age groups of under-16 and under-18, but then I seemed to be overlooked at under-21 and senior level. Indeed, despite scoring consistently since my debut at eighteen, I only picked up five under-21 caps before being over-age. I had been called up for the squad for a friendly against Holland in 1986 but was an unused sub alongside Gary Mackay. As I've said, the pool of striking talent available to Scotland throughout my career was remarkable, from Dalglish and Jordan in the early days to Speedie, McInally, McClair,

McAvennie, Mo Johnston, Black, Fleck, Shearer, McGinlay, Durie and, of course, Ally McCoist later on. There was a fair bit of competition to say the least. But I still felt that my record at Hearts merited me a chance, especially having won the Golden Boot. By this stage, however, I'd had to accept that it was not to be. Perhaps I wasn't seen as athletic enough for international football. Or maybe, like they said, me and Coisty were too similar in style, and he was definitely seen as the main man. So it was a real surprise to find out I had been selected for the squad for the opening European Championship match against a Romania side that had thrilled everyone with their third place finish in the World Cup in Italy.

I say surprised because I had started the season quietly and had indeed been in far more prolific form in previous seasons and been overlooked. Despite the mass retirements, I'd thought I wasn't on the radar, but Andy Roxburgh picked me for the squad alongside new boys Brian Irvine and Robert Connor of Aberdeen. In that pre-season, Doddie had reacted to the Hearts fans calls for a playmaking midfielder as they thought that was the missing piece of the jigsaw that would finally see us end our quest for silverware, so he had splashed out a club record fee of £750,000 for Derek Ferguson from Rangers, a very good player.

We had an unusual pre-season as we played Raith Rovers away, where I got my second of the game in the last minute to secure a 3–2 win before we flew off to Romania where Wallace had negotiated a handsome appearance fee for us to take part in a four-team tournament in Bucharest between the host side Dinamo, Brighton, RFC Liège and ourselves. After getting on our 'chartered' flight that took us down to pick up Brighton then via Belgium to pick up Liège, we eventually arrived in Bucharest.

The city itself was beautiful but the poverty was appalling and it was heart-breaking to see. The players of all three sides regularly handed out the spending money we received to the locals as there was very little we could have bought anyway. We played Liège in the first semi-final and another ex-Rangers man, Davie Kirkwood, fired us ahead, only for Liège to equalise with the last kick of the game and then knock us out 4–3 on penalties. The biggest factor of the day was the searing heat of the Romanian summer. We had kicked off in the early afternoon so a few kilos were shed. Dinamo disposed of Brighton 3–0 in the evening game and that meant we faced off against the English side a couple of days later, again in the blistering heat of the afternoon. I got both our goals in a 2–2 draw that saw us triumph 4–2 on penalties.

On the last night there was a tournament dinner and the food was dodgy to say the least, with some raw-looking meat dishes. This was to prove a correct observation as after our return, several of the lads, including myself, went down with food poisoning. I hadn't recovered before the team flew off once more to play in the Valencia tournament in Spain that saw us lose 3–1 to Valencia before drawing 0–0 with Levante. JC scored a great goal against the hosts and then it was back to a 1–1 draw with Spurs at Tynecastle before we started our campaign.

Victories over Cowdenbeath and St Mirren saw us into the quarter-finals of the League Cup where we were well beaten at Aberdeen by 3–0. In the League, we had drawn at home to St Mirren and lost away at Dunfermline before Rangers put us to the sword at Tynecastle, where a late George Wright goal was our only bright spot in a 3–1 defeat. It was after this match that I headed to Hampden as the squad assembled for the international match. In the six competitive games so far, I had scored only two goals so I wasn't in the greatest form.

We played a couple of thirty-minute practice games against the under-21 squad and we left for Troon on the Sunday evening as we prepared to face an extremely good Romanian side. On the Monday, we went through passing drills and finishing drills before Andy Roxburgh started to show videos of the Romanians in action and their style of play and formations. This was new to me as no one in domestic football did that at the time. Now, of course, video analysis is a hugely important part of match prep.

On the Tuesday, we went over more shape work and various formations but I was still not sure what our starting line-up was going to be as Andy kept switching positions about to keep us guessing who may or may not be playing. After lunch we went back to Troon Juniors ground and did set plays. Again we were split up into groups and finished with a round of shooting drills before heading back to the hotel where I was told the bombshell news that Hearts had sacked Alex MacDonald. I was gobsmacked as despite our poor start he had done wonders over his nine years in charge, taking us from the *Dad's Army* tag to gradually introducing younger players and more quality on a fraction of what the Old Firm, and indeed Aberdeen, were spending. But all the near misses had been enough for Wallace and with the record signing money being spent in the summer he had seen enough and the gaffer was axed. I was hugely disappointed. The press asked for my reaction and, of course, you can imagine I was desperately disappointed at the news and hit out, saying it was a ludicrous decision as the season was only three games old and that despite our Cup exit we could soon climb the table. I also said it was the last thing we needed with an away trip to Hibs the following Saturday and that the gaffer's record against Hibs should have saved him.

As you can imagine, the press went to town as it was a shock decision. And the Wednesday morning saw my comments hit the headlines. Giving the chairman stick on the back of the run-in about my Hands Off Hibs appearance was always going to be a problem. The chairman was livid and I was told that I would be getting dealt with severely on my return.

The morning of the Romanian match saw us take a leisurely walk by the famous Troon Golf Course and as we headed back for lunch, I was told to go and see Andy Roxburgh. He informed me he had received a call from Wallace Mercer asking me to be sent back to Edinburgh immediately, as, given my comments on the gaffer's sacking, I was obviously in no fit state to play mentally.

Andy looked at me and said, 'John, up until this morning I wasn't sure if I was going to play you or not but, given your admiration for Alex and then hearing that Wallace wants you back now, I have a feeling that with that fire in your belly you will do well tonight, so I am starting you up front with Ally.' I assured him I was ready to give everything and after lunch the team was named and I was to get my first cap at Hampden.

I then became extremely nervous as it suddenly dawned on me that I was going to realise every young player's dream to pull on the dark blue of Scotland. I always imagined it would be Chris who would achieve this first as I had used all his landmarks as inspiration to drive me forward. This was the first time I had done something ahead of him and suddenly it felt strange. On the way to the game, Ally jumped onto the seat next to me and asked what was up. I blurted out that I was feeling very nervous about playing for Scotland. He just laughed and said, 'Don't worry, I'll look after you. I'll talk you through the game and make sure you are okay, trust me. We'll do fine.' It was a line that would come back quickly in the game as Ally would indeed impart some advice very early.

As a kid I had grown up with the Hampden Roar and, of course, I had this vision that it would be packed to the rafters. Sadly this was the one thing that was a huge let down on what was a memorable evening. The Tartan Army had obviously had enough of the team and only 12,000 turned up that evening, much more in hope rather than expectation that we could get anything against such a highly rated side. I have to admit I did have a tear or two in my eye as we sang 'Flower of Scotland' and there was regret that my father was not there to see it. Chris was, however, as I had arranged a minibus worth of tickets for him, and despite them being for the West Terracing, I found out after that he had told his mates he wanted to experience the occasion away from them and asked a steward to allow him into the virtually deserted East Terracing. He too was thinking about our dad and what it would have meant to him to see his youngest boy pull on the dark blue at Hampden.

The first twenty minutes were a blur as Ally and I were doing doggies trying to shut the Romanians down from the front, but we couldn't get near them. They popped the ball around us with ease. They were all at their prime – players like Petrescu, Răducioiu, Popescu, Lăcătuş, Cămătaru, Lupescu and the imperious Gheorghe Hagi – and it was no surprise when Europe's top goalscorer Cămătaru put them ahead early on.

It looked like a case of how many goals they would get. Now, to this day I don't know if it was by design or by chance that Brian Irvine, with no one in his nearby vicinity, went down injured and required treatment. While this was being administered, I was looking around Hampden thinking, really, is this what I waited for all these years, and what I had dreamed of? A chasing by a team of top players and not even a kick of the ball except when we kicked off after they scored! It was then that I heard the shout and looked up to see Coisty walking over, telling me to join him just outside the centre circle.

As I got there, he asked, 'Wee man, how you feeling?'

I replied, 'Ally, to be honest, it's not quite what I expected. I've not touched the ball and we're getting a chasing!'

'Wee man,' he said, 'I told you I would look after you and I'm going to give you some advice, and in future I want you to remember who told you this and what was said, okay?'

I said no worries and as I waited to hear his words of wisdom, he blurted out, 'Wee man, I think we're gonna get fucked!' And he just walked away.

I burst out laughing, but it was probably what we both needed as a few minutes later I had a scissor kick effort saved before the dream moment arrived. Stewart McKimmie floated in a cross from the left, Coisty went up for it and he managed to outjump the centre-half. I did as I was taught, gambled on him winning it and got the sole of my boot ahead of Popescu to stab it home. We were level and I had scored on my debut. This seemed to knock the stuffing out of the Romanians and we picked up in the second half and got about them as the small crowd suddenly sensed we had a real chance. Sure enough, with fifteen minutes left Pat Nevin got to the byline, cut it back and Coisty bundled it over the line for the winner. From a difficult start, we were off and running in the group.

The elation was clear for all to see, and as I spoke to the press, I dedicated my goal to the gaffer. It was then that one of the press men had asked if I was feeling apprehensive about returning to Tynecastle as I had upset Wallace. It was then that some reality hit home. I had promised not to cross him just three months earlier and I had criticised his sacking of Doddie. I could imagine that even me scoring was not going to dampen his rage this time.

The following day I reported around noon and was told the lads were still at training but wouldn't be long. Sandy Clark, then the first team coach, had been put in charge for the derby against Hibs at Easter Road. I was relieved that the chairman hadn't come in yet but knew he was expected at some stage in the afternoon.

Sandy said he would try and keep the chairman at arm's length ahead of the derby; he wanted me to concentrate fully on that as it was a big game which would be followed by a midweek trip to Russia and the formidable Dnipro side. Thankfully there was still no sign of Wallace on the Friday as we prepared for the match against our deadly rivals – and this was no ordinary match, as the summer had thrown up a lot of hate and vitriol. The Hibs fans were baying for our blood and wanted their side to take suitable retribution against the continued threat of a takeover by Wallace Mercer. Easter Road was going to be a boiling cauldron as the green side of the city massed together to watch one of the most eagerly awaited derbies of modern times. It has gone down in history as the Wallace Mercer Derby, despite the fact he was not in attendance; the police had instructed him to stay away for his own safety. He watched from the STV studios as we set about getting our season started. And boy, this game didn't let anyone down!

The Friday of the game was the first chance I got to realise that this was going to be no ordinary derby. Having been away in the Scotland bubble all week, I was unaware of the way the Edinburgh media in particular had been reporting the build-up. The bad blood was caused by the summer's actions and it was clear from friends, neighbours and family that this was a real grudge game. It was going to be hostile, to say the least, and not for the first time in my life my older brother George had temporarily disowned me. Anyone of the maroon persuasion was dead to him due to our club's desire to kill his team.

Anyway, training was short and sharp and Sandy had the same talk on the Friday that Doddie used to have and told us that the hostility towards us was going to be higher than normal but that we would follow the same plan that we had adopted since returning to the Premier League. It had been successful in delivering the performances and results that were required, although this time we would arrive a little earlier than normal at Easter Road as he had some last-minute advice he wanted to share.

Going to the game early was strange as normally we would pass lots of Hearts fans in their colours. On the first part of the route, we always headed up Ardmillan Terrace, along Fountainbridge, down into the Grassmarket and down Holyrood Road, before heading to the top of the brae and down Easter Road. Then it was a right turn into Albion Road and the stadium itself. By the time we got to Holyrood Road there would normally be pockets of Hibs fans giving their customary two fingered salute to us.

Then the top of Easter Road was always swarming with Hearts fans as they took over the pubs at the top end of the street for the day. On reaching Albion Road, the vast majority would be bedecked in green. Today, however, there were virtually no Hibs fans to be seen and at the stadium entrance where normally a few hundred would be waiting to 'welcome' us, there were none. This was quite disarming because we were really good at taking the stick and just getting ourselves ready mentally.

We strolled onto the pitch and, with the gates still closed, it was very much the calm before the expected storm. It was early in the season and the pitch, as you would expect, was in tremendous condition. And it was a hot day so a big crowd was expected. We made our way into the dressing room, passing all the Hibs stadium staff whom we had seen over the years, all wishing us good luck for the game. This was something I always smiled at as it's a strange thing in football that we all tend to wish each other luck when what we really mean is 'I hope we batter you today'.

Sandy sat us down, named the team that saw us go with a standard 4-4-2, with JC on the right and Fozzy and me through the middle. But Sandy explained that when we had the ball, he wanted me to drift to an inside left position with Fozzy directly through the middle and he wanted JC to push up on the right to make it a 4-3-3 in attack but a solid 4-4-2 defensively. He then told us the extra piece of information that he had wanted us to hear, and the reason why we were so early. Which was that, in his opinion, the Hibs players in the first twenty minutes were going to be after blood as their fans would demand that they took out everybody they could. They would want their players to feel the hurt, pain and hatred they felt for Hearts and exact that revenge on the pitch. He reckoned that every fifty-fifty would be even more robust than normal and that the Hibs lads would be extra motivated to please their fans.

Our plan was simple. We had to match every single physical challenge all over the pitch and for the first twenty minutes in possession, to be prepared to knock the ball into the channels and just help it on to avoid opportunity for them to get near us in a tackle. The forwards would have to prepare for heavier than normal tackles from behind but after twenty minutes or so on a hot, draining day, and with the adrenalin starting to drain, we would then be able to get the ball down and play through and round them as they tired from their initial efforts. Also, if we won the toss (which we did), then we were to turn them and make them kick down the slope which we knew would instantly annoy their fans and create an even more seething atmosphere on the terracing.

When we walked out for the match itself, it was like a scene from the great war film *Zulu*. Where there had been empty terracing at the start and only a couple of thousand in for the warm-up, the place was now packed to the rafters, with the Dunbar End packed with Hearts fans. That stretched into the top third of the main stand and the seated terracing below, from where the rest of the stadium was crammed with as many Hibs fans as any of us had seen in a long time.

Sandy was right. They were hanging over the fences screaming blue murder and wanted their pound of flesh. It was toxic, and when we looked across at the Hibs players, they looked like the veins were popping out their skin. It was obvious that they had been wound up inside their dressing room and that they were ready for the battle to end all battles. It was then that I reckoned that referee Jim McCluskey may well be in for a busy day.

The opening exchanges were exactly as Sandy had anticipated. Tackles from the Hibs lads thundered in, but as we had been expecting it, we used our calmness to play in behind and squeeze them up the pitch facing their own goal. All was going to plan and we got the bonus of a goal inside fifteen minutes when I collected a long ball from big Craig and cut inside. Willie Miller had a quick look up and I decided I would try a cross-shot for the far corner. I caught it well and, en route, Pat McGinlay diverted past Andy Goram. In it went and off I went to celebrate with the fans behind the goal.

As we walked back, I had reached the eighteen-yard line when I felt a thump on my back just below my neck. I genuinely thought it was Fozzy as he had been known to be a bit heavy handed with his celebrations. As I turned round, I was astonished to see it was actually a Hibs fan. Before I could react, Andy Goram had raced from his goal and pulled the lad away. As that happened, a Hearts fan ran onto the pitch and punched the Hibs fan. Cue bedlam.

As the Hearts support taunted the home fans, it was too much for some and suddenly the Hibs fans on the east terracing spilled onto the pitch. The teams were taken off while Edinburgh's finest were charged with herding them back and about five minutes later we were off and running again. With tensions higher than ever, we stuck to the game plan and after thirty-five minutes we were two up as Craig Levein bulleted a JC corner towards goal. I had a swing at it and got nowhere near it but that seemed to help deceive Andy Goram, and Craig's header ended up in the back of the net for 2–0.

That led to another minor pitch invasion from the Hibs fans and there was one more before we put the match to bed with the best move of the game. Gary Mackay played the ball into JC who cut inside then played a great reverse pass to Fozzy who had got in behind the Hibs defence. Everything seemed to be in slow motion as I made a move towards the back post. I saw Gordon Hunter look over his left shoulder to see where I was and this gave me the opportunity to dart past his right and into space to meet Fozzy's cross and head us 3–0 in front. Having watched it back, it all happened in the blink of an eye. But I swear that at the time, it all seemed like slow motion apart from me.

The half-time whistle just a minute later, gave everyone from the fans, the players, the referee and the police a chance to breathe. The half had raced by but we had done the job that Sandy had wanted and the Hibs players looked burst as they trudged off. What happened next will go down in Edinburgh folklore as Sandy came in, let us have the usual few minutes to ourselves to calm down, talked about what wasn't right and what was, before he took control and talked about how we were going to go about the second half. Again he said to be prepared for a twenty-minute onslaught and a physical battle but said if we matched that, we would go on and dominate the last part of the game, especially as we were now kicking down the considerable Easter Road slope.

At that moment, there was a knock on the door and in came two police officers who spoke to Sandy first then addressed the players. Many versions of what they said have been put forward over the years. It's widely thought in Hearts fans circles that we were told NOT to score any more goals or they would abandon the match due to the possibility of Hibs fans rioting! My recollection was that they explained that there had been three pitch invasions already and that they feared if we scored again, especially shooting down the slope to the majority of the home support, that the Hibs fans would likely come on the pitch again and that they were not sure if they could continue to hold them. They left, and Sandy looked at us and simply said, 'Fuck that, get out there and stick to the plan. If we score again then they will have to deal with it, and when we score another, then, again, it's their job to deal with it.'

And, with that, we trotted out to resume the battle.

The second half mirrored the first twenty minutes of the first, other than we didn't get a goal. We could sense that the Hibs lads had retreated a bit to make sure that they were not going lose any more goals and we were increasingly comfortable the longer the game went on. I was replaced late on in the game as the midweek international game took its toll and, to be fair, the heat had taken a lot out of us as well. Normally, I'd have watched the rest of the game, but given the circumstances, I decided to get myself in the dressing room quickly and get out the way. It was obvious that my appearance at the Hands Off Hibs rally had been deleted from the Hibs fans' minds. And there was definitely no Hands Off Hearts Players campaign that day!

The weekend was great for the Hearts support and we had a good night as the squad celebrated, although I was still wondering what was in store for me as I still had to face the wrath of Wallace Mercer. I wondered what Monday would bring but, again, the chairman was nowhere to be seen. As we were heading out to Russia to play Dnipro the following day and he was staying behind to start the search for our new manager, I hoped our meeting would be delayed a little further.

We flew into Moscow on the Tuesday before a flight took us down to the city of Dnipro, which is now in southern Ukraine. We thought we were getting the usual behind-the-Iron-Curtain tricks, when, after landing, we were held inside the plane on the runway for an hour in sweltering heat. They explained that some military planes needed to finish a training exercise before we could disembark. We thought it was gamesmanship until we stepped onto the top of the stair to disembark and looked out to see hundreds and hundreds of Russian fighter planes lined up. Our trip into the city was confirmation that Dnipro was the biggest military base in southern Russia as every vehicle seemed to be an army one. Later that evening, our hosts confirmed that the majority of the crowd would be in their Russian army uniform supporting the local team.

The stadium was a massive old concrete bowl with a decrepit running track round it but held 60,000, and it was a good five-minute walk from the dressing rooms in the bowels of the stadium to the pitch. It was noticeable in the training session that once more, the heat was going to be a factor, despite the evening kick-off time. Sandy picked a similar formation for the game, but this time I was deployed in a wider left position in a more 4-5-1 formation as we hoped to utilise Fozzy's pace against their massive but quite cumbersome central defenders. We survived a battering in the first fifteen minutes from the very good, highly skilled side before we broke forward. George Wright did great to get forward from right back and threw a ball in from deep that saw Fozzy manage to head back across goal from the back post area. My natural instincts had seen me drift in from the left and past Fozzy to the near post, but as he knocked it back, I was there to bullet home a header and give us a vital away goal and the lead.

We actually might have sneaked a second but as we made our long walk back to the changing rooms, we were delighted and were again told to stay tight and give nothing away in the second half. We started well and looked like we could grab another before Hudymenko cut inside and hammered one into the top corner. The home fans were delighted and for us it was circle the wagons time. We got battered for the next twenty minutes and were rarely out of our half. Henry and the defenders in particular threw everything in front of the Russians and they hit the woodwork at least a couple of times before we broke again. This time a low cross to the near post saw me slide in and get a touch in front of the goalkeeper, only to see it strike the base of the post and rebound to safety. Despite a couple more near squeaks, we held on for a good away result.

As we left the pitch, I was confronted by this huge Russian shouting what I thought was the word STRETCHER and motioning to the side of the pitch and, to be honest, I just blanked him. But he kept shouting 'STRETCHER, STRETCHER' and grabbing my shoulder. I thought it was more intimidation tactics and kept walking away before a second guy stopped me and pointed towards the sidelines where one of the Dnipro players was standing with some dignitaries. It turned out that the Russian word that I thought was stretcher turned out to be Man of the Match and I was presented, along with the Dnipro player, a rather large hand-painted vase and a bouquet of flowers. As you can imagine there was great amusement and much stick when I finally reached our dressing room that seemed to be about a mile away.

With Wallace not there, it was down to Pilmar Smith to take control, and with Pilmar being a real players' type of director, he announced as we reached the plane that celebratory drinks could be had by the players and the small band of fans who had accompanied us on the plane along with the press. Once more we were delayed as the Russian Air force were still doing training, but with the drinks and my highly prized vase being passed around the plane, we were in very good spirits. I may not have seen the attraction of my newly acquired vase but it seemed the rest of my teammates did. By the time we arrived in Moscow, it had gained a fair few litres of liquid and how that vase survived the trip home was beyond me. I think it ended up at a relative's house where the hand-painted Ukrainian vessel was appreciated.

We had a light training session on the Thursday and the big games continued as we had to travel to Glasgow and face Celtic on the Saturday. I was just about to leave Tynecastle on the Friday when I was told by Yvonne, the club assistant secretary, that Wallace Mercer wanted to speak to me and that he was on the pitch. I think the colour drained from my face.

I made my way out, and, sure enough, on another scorching day, the bold Wallace was striding about the pitch. As he waved me over, I must admit I felt the worst was about to happen. He was scowling and once more read me the riot act about how dare I question his actions or his motives and that, while he admired my loyalty to Doddie, I was not to get involved in anything that did not concern me. And had I not taken his previous warning that I would be in deep trouble if I crossed him again seriously? I wasn't really sure what was coming next as he tore strips off me but then, suddenly, his brows narrowed and he said that I was the luckiest little bastard alive. He'd been all for putting me on the transfer list and selling me but having scored on my international debut then got a double in the derby and followed that up with a goal in Russia to help get one of Hearts best away results in Europe to date, he would get lynched by the Hearts fans if he did. It was bad enough getting death threats from the Hibs side of the city but to have the Hearts fans turn on him as well would be too much. He then informed me I had one more chance to escape punishment. Beat Celtic, and that would be the end of the matter. If not, it was a week's wages plus the bonus from the Hibs game in fines. We got double bonuses for Hibs and Old Firm games so it was a few quid we were talking about.

I apologised and said I understood. Unfortunately for myself, my dream ten days finished with a 3–0 defeat as, despite losing an early goal scored by Joe Miller and giving as good as we got, our midweek game and travels caught up with us when Creaney and Miller (again) scored very late in the game to give Celtic the points. And lo and behold, Wallace did indeed remove a week's wages and the double bonus for beating Hibs. Losing the wages, despite them being less than the bonus, was a blow. The double bonus for beating Hibs was less so as I knew there were going to be plenty more of them in the future.

Sandy was still in charge as caretaker manager and the lads made it three games without defeat as Eamonn Bannon scored the only goal against his former side Dundee Utd to get the points, before Wallace announced the sensational news that our new manager was none other than Scottish footballing legend Joe Jordan. It certainly was a major appointment for Hearts as here was a man that had left Scotland at an early age but had gone on to play for Manchester Utd, Leeds Utd and then on to AC Milan to play with superstars like Baresi and Maldini. There was real excitement as he was introduced to the crowd before the second leg against Dnipro but they left Sandy in charge for the game and we rounded off that spell with a great 3–1 win, with big Dave MacPherson stooping to head us in front before I got the second from the spot. Shakhov pulled one back but less than a minute later, Alan McLaren flicked on a corner at the near post and I headed home to give us a two goal cushion. To be honest, I could and should have gone on to score more as I had three great efforts, one saved and two narrowly past the post. But it was an impressive 4–2 aggregate victory and heralded in a new era for the club with Joe Jordan at the helm.

20

The Italian Way to Conspiracy

Joe Jordan's appointment was a major coup and despite the sadness at the loss of Doddie who had shaped our careers thus far, there could be no doubt that Wallace had decided to go big on his replacement. It was a bit of a stir as his playing CV was sensational and he had a very good reputation as being a brilliant coach and tactician.

On the international front, I made it two goals from two games as I scored a penalty ten minutes after Coisty had missed one, and with Gary McAllister adding a second we hung on to record our second win of the group. In the third game, also at home against Bulgaria, I found myself injured and out of the squad as Andy Roxburgh changed to a 4-3-3 formation. But we came away with a 1–1 draw and were still unbeaten in the group. A 2–0 win in San Marino followed by a 2–2 draw in Switzerland saw us stay ahead, before we lost 1–0 in Romania. Defeat there meant the group was wide open again.

At home, we drew Joe Jordan's first game in charge and I picked up a hamstring injury as we went down 3–2 at home to St Johnstone. I missed the next four games including the first leg of the second round UEFA Cup game where we raced into a 3–0 lead before Henry stepped out of his area with the ball and conceded a free kick. From this, the Italians grabbed an undeserved away goal that ultimately proved decisive as they beat us 3–0 in the second leg, with two of their goals coming in the last fifteen minutes. That sent them through 4–3 on aggregate.

We bounced back with a John Colquhoun wonder goal which was described as a fluke by the Celtic manager in a 1–0 victory that gave Joe his first domestic win, but draws with Dundee Utd and Hibs and a 4–0 defeat at Ibrox left us well off the pace and meant that the Scottish Cup was our only real hope of rescuing the season. We hammered Hibs 4–1 in the first Sky TV game in the New Year and Gary Mackay scored at both ends in a match where we could and should have scored more.

In the Cup, we had drawn Airdrie away at Broomfield and knew it was going to be a tough tie. We went ahead early through Gary Mackay and looked to be in control before goals from Paul Jack and John Watson against the run of play had the hosts in front. Try as we may, we could not force an equaliser and we were out to the Diamonds and out the Cup at the first time of asking, our earliest exit in a long time.

Joe decided that he had seen enough and immediately told us that the training, tactics and formation would start to change and that he was going to change our style of play into something like he had seen up close and personal in Italy. We would be playing a back three with offensive wing-backs, two sitting plus one attacking midfielder and two strikers up front.

I was now feeling completely free of injury and managed to double my tally for the season to sixteen as I scored in another victory over Hibs that saw a remarkable performance from

Andy Goram who made saves into double figures to keep the score down to 3–1. Indeed, his performance was so good that even the Hearts fans were singing his name at the end. It was heart-breaking for Crabbo as, being a dyed-in-the-wool Jambo he was desperate to score and had half a dozen attempts at goal saved by the goalie, one in particular from a scissor kick which defies belief even to this day.

We finished off the League campaign with a win over Dundee Utd, with goals from myself and Eamonn Bannon, before taking part in Gary Mackay's well-deserved testimonial. Everton were the visitors, and it was a fairly typical game of its type. In the first half, both teams were content to knock the ball about on a pleasant evening. However, all that was to change when the gaffer decided to bring himself on at half time to replace Crabbo. Joe was still as fit as a fiddle and he should have scored with his first touch but miskicked a George Wright cross in front of goal. He did then put us ahead on fifty-five minutes when I got clear on the left, cut inside and chipped Neville Southall from twenty yards. The ball hit the bar and went up in the air, and, as it dropped, Neville, facing his own goal, and Martin Keown next to him, were waiting for it to drop into the keeper's hands. But big Joe was having none of it. He launched himself at the two on the line, clattered them and the ball into the back of the net where all three ended up in a heap! Jimmy Duncan, the ref, didn't know what to make of it but he gave the goal, which upset Everton as he had given a soft penalty earlier which Southall had saved from Gary. Everton were fuming and things got spicy when substitute David Unsworth clattered the gaffer and was booked. Then the gaffer exacted revenge by giving him what is known in the trade as a Spanish Archer (elbow) and for a while it got very tasty. In the end, the gaffer smacked home a second to win the game 2–0 and show off his famous toothy grin.

That summer, there were major changes. Six players were brought in for the start of the season, with Ian Baird, John Millar, Graeme Hogg, Steve Penney, Ian Ferguson (Raith) and Glynn Snodin joining the club. We knew that things were changing as John Colquhoun and Iain Ferguson had left.

It was sad to see JC go as I had a tremendous understanding with him on the pitch and a great friendship off it. I felt that despite being tagged as similar, Fergie and I had shown we could play together well enough but the gaffer was changing the system and there was no room for sentiment. But losing JC was a big blow as without doubt he was one of the finest players I had played with and, considering the punishment he took from full backs, it was amazing he played as many games as he did. He had shown what a precocious talent he was and was severely underrated. His meagre haul of just two caps for Scotland was a disgrace for a man of his ability and his consistency.

Pre-season was done the Italian way, with the gaffer taking the lead, and consisted of lots of mobility, stretching and movements designed to make the body as supple and flexible as possible but also to make it stronger. Running was shorter but done on hills to improve the strength of the thighs and calves but with usual circuits thrown in so that the core aspects of the body were also catered for. This was totally new but readily accepted by the squad and was completely different to previous years. But Bert and George were still retained so we had a good mixture to ensure we were at our peak for what the gaffer wanted.

As the ball came out, nothing greatly changed regarding

the passing, movements and crossing and finishing sessions. Obviously there were a few we had not seen before and subtle differences to others, but the real change came with the shape work, which the gaffer took. This was different and we were on the pitch for one to two hours as he painstakingly went through how the system worked and what the key elements of it were. The keeper had to be in contact with the sweeper, Craig Levein, but Craig was in charge of his two central defenders and would dictate when they pushed up or dropped back. He would also tell the wing-backs when to drop deep and also keep the three midfield players in front of him to make it a solid defensive formation that would be complemented by two strikers dropping off when the opposition had the ball. We spent hour after hour and day after day going over and over the formation.

Three pre-season games saw us play and beat Morton (the gaffer's old club) 3–0, Raith 4–1 and Real Sociedad 3–1 and I scored in all three games. I felt fresh and sharp for the start of the season and the new formation was bedding in nicely. The only real surprise to begin with was who the gaffer had picked at right wing back – Gary Mackay. That raised a few eyebrows as he was seen as our best attacking midfield player and not one you would have thought would want to be going from box to box covering the whole pitch, but he took his directions, and, as the season went on, did very well there.

The make-up of the team was pretty regular with McLaren, Levein and McPherson being the three at the back (Hogg deputised for injuries or suspension). Gary and Tosh McKinlay were wing-backs with Derek Ferguson and Johnny Millar being the midfield men. Initially, Scott Crabbe was just behind Ian Baird and myself up top, but we had a good squad with Eamonn

Bannon being able to play either wing-back position as he was still insanely fit, and Glynn Snodin could play left wing-back as well, with big Fergie and Fozzy as back up strikers. George Wright, Chuck Berry and Steve Penney bolstering the ranks.

We got off to a flier with victory at Dunfermline where Crabbo and I scored, then I got a brace in a 3–2 win at Airdrie before Crabbo scored a wonder goal to sink Rangers at Tynecastle and a Craig Levein header saw us take maximum points from the first four games. We added to this with victories over Clydebank and Hamilton in the League Cup which saw us to six straight victories before Hibs held us 0–0 at Tynecastle. We also went out in the quarter-finals of the Cup, 1–0 to a Coisty goal, and in the end were unlucky as once more it was a game we should have won. We added wins against Motherwell, St Mirren and Falkirk and a draw against United and headed to Celtic Park top of the table.

After an early setback, I equalised before a hotly disputed Charlie Nicholas penalty put the hosts in front. Cascarino scored a third and was sent off almost immediately, conceding a penalty which I missed. As Bonner denied me, and despite piling forward, we could not get back into the game. I felt I had let the lads down as, had I scored, we would have been just one behind with twenty minutes left. My mindset was that I should never miss a penalty.

We lost to Rangers a fortnight later but then went fifteen games unbeaten (eleven wins, four draws) and were top of the table again before we were thumped 4–0 by Aberdeen. Then our nemesis, Airdrie, beat us 2–0 but it was mid-January and we were right in the fight for the title with Graeme Souness and his dominant Rangers side.

Rangers, however, inflicted a third league defeat on the spin when, yet again, a Coisty goal late in the match gave them points they didn't fully deserve. We responded with two more wins before Celtic beat us 2–1 in a tight match, and then after three more wins, Aberdeen beat us up north as Rangers started to stretch away. Despite losing only one of our last seven games, three draws meant we had to be content with the runners-up spot again, finishing a point ahead of Celtic.

In December, my second son Liam arrived safe and healthy and so there was another boy added to the Robertson Clan.

Once more, I scored the winner in the following game to clinch a 3–2 win against Motherwell to celebrate his arrival. If the League had been seen as a success then the Scottish Cup would once more prove a frustration. We seemed to find new ways of shooting ourselves in the foot in search of that elusive silverware. We had drawn St Mirren away, the only notable thing in a dour game being the red card for big Bairdy, who played in a similar style to Joe Jordan. He was a nice guy off the pitch and I got on very well with him, but on this occasion there was nothing subtle about his charge on Campbell Money. He saw red as he clattered him into the middle of next week.

The replay was a personal highlight for me as I scored a hat-trick in the second half to see us through to face Dunfermline away. Crabbo got a late winner there to ease us into the quarters where goals from Fergie, myself and Gary Mackay saw us through to a Hampden date with Airdrie and Alex Macdonald.

The semi-final at Hampden was a non-event as both teams matched up. There was no doubt Doddie had got his Airdrie team super fit and organised, as he had done with us. It was hand to hand combat all over the pitch with neither side really looking like scoring in the first eighty minutes.

Then there was an incident that cost us the chance of winning the match. Big Davie had stormed forward as was his manner and after a couple of one-twos he found himself in the box. As Paul Jack came hurtling in to tackle him, the big man knocked it past him and took a couple of steps before collapsing to the deck like a Z-bed. There was no doubt in the ref's mind that it was a dive and Jim McCluskey correctly waved it away, booked Davie and gave him a real talking to. No one batted an eyelid, but just two minutes later we won a free kick. When it was floated in, big Davie rose above Evan Balfour and bulleted a header in from about twelve yards in textbook style. We took off, only to see the referee disallow it for what he had claimed was a push. We immediately surrounded him, protesting and saying it was perfectly fair, only for him to snap and say that he shouldn't have tried to con him earlier. He was obviously still raging with the dive. More heartbreak was to come as I scrambled one that I thought had crossed the line before John Martin clawed it back, but the linesman said no. And so the game ended goalless and a replay was required.

The replay was ten days later and this time there were goals. Henry Smith fell foul of the new rule that keepers couldn't pick up passbacks or throw-ins and Kenny Black rubbed salt into the wound by smashing it home. It looked likely that that would be enough until Alan McLaren popped up in injury time and levelled, to send us into extra time. I hit the underside of the bar with ten minutes to go before, a few minutes later, John Martin hit a goal kick straight at me and I chested it forward before deciding to hit it early from twenty yards. It looked in all the way only to crash back off the post to safety.

If that was disappointing, the pain in my groin added to the agony and was about to cost me an opportunity that would not come around again in my career. Penalties it was and I was in so much pain that I genuinely thought I would have to take my kick with my left foot. I watched on as Crabbo and big Davie missed their spot kicks. I needed to score and just side-footed it down the middle as I couldn't be sure of powering it, and so I rolled it straight down the centre of the goal and into the net. Kenny Black then stroked home to send Airdrie into the final to face Celtic and, once more, we were out at the semi-final stage. I only managed one more appearance for us that season, scoring in a 1–1 draw with champions Rangers, as the pain in my groin continued. I had to rest and see if it cleared up without needing surgery in order to keep my dream alive of representing Scotland in their first ever qualification for the European Championship Finals in Sweden. All the more appealing as our group was right out of the top drawer and comprised Russia, Holland and Germany.

The last games of our group meant that Romania were in pole position and a win in Bulgaria would see them win the group. If they lost and we didn't win, then Switzerland could also finish top. If Bulgaria beat Romania they had an outside chance but we had San Marino at home and if we could win by four or more that would mean Romania had to win in Sofia to pip us.

I was recalled for this game in an attacking line-up and while we achieved the bare minimum we needed with goals from

McStay, Gough, Durie and McCoist, I was personally disappointed that I had passed up a golden opportunity to add to my Scotland total. I really should have walked away with the match ball as I had a couple of good chances saved, I headed one just past, blazed another over the bar and then had one knocked off the line by a defender. It was one of those games where I was simply not destined to score whatever I did.

A couple of goals early in the tournament had cemented my place in the squad but we now had to wait to see if Bulgaria could do us a turn. Having already turned Romania over 3–0 in Bucharest, we knew a draw would see us through, and just a week later that's what we got as Bulgaria drew 1–1 with Romania. Despite a tense last fifteen minutes, we were there. We had qualified for Sweden '92.

But now I had to get fit.

The physio Alan Rae felt that the initial injury, while painful, would hopefully only require rest and I was included in the squad to travel to the USA for our preparations. Andy Roxburgh told us that barring injury, this was the final squad for Sweden. All seemed well as we arrived in Chicago and then right at the end of our first training session I felt an uncomfortable pain just above my right groin. Once the SFA physio and doctor had looked at it, they said that with three games in seven days it was best to send me back to Tynecastle to receive more treatment rather than just sit about getting treatment there, particularly as the squad would be flying to Canada as well. It seemed the right way forward so I was flown back overnight to Glasgow but was unprepared for the 'welcome' I would receive. On touching down, I was met by dozens of photographers, journalists and TV cameras as they wanted to know why I was suddenly sent home from the squad. In their haste to get me back, the SFA PR team had failed to tell anyone that I was returning for treatment. When they found out a player was heading home, they assumed I had broken a disciplinary rule or something along those lines and that I had been sent home in disgrace.

Fortunately, Bill McMurdo was there as I had asked him to pick me up and drive me through to Edinburgh, but we were shadowed all the way home by press. One photographer even decided to climb over my back fence to get a photo of the 'shamed' Scotland player. Thankfully, Andy Roxburgh then told everyone at his press conference before the USA game that I was injured and would be receiving intensive treatment ahead of assembling with the squad before we departed for the tournament.

Alan Rae worked away for the following fortnight and did a great job with getting me right. I had done plenty of running and ball work, testing the injury, and felt sure I would be able to take my place in the squad to travel. All that was required was to get through a squad training session at McDiarmid Park in Perth where the squad would get the final details of what would happen, where we were staying in Sweden and when we'd be training and playing in the tournament. It was exciting and the session went well with no pain or discomfort. We finished off with a twenty-minute game that was to allow the press some coverage and it was in the last minute of that game that my dream ended.

As I cut inside and fired a shot from twenty yards, I felt that someone had stabbed me just above the groin. The whistle went and as we walked off I knew then in my head that it didn't look good. I put some ice on it in the dressing room and as we headed back to the hotel for lunch, Dave Bowman spoke to me, asking if I was all right, as I looked white as a sheet. I told him my injury had flared up and that I was going to have to withdraw and he went quiet before saying to me, don't tell them, just go to the tournament as it's too big an opportunity to miss and it might settle down again. He was right when he said it looked like Jukey and Coisty would be starting the games, but I had a chance of coming off the bench and playing a part, so my injury would be okay for that short spell. He wasn't that far off the mark but I told him I had a decision to make after lunch.

I phoned Chris, and like Bow, he asked if I could manage to sit tight and get through the tournament as the likelihood was I would be coming off the bench a couple of times. I got where they were coming from, but Chris also said I had to do what I felt was right and, having spoken to Alan Rae, I knew if it broke down I was looking at eight weeks out with an operation and recovery and if I needed surgery then I would miss the start of the season with Hearts.

In the end I decided deep in my heart that I needed to do what I felt was right, return to get the op and be ready for the new season. I couldn't cheat my country and I couldn't cheat my club or myself. I was tearful as I spoke to Andy privately and told him that it had flared up at the last minute and that I would have to withdraw. He even got the doctors and physios to take another look after lunch but I knew it had torn. He then pulled a squad get together and announced that I was incredibly brave and honest and that I could have hidden it but had chosen not to. I was out and Kevin Gallagher was called in.

Like everyone else, I watched as Scotland started the tournament against the Dutch where we lost to a solitary Marco van Basten goal. To be fair, there were not many chances created for either side. It was the next match that frustrated me as, despite passing up lots and lots of chances, we lost 2–0 to the Germans and were out the tournament. But there were chances I felt that, had I been there and come on, I might have managed to score. This was compounded when Andy Roxburgh said in the press that it would have been the ideal situation for me to have been involved! Scotland beat Russia (then CIS) 3–0 to finish the tournament on a high, but it was with huge frustration and sadness that I spent the rest of the summer recovering from a hernia operation.

There was more drama over the summer as Aberdeen manager Willie Miller first made a £700,000 bid for me, then upped that to £800,000 plus Peter van de Ven. I wasn't told this until after Peter van de Ven arrived in a separate £100,000 deal. Wallace had stood firm so I think he had forgiven me. Ally Mauchlen came up the road from Leicester and we had an exciting clutch of young lads knocking on the door in the shape of Kevin Thomas, Gary Locke, Allan Johnston and Paul Ritchie.

I missed our first three games of pre-season as our customary game against Raith Rovers was won 2–1, before Hamilton were beaten 2–0 and Tottenham won 2–1 after big Craig had put us in front. Two Gordon Durie goals won it for the visitors. I was then passed fit enough to play for an hour, which was great as the visitors were Newcastle and it was the occasion of a testimonial match for myself, having now started my eleventh season at the club, despite eight months' time off for good behaviour in Tyneside. I was delighted that Kevin Keegan not only agreed to bring Newcastle up but, such was his delight at Doddie's testimonial, he asked if he could play in the match for a short period. That was fantastic and it generated a crowd of over 11,000 as an Ian Baird goal gave us victory. I got the sixty minutes under my belt without incident but was still short of match fitness as the season opener against Celtic loomed.

I didn't make it and once again we were unfortunate to lose 1–0, with a Levein own goal ten minutes from time. But I was back for the following game and scored twice as, along with another Crabbo goal, we won 3–0. We then had a draw against Hibs as we took our unbeaten run against them into double figures. Despite beating Clydebank at home and Brechin, where I got a winner in extra time, it was Celtic once more that stopped us in the quarter-final with another fortunate victory. Gary Mackay got an equaliser but we went out to a Gerry Creaney winner in the second period.

Three straight league wins saw us fly to Prague to play Slavia in the UEFA Cup where we lost 1–0 to an outrageous free kick. We had sold Scott Crabbe, which was a real disappointment as I had an unbelievable relationship with him on and off the pitch, and my protégé had gone to Dundee Utd in a cash plus player deal with United winger Allan Preston coming in exchange.

The second leg was one of the great European nights at Tynecastle as a crowd of 16,000 saw us level the tie after just eleven minutes as Gary Mackay played a one-two with me before crashing us ahead. Before we could settle down on our lead, the Czechs drew level through Jaroslav Šilhavý four minutes later but in a rip-roaring first half, Bairdy and Craig headed us into a 3–1 lead on the night and 3–2 on aggregate. We had chances to increase the lead early in the second half before Pavel Kuka levelled the tie 3–3 on aggregate and put the visitors ahead on away goals. Throughout the game I had come under special attention of the Prague defence and they systematically took their turn in kicking the living daylights out of me. Then, as I ran for another ball over the top, I received an elbow in the face from Panenka and he received his second yellow.

It then became more frantic as Kuka passed up a glorious chance to level the game on the night, before we were given a free kick twenty-five yards out, slap bang in the middle of the pitch. I was never shy in fancying my chances but on this occasion, as the wall had taken up position on the goalie's left side, Glynn Snodin ushered me away and said he fancied it. Trust me, when a lefty tells you he fancies something you let them be as they have this insane way of delivering a dead ball better than a right-footed player. Glynn strode back and while Ian Ferguson's thunderous strike against Bayern Munich will live long in the memory of all Hearts fans, this one was arguably even sweeter as he hit it into the top left-hand corner. The Slavia keeper had no chance and the Shed went wild. We held on nervously to make sure a talented ten-man Slavia did not get another away goal before the end.

The second round saw us up against Standard Liège, a Belgian side of good pedigree, and they scored a scrappy goal from a corner after just seven minutes at Tynecastle. While Slavia were undoubtedly a better technical side, Liège were disciplined and strong and afforded us very few opportunities to get an equaliser. We lost 1–0 on the evening and had everything to do in the second leg.

The second leg was a great match, and roared on by 3,000 of our fans in the stadium, we created lots of chances in a very open game. Their goalkeeper, Bodart, was outstanding as he saved a couple from myself early and late in the first half and made two outstanding blocks from Tosh McKinlay as the tie hung in the balance. But just as we had the home fans starting to worry, the Belgians broke and it was Marc Wilmots who finished well. We had nothing to lose and felt if we could just get the equaliser we could still get the two goals we needed. But the home side retreated to their box and snuffed out our threat to progress to the next round. It was disappointing to go out as we had played really well but we just didn't take our chances and once more the fine line in football had seen us lose out.

We were lifted domestically as Ian Baird headed the winner at Tynecastle to beat Hibs, but that preceded a poor run of no wins in six as we drew and lost three league games, including a 6–2 thumping from Aberdeen at Pittodrie. We'd levelled from 2–0 down but then lost heavily.

Once more we turned our attentions to the Scottish Cup and once more it turned out to be frustrating as we beat Huntly 6–0 in a game that saw Aidy Boothroyd score a solo goal that won Goal of the Tournament. I suffered the agonising yet ecstasy-filled moments of a striker's life when, in the final moment of the first half as we led 3–0, the ball was cut back to me past the keeper by Derek Ferguson. It left me the simple task of knocking it home and to my disgust, as I went to tap it in, it bobbled through my legs (honestly) and flashed across the goal beyond the far post. I ended up running into the empty net to the cries of disbelief and some laughter from the fans behind the goal. Fortunately for me, Biscuits (Allan Preston) had retrieved it and fired it back into the middle where this time I knocked it home and cheekily waved a finger to the lads behind the goals to shoosh, which they loved. Added to the fact it was my two hundredth competitive goal for the club, it was a strange way to get it but welcome nonetheless as I hadn't notched for a while.

Dundee were next at Tynecastle. It was a tough match, with goals in the last minute of both halves by big Fergie and me that saw us through to the quarters and Falkirk at home – where Biscuits and I scored just before and just after half time to ease us into the semi-final against Rangers at Parkhead.

I notched another winner against Hibs when my cross-shot deceived John Burridge in the visiting goal and another season without defeat to our city rivals passed in a fixture that we knew we were dominating since coming back up a decade previously.

There were 41,000 fans at the semi-final to witness a dour first half with few chances on a wet, blustery day before we made the breakthrough. As I went down the right-hand side and against one of the quickest full backs in the game, David Robertson, I used my 'blistering' pace to get past him. I fired in a cross towards the middle where, from the left flank, Biscuits had floated in and met it with a tremendous header from about fourteen yards away. We were ahead and in control before a mistake from the referee led to Rangers equalising. As a shot from McCoist went flying over the bar, referee Douglas Hope signalled it had taken a deflection, and despite immediately being surrounded by our players in protest, he stood firm and awarded the corner. As it swung in, it was former player and good friend Dave MacPherson who met it six yards out with his head. Johnny Millar stopped it on the line but it rolled back to big Slim and he sclaffed it through a crowd of players and in for the equaliser.

We were furious and Hope realised he had blundered, but before we could gather ourselves, Rangers struck again. McCoist raced through and lobbed Nicky Walker, and despite it looking as if it was going to drift past, the spin on the ball took it just inside the post. Rangers were ahead, and once more, despite us pushing everything forward, Walter Smith's side stayed in front and out we went. We'd had the best of the game and the chances in a match bossed by our Derek Ferguson but once more our failure to negotiate the semi-final hit hard and deep. It was nobody's fault but our own as our frustration grew, no doubt felt ten times worse by the supporters.

A draw against Dundee and further defeats to Rangers, Aberdeen and Motherwell saw us head to Falkirk and a match that to this day is controversial. As I have said previously, the players had huge respect for Joe Jordan – his detailed coaching and preparation were excellent. The one thing lacking was his man-management. It was completely different from Alex Macdonald in that he didn't really do one-to-one, of-the-moment conversations with players. If he had a problem with your performance, this would be rectified later in the week when he would give you a tap on the shoulder and ask you to his office for a discussion.

I had only been seen once when, after a 3–0 victory over Clydebank, he had asked me in and said that in his opinion I wasn't in the box enough in the first half and that I needed to be in the box more, to which I replied that I thought I had been as that was the strongest area of my game. He said no, I hadn't been in the box at all in the first half and given that I had scored a header, this seemed pretty strange. He handed me a videotape of the game and told me to take it home and watch it. When I did, I noted that I was in the box several times before and after my goal and I thought maybe it was a test, so I wound the game forward. It was indeed the whole game, so I noted the times that I was in the box in the first half and went in to see him where, despite my pleas to watch the first twenty minutes of the tape in the office, he refused. He said he had watched it and his opinion stood. I knew from the tone he was not for debating it. That was the only time I had cause to be there, unlike some others, but generally no one had any problems with his analysis most of the time.

It had been circulating that he had been given assurances from Wallace that he would have money to spend and that we would get a proper training ground. At this time, we were training on the rugby pitches at George Watson's College, but that money had not been forthcoming and even after selling Crabbo he had not been given the funds. He said that had he known that, he would not have sold him.

The training was also a source of frustration at times as Joe loved the shadow play, and we spent hours on a Monday, Tuesday and Thursday going over the shape and positions. It was very repetitive and despite the fact that everyone knew what their role was, this continued week in and week out. Generally it was fine for the defenders and midfield players as the defensive shape was what we always worked on, but it was stop-start and even if you were injured you had to come to training and watch everything that was happening.

We had been doing well enough but there had been a few players who had gone to his assistant Frank Connor asking if there was any chance of doing some more dynamic stuff from time to time. Frank, despite his best efforts, could not get much changed so there was plenty of frustration from all parties. It was known to the players that the gaffer and Wallace had fallen out and all was not well, and I could certainly understand why the gaffer would be upset and frustrated. Adding to that, our semi-final defeat had seen another opportunity gone.

We hadn't won in five games ahead of the match and were not in good form as our hangover from the Scottish Cup seemed to linger. We started the next game at Brockville well enough and had a few chances. I hit the post and had a couple of efforts saved, as did Gary Mackay and Ian Baird, before Davie Weir scored on a rare Falkirk attack after thirty-three minutes. That was quickly followed up by Fraser Wishart four minutes later and I missed a sitter just on half time that would have seen us right back in the game.

The gaffer and Frank tore strips off us at half time as the frustration from the previous five games kicked in and they told us in no uncertain terms that we had to get back into this game quickly. Despite the chances created, our performance was way short of what was expected and we knew ourselves that a quick goal and we could turn this around, especially given the chances we had made but missed in the first period. Falkirk came out strong and a mistake at the back allowed Crawford Baptie to make it 3–0 after just two minutes. Brian Rice and Baptie again made it five after fifty-seven minutes. They had scored from their first three attacks of the second half and we were stunned and reeling as the Brockville crowd smelled and tasted blood. Richard Cadette made it six after seventy minutes and we continued to miss good chances on the break to save some kind of face that we scantly deserved. The stick from the terracing was deserved as we trooped off after a tanking.

Nothing was really said after the game other than we would look at it on Monday and that all the players were to have a good look at themselves as our winless run was now seven and could not continue. Wallace was in France but suffice to say that Joe Jordan was sacked, and then the conspiracy theories surfaced that we had deliberately lost the match so that we could get rid of him. The rumours were of a Hearts 'mafia' of senior players who wanted rid of the manager and therefore chucked the game. The gaffer himself came out claiming the same sort of thing as speculation grew about what had happened.

My view is simple: if any person thought I had deliberately thrown away a game, they do not know me. I had to take my share of the blame for the defeat as I missed several opportunities during the game that might have made a difference, especially before Falkirk's opener. We had been very poor, but to say we deliberately lost 6–0 to get rid of a manager is way, way off the mark. Were we poor? Yes, absolutely. Did we miss chances? Absolutely. Did we defend badly? Hell, yes, we did. But not one of those players played to lose that game and Falkirk scored with their first five attacks.

It would also be wrong to dismiss just how well Falkirk played and how clinical they were in a game where they hammered us, but to this day, people still think that the team lost this deliberately. I can now categorically assure every Hearts fan out there that that was not the case and that none of the players would disrespect the fans, the club, the badge, Joe Jordan or their family and friends in this way. And while you can say it was just one of those games, which it was, the ramifications after with the gaffer's sacking has led to conspiracy theories to this day of what went on. There are still fans who were there that genuinely believe we didn't try, and no matter how hard you try to convince them – I have had this conversation thousands of times – that there was no more in it than a horrendous performance from us and a terrific performance from Falkirk, many still do not accept this and believe other scenarios. I have met Joe several times since then and if he thought that way, he certainly hasn't said anything about it to me.

Our winless streak stretched to ten as we ended the season under Sandy Clark in caretaker charge and he brought in a raft of youngsters who had won the Youth Cup. Kevin Thomas, Allan Johnston and Tommy Harrison all scored in the final three games that saw us lose to Aberdeen and St Johnstone away and draw with Airdrie at home as we finished a poor fifth, twenty-nine points behind champions Rangers.

21

Sandy Clark's Kids to Tommy McLean Mayhem

Sandy Clark was given the permanent job as manager after his previous spell in caretaker charge had gone well prior to big Joe's arrival. And while he wasn't able to turn around our losing run in the last few weeks of the season, there was no doubt he had earned the opportunity. He had been very successful with the Hearts youth teams, had won the BP Youth Cup and had produced a marvellous clutch of young players who had been given some game time. In Sandy's view, these players were now ready to really push on. A fair part of his interview would no doubt have been based on the fact that he wanted to continue with these players and there would be no need for a mass of players to come in.

The young squad had two good goalkeepers in Roddy McKenzie and Myles Hogarth, and defenders in David Murie and Paul Ritchie. We also had midfielders Tommy Harrison and Mark Bradley and the talented Allan Johnston and Kevin Thomas up front. Bearing in mind there was the likes of Alan

McLaren, now a fully-fledged internationalist, and Gary Locke who was just slightly older, we had no shortage of burgeoning young talent at our disposal. He also added Stephen Frail at full back from Dundee alongside Jim Weir from Hamilton and midfield pocket rocket Scott Leitch from Motherwell, as well as the high profile signing of Justin Fashanu who had had a fantastic career down south including million-pound transfer deals. Justin had also blazed a trail by becoming the highest-profile footballer to come out and say he was gay.

I was roomed with Fash and we got on really well. He broke the ice immediately by teasing me that I was nowhere near good looking enough to be on his radar! That was the start of our friendship. He had the wickedest sense of humour ever and a heart of gold that was as deep as you can imagine. He was a great guy to be with and, in a macho sport, his bravery was unquestionable. On the pitch he was as hard as nails with an incredible physique. And although bad knee injuries had taken their toll, he was still a real handful for defenders and they knew it.

Pre-season was in Holland and we had five matches with various results that ended with two defeats to Borussia Mönchengladbach (3–1) and Twente (2–1), but it had been a good tour with the new signings settling in well before we finished with a third defeat on the spin as Everton once more provided the opposition, this time for Henry Smith's testimonial match. Matt Jackson and Tony Cottee scored either side of half time to give the Toffees a 2–0 victory and the following Saturday we lost 2–1 at Ibrox as Rangers raised the flag with a big Fergie goal coming just too late to allow us to complete an unlikely comeback.

Sandy Clark's Kids to Tommy McLean Mayhem

I scored both goals in our victory over Stranraer in the League Cup and I got the winner against Raith before Allan Johnston scored a great goal to maintain our ever-rising unbeaten tally against Hibs. A late Eddie May goal gave Falkirk, managed by Jim Jefferies, a smash and grab victory to send us undeservedly out the Cup on the night, and once more the frustration of the fans was there for all to hear. This sparked immediate changes as Sandy publicly said he was going to start playing the younger players and that the senior pros had a fight on their hands if they wanted to stay in the side. He also signed another high-profile striker, who I got on very well with, in Maurice Johnston from Everton, which was a huge coup for Hearts.

I was dropped and Mo and Fash started. Kevin Thomas was going on before me as well so it looked like Sandy had decided to make an example of me. We had played together but he wasn't afraid to make hard decisions, leave senior players out and promote the youngsters. I was fine about that as I had never been scared of a challenge from anyone for a starting place. I knew and believed that my ability and goals would come good.

I was out of the starting line up before a recall for the UEFA Cup first round with the mighty Atlético Madrid on a blustery night in Edinburgh. It looked as if we were going to get an unbelievable first leg victory as I bundled us ahead before JC, who had re-joined us from Sunderland, rifled us into a two goal lead with just fifteen minutes to go. But Atlético, who had looked subdued for most of the evening, then capitalised on a bit of slackness at the back to snatch a vital away goal through Roman Kosecki, to turn the balance of the tie in their favour. It was still a good victory and gave a glimpse of what we could be capable of, but our up and down form continued as we lost

1–0 at home to Kilmarnock then beat Celtic as I scored the only goal of the game.

We headed for the return in Madrid at the Vicente Calderón stadium, which was looking the worse for wear but still impressive. A crowd of 35,000 turned up and saw us miss two decent chances from Fash and me before a deflected Martinez effort tied the aggregate scores but meant we needed to score to have any chance. The Spaniards retreated back to their own half and invited us on to them, and the more we pushed forward, the more they used their experience to hit us on the break. They added two goals in three minutes through Manolo and Postigo in seventy-two and seventy-five minutes to take the game away from us and allow them to showboat to a chorus of *Olé* from their fans.

This game was to start a run that would see us win only once in nineteen matches (lost nine; drew nine; won one). The solitary win was once again over our city rivals as JC scored two fabulous goals to maintain the stranglehold we had in the derby clash, but Sandy had continued his decision to play younger players and leave the experienced lads out. Despite this poor run, a late Johnny Millar equaliser at Tynecastle kept Hibs at bay once more and the same player scored the only goal as we entered January with only six wins in the League and now embroiled in a relegation fight.

Mo Johnson got our winner in an ill-tempered Cup game at Firhill, where he was taunted by the fans on his return, and as we left the stadium, there was a hushed silence as we listened to the draw on the bus. Out it came: Hibernian versus Hearts, so Easter Road it was. It was not lost on us that it would be catastrophic if we were to get knocked out the Cup by our city rivals and lose our unbeaten run that now stretched to twenty games. The clubs had not been drawn against each other since 1978 so this was a game that was suddenly much more than just a cup tie. Hibs fans had made it known that beating us in the Cup would, in their minds, make up for not having beaten us in the League for nearly five seasons. In my brother George's head, it would be far more significant than our Mickey Mouse league run against them, such is the mindset of local rivalry.

The Hearts fans were not fazed in the slightest, as going to Easter Road to make it twenty-one undefeated was a sure thing, so sure they were taunting the Hibs fans with an invitation to come and celebrate a special twenty-first party. Already this game was shaping up to be the most talked about derby since the Mercer game a few years earlier. It was not going to be a game for the faint-hearted and it most certainly was not going to be a game for the kids, talented as they were.

My third son Scott had arrived in late January, and once more his birth was celebrated as I scored in a 1–1 draw against Kilmarnock, but all the attention was now on the Cup game between ourselves and Hibs.

The game didn't lack drama, that's for sure, but the real drama, for me anyway, started on the Saturday as we trained round at Roseburn. The game had been picked by BBC for live broadcast as it was the undoubted tie of the round. It was no different to most days before the game with a warm-up, some possession boxes before some sprints and some shooting then a small-sided game to finish. Just as we were about to finish, I rolled my ankle in the act of shooting and hobbled to the side. Alan Rae had a quick look and I said it was nothing serious and a bit of ice on it and I would be fine.

Back at the stadium I had a quick bath and went through

for treatment and, although it had swollen up quite quickly, I didn't think it was going to cause any problems. At worst, a small support strapping would be enough to give it a bit of added protection. Alan gave me ice to take home and some anti-inflammatory tablets and told me to phone him if there were any problems but we were both confident all would be well for the following day and I told Sandy that I would be fine.

Overnight, however, the swelling would not go down and it was steadily getting more painful. At 9 a.m., I phoned Alan Rae and said we had a problem as my ankle was up like a balloon so he told me to come in an hour earlier and we would have a look and that he would tell the gaffer that I was a doubt. I hobbled in, and Sandy was obviously concerned, but when I took my sock and trainer off the ankle was complementing the club blazer and flannels! He could see the purple bruising and the puffiness of my entire ankle. It was not looking good. Doc Melville was brought in, and in the end, my only option was to take an injection (I think it was cortisone) to numb the pain and bring the swelling down so that I might be able to play part of the game. Obviously I agreed as I didn't want to let the gaffer, the team or the fans down and miss the first cup-tie derby since 1978. When we got to Easter Road I somehow managed to get my boot on after a strapping to give more support, but despite some painkillers, my ankle was agony. Sandy said to see how it went in the warm-up.

It didn't go well. I hobbled through it and genuinely thought that my game was over before we even started. I said as much to Sandy who took me to the side and asked me if I thought I could start the game and maybe play fifteen minutes or so as he didn't want to give Hibs or their fans the boost that I was out injured. I agreed as I could see where he was coming from and really, given the pain, I couldn't see it being any worse. That decision seemed totally warranted as after just eighty seconds (my second quickest derby goal after the 27-second one at Tynecastle), I had us ahead when JC fought for position and fired a pass-cross along the eighteen-yard line that eluded everyone and allowed Tosh McKinlay to get on the end of it and take a brilliant first touch, knocking the ball past Willie Miller to the byline. Once again this is where, in my mind, the game went into slow motion. I sensed Tosh was going to play it first time towards the near post and I made my run there. Tosh did what I had anticipated; I got there ahead of Steven Tweed and just flicked it past Jim Leighton to the delight of our fans at the Dunbar End. The Hibs fans were stunned into silence.

Sandy had gone with experience for this crucial game with the only young player in the thirteen being the matured and brilliant Alan McLaren who was our captain. He was being watched by a host of clubs that day and we circled the wagons to do our usual derby job of keeping Hibs at bay whilst looking for the quick break, with Scott Leitch and JC supporting Mo and me up top. Gary Mackay and big Chuck were sitting protecting the back four and we were in control when, out of the blue, Keith Wright rolled in an equaliser. Suddenly we were all square, right on the half-time whistle and with everything to play for.

Now whether it was the injection, the painkillers or adrenalin, I had hardly noticed my ankle, but on the return to the dressing room the throbbing was back. Another couple of painkillers and Sandy said the same again – can you give me fifteen minutes – and he got the same reply.

Hibs, buoyed by the equaliser, had their tails up. McAllister hit the post and they were swarming down the slope. Henry had to make a couple of smart saves and it was evident our back four plus Henry and Chuck were digging in.

After sixty-three minutes my race was over. I simply could not move so I was replaced by Wayne Foster, and while I was booed off by the home fans, inexplicably they roared Fozzy on as he was seen as no real threat by the Hibs fans. That was about to bite them big-time as, due to the back four and Chuck and Henry being at their best, we got a grip of the game. We didn't look like we were going to score but our defensive lads had re-established control of the game. We had weathered the storm and it looked a stick-on that we were heading for another derby at Tynecastle.

I had watched the whole second half with my foot in an ice bucket, much to the delight of the Hibs fans behind the dugout who, as usual, were questioning my parentage. Then, with just two minutes to go, Gary Mackay took possession about halfway in our half of the pitch, looked up and played a long ball over the top of the Hibs central defenders for Fozzy to chase. Now, while Fozzy had his critics as he tended to be erratic in front of goal, the one thing he was particularly good at was going in behind the defence as he was very quick and was only just behind JC and Craig Levein pace-wise. He took off in pursuit, got there first about thirty yards out and knocked it forward. He went a couple of yards clear before knocking it further forward with his shin. Now, at this point, no one on our bench was getting too excited as we thought either Beaumont or Tweed would just chop him down, take the red card but be eligible for the replay. But neither did. They both paused and allowed Fozzy to get to the eighteen-yard line where he rolled it through Jim Leighton's legs and into the net to put us ahead and ultimately through. This, of course, sparked delirium on our part of the terracing as he decided to join the fans by leaping onto the fence in that now iconic photo. We were through, we had nicked it and we had now gone twenty-one matches without defeat to our rivals. It was, quite simply, a phenomenal day for Hearts.

Our run was stretched to twenty-two when we returned in the third last game of the season and ground out a goalless draw. I was out for three weeks with ankle ligament damage and was on the bench as goals from John Brown and Mark Hateley saw Rangers once again end our silverware dreams. Our run-in saw us win three, lose two but draw seven, and that was our problem. We drew twenty matches of our forty-four, winning eleven and losing thirteen, which meant that going into our last home game, played with the Shed demolished in readiness of the new Wheatfield Stand, we were in relegation danger. Thankfully, goals from Stephen Frail and Craig Levein meant we just needed to avoid defeat at Partick in the last game, or hope that other results went our way. It looked like, with just a few minutes left on the clock, both clubs would get the draw that saw us safe.

Then Alan McLaren knocked a ball into the corner flag area that was poorly defended and gave us a corner. Craig, Jim Weir and Neil Berry all decided to stay back as the draw was enough and the game had virtually been played in the middle third of the pitch as neither team's strikers were applying pressure. With thirty minutes to go, it was clear that neither side wanted to take a chance and so it was an 'after you, Claude' situation. With the ball periodically knocked behind the opposition defence, just to appease the fans who, while happy enough, were still wanting some attacking intent from their teams.

So only Alan McLaren ventured forward and despite being outnumbered by the big lads of Thistle he threw himself at my clipped-in corner and thundered it past the keeper to give us the lead. It stunned everyone in the stadium and gave us the points. Fortunately, the other results went both our and Thistle's way. By winning, we finished seventh behind Dundee Utd on goal difference with forty-two points. Kilmarnock, Thistle and St Johnstone all finished on forty and Thistle stayed up by one goal. Saints, Raith Rovers and Dundee were all relegated with Falkirk being promoted, as the Premier League returned to just ten teams.

Our topsy-turvy year with Sandy blooding a lot of the successful young players had started to look like paying dividends as he realised he may have played too many too quickly but had got the balance much better as the season drew on. However, it was not the season that new owner Chris Robinson who, along with Leslie Deans, was now in charge of the club, wanted. They dismissed Sandy and replaced him with one of the most famous managerial family names in Scotland, recent Scottish Cup winner Tommy McLean from Motherwell. I felt Sandy was really unlucky. Our form was erratic but we were slowly bringing through a good crop of players from the youth team but progress wasn't quick enough so in came the new gaffer.

To say Tommy McLean's era started off with a bang was an understatement.

We had headed north to play a couple of friendlies after a pre-season using the facilities at Heriot-Watt University. We'd done a lot of 1,500 metre runs that the gaffer liked alternating between a six-minute and seven-minute mile pace and, while I was not a great admirer of pre-season generally, I got through it. Afterwards I was feeling a bit under the weather as I felt I was not one hundred per cent but I scored in both matches against Inverness Clachnacuddin 5–0 and Forres 9–1, and then again in a win at Morton 3–1. I also scored a late goal as a sub when we lost 3–1 at Ayresome Park against Middlesbrough but was struggling with my health.

Alan Rae discovered that I had an infection caused by my wisdom teeth and so I was whisked off to the Murrayfield hospital to have them removed straight away to give me time to recover for the opening League game against Aberdeen away.

I was still in my room the following morning when the phone woke me and, still a little bit groggy from the operation, I was surprised to hear Mo at the other end asking if I'd heard about last night? Obviously I hadn't and all he muttered was that he was injured and hadn't travelled but that Craig Levein and big Hoggy had been sent off. I assumed it was perhaps a naughty game (although Raith was a regular pre-season game for us and had never been a kicking match) or maybe an over-zealous young referee had got a bit card happy. It was then he had said no, they had been fighting each other and Craig had knocked Hoggy out!

So for the next few hours as I waited to get the all-clear to leave, I was reading the papers and calling a few lads to find out what had happened. It had started because of the same flaws that Hoggy had playing in a back three, which went back to the time with Joe Jordan. Craig dictated the line and when he pushed up, everyone was supposed to, but Hoggy had the tendency to drop back as he had been used to doing in a back four. It had led to many harsh words between Hoggy and the rest of the defenders at times. Raith had taken the lead through a Dalziel goal right on half time and Craig had pushed up and out with the rest of the back five only for Hoggy to stay deep and play Dalziel onside. Despite scrambling back to prevent the goal, the whole defence, and, in particular Craig, had had a go at Hoggy with Craig barking something like, 'Jesus Hoggy, are we going to spend another fucking pre-season going on about you pushing out!' As Craig approached him, there was an altercation and Hoggy stuck his head in Craig's face before Craig knocked him out with two blows that an accomplished boxer would have been proud of. All hell then broke loose, and both were sent packing, leaving the lads to play the whole of the second half with only nine men.

Now I had got all this second-hand, but it was on the news that night and was an explosive incident that the SFA jumped all over. In the end it cost them both a twelve-match suspension and some raised levels of tension in the dressing room as Craig was not happy that Hoggy had gone to the press with all sorts of allegations at the time. Not the midweek you wanted before heading to Pittodrie!

At Aberdeen in the season opener, JC levelled after their opening goal but we lost to two more goals from Billy Dodds and Scott Booth in a 3–1 defeat. Despite a 4–0 victory over Dumbarton in the League Cup, we then drew 1–1 against McLean's previous club, Motherwell, before our first home game of the season arrived against Hibs. This coincided with the opening of the massive Wheatfield Stand, replacing the old Shed and terracing and, of course, we were looking to extend the five-season unbeaten run against Hibs and the 22-game run that went with it. Alas, it was not to be as a goal by Gordon

Hunter gave Hibs the win. Despite dominating most of the game and laying siege to their goal for the last thirty minutes, we could not force the equaliser to keep the run going and Hibs celebrated a rare victory against us. It was annoying as we had clearly been the better side, but when you look back at the two runs we enjoyed against them, they could have won two or three matches but, this time, the luck was on their side. Jeebsy wrote his name into derby history as the man that stopped that incredible run.

Worse was to come for us. After racing into a comfortable 2–0 lead against St Johnstone in the Cup, an unfortunate slip at the back by Nicky Walker saw Stephen Frail punch the ball off the line and he was red carded. Despite Nicky saving the spot kick, we were down to ten men, and within thirty seconds of the second half, Saints had pulled one back. The gaffer had put on Tommy Harrison and when Saints first equalised and then went ahead with ten minutes to go, he took Tommy off again. This was devastating for the young lad and something I don't think he fully recovered from. Despite pouring everyone forward, Davie Irons clinched victory with a couple of minutes left. We were out the League Cup and the following Saturday we were thumped 3–0 at Ibrox as a Mark Hateley double and a Gordon Durie goal gave Rangers a comfortable win.

There was then a raft of changes as Jim Bett and Colin Miller arrived and Nicky Walker and Wayne Foster departed. At Christmas time, Willie Jamieson, David Hagen, Craig Nelson and Brian Hamilton arrived, with Mo being one of the Hearts lads to leave in exchange, and there was more change with Colin Cramb and Fraser Wishart arriving as the gaffer rang the changes.

Earlier in the season, there was a totally bizarre moment when Mo and I were both called out the dressing room to see the gaffer before the start of the Partick away game. We were told that he had decided to give Kevin Thomas a real run in the team and that one of us would have to make way for him but he couldn't decide which one it was going to be. Mo and I looked at each other and were dumbfounded by what happened next as he said that because he didn't know which one to drop he was going to flip a coin and the loser would be on the bench.

We couldn't believe it but he was adamant that this was his way of determining who was going to start with Kevin, at which point Mo stood up and said, 'Right, boss, I'll call.' The gaffer flipped the coin, and as it was in mid-air, Mo shouted heads, grabbed the coin, put it in his pocket and said it was 'tails so Robbo, you're playing,' and walked back to the dressing room with the coin in his pocket.

It was an odd way to decide the starting line-up but Mo's call was spot on as I scored the only goal early in the first half. But you could see that he knew he had riled the gaffer who, later in same game, berated him for warming up in his training shoes rather than match boots, despite Mo saying he would be ready when asked to come on.

Just a few weeks later they had another incident as Mo came in one day with designer jeans on. The gaffer, like Doddie before him, had a no blue jeans dress code and fined Mo £20, to which Mo argued that his designer jeans were probably worth more than everyone else's tracksuits put together. He was probably right but the gaffer stood his ground, so Mo walked over to his place, took out his wallet and handed the manager £100 in cash. McLean asked why he'd been handed £100 as the fine was only

£20? To which Mo gave that cheeky grin and said, 'Keep it as I'm wearing them for the rest of the week.'

I scored the winner against Celtic the following week before netting again in a 2–0 win against Aberdeen as we recorded three wins on the bounce. But that was stopped by Hibs again as they scored twice through Darren Jackson and Michael O'Neill in the first fifteen minutes. I pulled a goal back ten minutes from time before both myself and Dave MacPherson had headers blocked and our rivals made it two wins from two.

Mo had left, but the arrival of Jim Bett was tremendous and I have to say he was one of the finest midfield players I played with in my career. His composure on the ball and his ability to spot a pass was as good as anything I had seen. He was superb for us in this challenging season that had seen the twelve-game bans, the derby run ended and us losing our young captain, Alan McLaren in a million pound move to Rangers.

There was the Edinburgh derby coming up, a game that is still the subject of one of the weirdest conspiracy theories in the fixture to date. As we approached the New Year game, we had won only one game in eight. We had just been beaten 3–1 at Aberdeen on the Saturday and were due to play Hibs on the Monday when the game was called off due to a 'waterlogged' pitch. Even to this day, Hibs fans are convinced that the gaffer had ordered the pitch to be watered and, with snow coming, it would be unplayable. I can honestly say I have no idea if that is true or not, but the game was cancelled. We instead played a few weeks later and we beat Hibs 2–0, with Dave MacPherson and Johnny Millar goals restoring what we considered the natural order of things in the city rivalry.

There was discord in the dressing room as the gaffer and

his assistant Tom Forsyth were pretty volatile and the results were not what they wanted. We had continued to struggle in the League and were in the bottom half of the table and there were more than a few players who felt that the tactics employed were extremely negative and based on defence. That was not something we were used to, but it was the manager's way and the Scottish Cup again offered us a chance to salvage something from the season. After a postponed game, we drew 1–1 at Clydebank where my penalty was cancelled out by Ken Eadie before Kevin Thomas and I earned us a place in the next round in the replay and a home game live on Sky against Rangers.

The game was played on a Monday evening and was an absolute classic, well worthy of the UK audience that tuned in. As a sideshow, it pitched me against the recently departed Alan McLaren and I was looking forward to the battle. I knew he would be too, and, boy, what a battle it was. Colin Miller fired us ahead with a free kick before big Dave (who had arrived back as part exchange for Alan) headed us two in front. Then Brian Laudrup and Gordon Durie levelled it up in fifty-eight minutes before I scored just sixty seconds later as a Jim Bett shot was parried out to give us the lead. Both teams went toe-to-toe for a last half-hour that was eventually settled in the final minute. Big Dave went on one of his iconic runs up the park and played a couple of one-twos before releasing Kevin Thomas to blast in a fourth and clinching goal. The Hearts fans went wild and spilled out after the game to celebrate a famous Cup win.

We were given two days off with it being a Monday evening match and we headed to our after-match destination, Montpeliers in Bruntsfield. It was on the way that big Dave and I realised that there was an added bonus awaiting us on our arrival. After the Clydebank replay we had been in Monty's and had bumped into David Wither and his wife from the group that owned not only Montpeliers but also Tigerlily and Indigo Yard, among others. David was a big Rangers fan and, as the draw had already been made, we knew that Rangers were waiting for us in the next round.

There was a fair bit of banter going on and with a few drinks down us and getting a bit braver, we jokingly asked David – who was sure his team would advance – to put his money (or in this case his drink) where his mouth was. Initially we were saying a couple of bottles of red wine, but David was having none of it. He wanted to bet champagne and was laying down a bet of six bottles (three each for me and Dave), so with the drink taking effect, we thought we would call his bluff and say, 'Okay, how about six each from us against a case from you?'

He countered by saying, 'You must fancy your chances, so it's a case from you guys (twelve) against two cases from me,' which, to much laughter from the rest of our party, was agreed. By the Thursday, we were a little bit sheepish about our bravado but, fortunately, in the end, we won our wager. I have to say that over the months and years that followed, we not only collected the entirety of the bet but also a few extra bottles as we were never great counters anyway!

Two Johnny Millar goals gave us a win over Dundee Utd in the quarter-finals and once more we headed to Hampden and another opportunity to get to a final. And once more it was Airdrie that stood in our way. We didn't need reminding about how well Alex MacDonald had done with them and we again headed into the game in poor form, on the back of defeats to Falkirk and Partick Thistle.

The game, as usual, started off like a hurricane and inside three minutes I chased a long ball forward and headed it on. As I did so, Paul Jack attempted a hooked clearance and caught me on the head and off I went, dizzy and requiring six stitches in a head wound. I was soon back on the pitch, unaware until the following day that in my fall I had also broken my arm about five inches above my wrist. Only the pain from the head wound had stopped me realising this. The pain was not helped when Stevie Cooper headed Airdrie in front and once more we needed to pierce their well-drilled defensive set up. We went close a few times, with Johnny Millar clipping the bar and John Martin pulling off a few saves before, in the last minute, I went to make a run for a throw-in and got an elbow in the face from young Anthony Smith – an ex-Hearts player. It was totally unlike him. I instinctively lashed out and caught him but, unfortunately for me, Hugh Dallas, after talking to his linesman, decided to book Tony but I was sent off for retaliation.

As I sat in the dressing room, I was gutted. Having played well, I felt I had let the team, the fans and my family down and that I was fast running out of chances to win something. Another glorious opportunity had passed us by. My mood was worsened when it was confirmed I had broken my arm and would be out for the next few games with the club deep in a relegation battle.

While I was upset at my own injury, young Kevin Thomas had suffered a cruciate knee injury when, incredibly, he was allowed back on to the pitch for a few minutes after suffering the initial trauma. Kevin recovered well enough after a period of months out the game but he never really recaptured the promise he showed early in his career. There is no doubt in my mind that he could have gone on to achieve far more if he hadn't suffered this cruel injury at such a young age.

With defeats to Kilmarnock away and Thistle at home, David Hagen grabbed a late winner as we beat Celtic away. It was needed. Defeats to Aberdeen and then Hibs, where we led 1–0 before collapsing to three goals lost in seven minutes, meant we needed a point at home to be sure of staying up against, of all people, the gaffer's old club Motherwell.

In a tense and nervous game, Brian Hamilton put us ahead before I scored a late penalty that moved us up three places and to safety. But it was clear that the players were struggling to play in the gaffer's negative style and the fans were not happy with what they saw as a defensive system. They wanted change and they made it clear there was only one man for the job, and that was former player and club captain Jim Jefferies. He had been doing great things at Falkirk, having arrived there from spells at Gala and Berwick Rangers, and after plenty of speculation he was finally prised away from Falkirk back to his spiritual home in Gorgie. He would see the club finally break their semi-final hoodoo.

On the Scotland front, I had not been involved for about eighteen months and it looked like eleven caps was all that I would attain for my country. Duncan Ferguson, Duncan Shearer, Eoin Jess, Scott Booth, Darren Jackson, Gordon Durie and, of course, Coisty were all deemed better options, so when Scotland announced a huge squad for the Kirin Cup in Japan it came as no real surprise to me that I was once again overlooked. That appeared to be that in terms of international selection.

Having not made the initial thirty-man squad, all of whom Craig Brown had asked to send in their passport details to get visas, I had looked at getting a break before doing my usual pre-season training with George and Bert down at Meadowbank. I went in to Tynecastle to find out when we would be returning to training and was informed by Les Porteous that they had just received a call from the SFA asking for me to report to Slaters in Glasgow the following day to be measured for a suit and that I was travelling to Japan as part of the squad! I assumed Les was at the wind-up as given they had selected thirty players and only eighteen were travelling, there was no way there could be that many call-offs, but he assured me there had been a few Old Firm players and English based players who had called off 'injured' and that myself and the uncapped Paul Lambert had been called up. That meant they were busy applying for visas for us to travel.

The fun started when the squad met up. Craig Brown went through the details and handed out little baseball cards of the players, saying the Japanese people loved collecting them and we were to hand out these photos at training. Each player would have a hundred with the new Scottish strip. Paul Lambert and I exchanged a wry grin as we had not been privy to being photographed in the kit. It was of great amusement to the squad when Craig apologised to me and said the best they could do was superimpose my head onto Duncan Shearer's body. It made me look like something out of the mutant team in the movie *Space Jam* but sent the rest of the squad into hysterics.

The three-team tournament saw us play the hosts Japan first, and John Spencer and Darren Jackson were selected to start up front. Paul Lambert finally got his well-deserved first cap. It became apparent that the Japanese football team was tough: they battered into tackles and were extremely physical, if not downright dirty, with elbows off the ball, late tackles, shirt pulling and body checking going on from the off. After about thirty-five minutes, John Spencer had had enough and retaliated with a wild kick, to be promptly sent off by the 'neutral' referee who had turned a blind eye to most of what was going on so far.

I was summoned from the bench, told to strip and replaced the luckless Paul Lambert as Darren Jackson dropped into midfield. I was instructed to put myself about up front and give us a platform to play from. I actually did very well as the lone striker and had a couple of half chances that brought decent saves. And I also had a free kick deflected just wide before Darren nearly won it for us after a wee one-two between us, only to have his shot blocked by the huge Japanese keeper. Both teams were down to ten men late on as I drew another foul from their centre-half and made enough of it to earn him his second booking. But the bruising encounter finished 0–0 on goals, 1–1 on red cards and about 7–7 on yellow cards. It was not a classic but was a decent result considering we were down to ten for around fifty minutes of the game against a team that, while overly physical, actually possessed a number of talented technical players.

A few days later we played Ecuador and I was selected to start alongside another debutant, Stevie Crawford. We played well together as a pair, mixing up who went short, who went in behind and we had lots of little step-overs and round the corner passes. Eventually our link-up play paid off as I slipped him in to fire us in front with eighteen minutes to go before Hurtado equalised from the penalty spot just two minutes later. I then backheeled us in front and both Stevie and I hit the woodwork before the final whistle. We had recorded a victory which meant that Japan had to beat Ecuador by two or more to win the Cup. They did that and more with a couple of late goals giving them a 3–0 win. The trophy remained on home soil but it had been a great experience and I had added two more caps to my tally. The same squad travelled to the Faroe Islands on our return and I was a late substitute in a game where we won 2–0 to keep European qualification on track.

I made my final appearance for Scotland in a friendly in Sweden in a 2–0 defeat and I did well enough, being unlucky not to score on a couple of occasions, but I was never picked again. So my lot at international level consisted of sixteen full caps and one non-cap appearance for Scotland against the Scottish League. I loved every minute of playing for my country as, once more, I reminded myself of the 'too small, too fat, too slow' jibe I'd had to put up with. Looking back, I don't think anyone would disagree that I deserved more opportunities for my country given the domestic totals I scored every season. However, I suppose a mixture of some top class strikers in my early years and then just a probable lack of belief from Scotland managers that my style would be suited to international football, plus the much trotted-out excuse that McCoist and I were too similar, saw the total remain meagre. But, to be honest, I haven't lost much sleep over it as, while I wasn't perhaps fully appreciated in the west, that was definitely not the case in Gorgie.

22

Breaking Records and Hampden Horror

There was a prolonged battle to prise Jim Jefferies away from Falkirk. And as we continued our pre-season, it seemed to be dragging on endlessly. Then, late on in pre-season, Jim and Billy Brown were eventually unveiled as the new management team.

Jim and Billy had us back to more familiar surroundings as we battled round the Braid Hills Golf Course and the Queen's Park in the first few days of their pre-season. They made it clear that everyone was under scrutiny as they felt the club had been underperforming. You could see from the off that the gaffer had a huge passion for the club and that he was determined to be a success. And, like Alex MacDonald, the basis of that was going to be down to fitness and an attacking brand of football that they had used at their previous clubs. No one was safe and changes would be made.

They were prepared to play the outstanding youngsters we had and bring in new faces if required, and almost immediately David Winnie and Alan Lawrence were added to the squad. The first game they took charge of was Derby County away, after we had beaten Peterhead and Elgin 6–0 and 4–0 respectively – the Elgin game being played in the hottest conditions I have ever seen in Scotland. Then a 3–3 draw at Montrose saw us travel south after a quick introduction to the new management team. We started the match at the Baseball Ground and in the blink of an eye we were 3–0 down and getting berated by our new boss on the touchline. Fortunately David Hagen and I grabbed a goal each in the final sixty seconds of the first half to slightly ease the half-time team talk, but we were still given a reminder of the gaffer's standards and that much more was expected in the second half. We grabbed an equaliser with thirteen minutes to go, through an own goal, which slightly appeased our new management team.

We then lost 1–0 to a Peter Beardsley goal for Newcastle at Tynecastle before thumping Manchester City 5–1 in a testimonial game. But it was clear that the gaffer and Billy believed changes were required and were bemused to say the least as to why there were still players here from his own spell as a player. Many had been at the club for a long time and more new blood and fresh faces were needed going forward.

We drew 1–1 at Motherwell before Nipper Lawrence, a JC double, and I saw the gaffer win his opening League match at Tynecastle. And, with Alloa and Dunfermline dispatched in the second and third rounds of the League Cup, we were sitting in the quarter-finals when a week from hell was unleashed. Determined to mix up the team and introduce change, the gaffer and Billy snapped as we lost 2–0 at Partick Thistle. We then travelled to Dens Park for the chance to make the semi-finals of the League Cup and a game that was astonishing to say the least.

Breaking Records and Hampden Horror

No one could have predicted the drama of the evening when, after a dour battle, the game remained goalless after forty minutes. Then, suddenly, George Shaw scored twice in as many minutes and we went into the break 2–0 down and teetering on the brink. We were lambasted by the gaffer and Billy for what they saw as a lacklustre performance and came out for the second half with their words ringing in our ears. We were going down the slope, and began to take control. Big Dave pulled one back before JC bundled in the equaliser only for us to go behind less than sixty seconds later to a Paul Tosh header. It looked all over before Alan Lawrence scored to square the match 3–3 and take us into extra time. A sublime Morten Wieghorst chip put Dundee ahead once again and after I was bundled over, I converted the spot kick to make it 4–4. Both teams then had chances to win it before the final whistle went and it was down to penalties.

The gaffer asked for names to take the kicks, but only JC and I put ourselves forward. Looking about, a lot of lads' heads dropped. David Hagen and Alan Lawrence finally said they would take one, with Hagey's proviso that if he was taking one, he wanted to be first. But that left us with a problem as we still needed one more. With players still not stepping up, Big Henry said he would take one! Now Henry took them after training with the players and was actually really good, with his technique being to take one step and side foot it high to either side. But that was training and this was to reach a semi-final. However, with no one else prepared to take one, he was given the go ahead. Having been at fault for a couple of the goals, maybe this was a chance for redemption.

After Hagen and Nipper had cancelled out Dundee's first two

penalties (Hagey taking his with his weaker foot as he felt more confident with that one), Henry pulled off a save from Tosh and signalled he would take the third spot kick himself. With all the excitement, he probably felt the adrenalin would help and he then set himself up, took one step, and side footed the ball high to the left as the Dundee keeper dived to the right. Unfortunately for Henry, the ball smashed off the junction of the bar and post. Duffy and Anderson scored for Dundee and JC for us, then I was left with the last kick, sending the keeper the wrong way to square the score 4–4. Then Wieghorst scored again and we looked around to see that no one was putting themselves forward for the next kick. Big Willie Jamieson eventually said he would take it and, despite putting the keeper the wrong way, his shot came back off the post and we were out. It dawned on me, as the Dundee lads charged towards their keeper, Michel Pageaud, that he had gone the wrong way for every one of our penalties and yet they were through.

The gaffer went nuts after the game and vowed changes – and plenty of them. He felt there was obviously a problem with our mentality and that there were too many losers at the club. His mood was not helped as we were thumped 4–0 at home by Celtic on the Saturday, and with Hibs on the horizon at Easter Road, 'trialists' started to appear at training as the threatened changes accelerated.

The game at Easter Road ended up being a landmark one for me as we started the match well and eventually the pressure paid off. Big Dave headed in my cross to put us in front at half time and we were well in control before we had a mad few minutes that saw Graeme Donald bundle in an equaliser. We then lost Gary Mackay to a stamp on Gareth Evans and with us up against it, Hibs took the lead through Pat McGinlay. It was still 2–1 when we approached the third minute of injury time and were awarded a free kick. We threw everyone into the box for one final assault. JC, on as a sub, clipped it towards me and I flicked it on before a scramble that saw the ball fall to me fifteen yards out. I cracked it low past Jim Leighton and into the back of the net. It sent the fans behind the goal into delirium and rescued a point. The Hibs fans were in despair once more as their victory songs were silenced.

After the game we were told by the manager that the police had asked for us to be away from the ground sharpish. They wanted to escort us up to London Road and away from any potential trouble. As I headed off to the press, I was told to be no more than two minutes or I was getting left behind. It was that warning that led to the following day's headlines and the subtitle of this book. The press were obviously asking the usual questions like, 'did we believe we had blown the chance to win having controlled most of the game', and 'how was Gary feeling after being sent off', and 'did I still believe I would get the chance to equalise'. Having answered them, I apologised and said I had to go as the bus was leaving.

Jim Kean of the *Daily Record* said, 'So the show's not over till the fat lady sings?'

And I instinctively replied, 'No, Jim. The game's not over till the fat striker scores.'

It's a phrase that was hammered out in the tabloids and brought many a smile to the Hearts fans as I had been teased relentlessly on what many people saw as a chunky physique. I was no Charles Atlas, but I always felt it was a bit harsh and never thought that I carried that much weight, but this was not a view carried by opposition and indeed some Hearts fans.

In the aftermath over the next few days, that goal became an important one for me personally as it took me one past Willie Bauld in terms of League goals scored; now only Jimmy Wardhaugh on 206 stood between me and the ultimate target of becoming the club's all-time leading League goalscorer. It was very much in my sights.

Beating Willie Bauld's record was huge. I was friendly with the Bauld family, and his son, Willie Jnr, was immediately on the phone congratulating me on my achievement. That meant a great deal to me as Willie Bauld was, and will always remain, the 'King of Hearts'. It was an emotional moment as, while my dad had always loved Freddie Glidden and admired his grace and play, like all Hearts fans he revered the Terrible Trio and adored Willie Bauld. I felt that at long last I had achieved something that would have made my dad proud.

I wish he could have seen his little boy score the goal that took him past one of his heroes and the greatest striker that ever wore the famous maroon jersey. Then afterwards, I could have bought him his favourite tipple, a rum and coke, to celebrate. But, of course, it was not to be. So I was hugely proud but also sad, and I now knew that I had to strive and score more to break the record held by Jimmy 'Twinkle-Toes' Wardhaugh, a record that I'd always been told would never be broken.

Within a month, the sweeping changes were starting at the club and I wondered if even I could survive the brutal cull the gaffer and Billy deemed necessary. The mercurial Stevie Fulton arrived alongside Neil Pointon and Paul Smith, and from abroad, striker Hans Eskilsson, goalkeeper Gilles Rousset and the fearsome Pasquale Bruno were signed. With youngsters Paul

Ritchie, Alan McManus and Allan Johnston getting more and more game time, it was clear that the management were determined to get rid of what they saw as dead wood. There would be no room for sentiment as players like Henry and Neil Berry were let go to make way for the new recruits.

Wins were still hard for us to find as the new recruits settled in and only Raith and Partick were beaten in a run of ten matches from the Dundee League Cup exit. We came from behind against Partick with two late goals from JC and Allan Johnston and headed down to Easter Road in buoyant mood to face a Hibs side that had been battered by Rangers on the Saturday and looked very fragile. Having followed up our last gasp draw earlier in the season with victory at Tynecastle against them, we felt that if we could get an early goal, Hibs would be there for the taking.

After a nice interchange, Neil 'Disa' Pointon fired us ahead in only seven minutes. We smelled blood and poured down the slope looking for the goal that could open the floodgates, and after twenty minutes we should have had it as I squirmed my way into the box. Being at a tight angle, I sensed and hoped someone was coming in more centrally and squared the ball across the goal where, to my delight, Hans Eskilsson was arriving. With an open goal gaping, it looked like we were going two up when, inexplicably, he somehow screwed his shot wide of the post, missing an absolute sitter. No one in a maroon jersey could believe it. To make matters worse, Hibs sensed the reprieve and went on to lead at half time, against the run of play, with goals from Kevin Harper and Michael O'Neill. Incredibly, despite pinning them in their own half for vast swathes of the second half, they kept us at bay. The New Year derby was theirs, much to the disbelief and annoyance of the gaffer and every Hearts fan attending. Once more he let us know that our yo-yo form was not acceptable.

We rallied and won four of the next five, with only a defeat to Celtic. That run included a simply brilliant hat-trick from Allan 'Magic' Johnston at Ibrox as he continued to flourish in the first team. And when we followed that up with a Paul Ritchie winner in the Cup at Partick, we felt once more that we could go deep into the tournament. Back-to-back victories at Kilmarnock in the League and the Cup showed we were still coming on strong in the second half of the season, and another victory away from home over St Johnstone in the quarter-finals saw us head to Hampden where Aberdeen awaited us.

I had been in and out of the team as the gaffer had persisted with Alan Lawrence, JC, Magic Johnston and Hans, and it was frustrating. Privately, I backed myself as I had seen other managers come in and decide to try something other than me, but I always knew that, given the opportunity, I would score goals and show that I was still the best finisher at the club. So, during this run, I made sure I supported whoever was starting and did my best to make an impression when given the opportunity. It was during this spell that, even at the age of thirty-two, I found I was still capable of taking on advice and key lessons.

We had travelled midweek to play Kilmarnock in the reserve league. As I had not started a game for a while, I was told to go and get some match fitness under my belt. I was then named up front by Paul Hegarty who, while being first team coach with the gaffer and Billy, also took the reserve team. After twenty minutes or so there was a clatter from the sidelines as the substitute boards went up and the number 9 appeared. I turned round to young Kris O'Neil and said, 'You okay?'

He just looked at me and said, 'Robbo, YOU are number 9!'

I was shocked, embarrassed and absolutely livid as I jogged off and shook hands with the sub. As I headed towards Paul, he just said, go for a shower, watch the game and we will chat later on in the bus.

The game finished 0–0 and I was still livid so I took a seat midway up the bus while I waited for the rest of the team. Eventually we left for Edinburgh and after about twenty minutes Paul asked me to come down to the front. Paul Hegarty is a man I had, and still have to this day, a huge amount of respect for as a player, a coach and as a person, but I don't mind admitting at this point I was still raging. He sat me down and asked if I was prepared to listen to what he had to say before coming back at him. He then asked me how I thought I'd played.

I said, 'Yeah, I thought I did all right and was doing okay in the game.'

He replied, 'Yes, you were doing okay, but when you are John Robertson, an international player and top goalscorer year in, year out, at the club then all right is not good enough!'

He proceeded to tell me that 'doing okay' and chasing a ball here and there, holding it up and generally being bang average was not going to get me back in the team. He explained that shortly the gaffer would be phoning him, and he could guarantee the first question would be, 'How did Robbo play?' and if that answer was okay or all right, it was not going to get me back in the team on Saturday.

'Imagine,' he said, 'if I told the gaffer, "He was unbelievable, boss. He chased lost causes, he bullied the centre-halves, he ran himself into the ground and looked really sharp. And although he didn't score, he worked his socks off and showed the young players the standards they have to reach if they are going to get in the first team!" You think he wants to hear that? Or he did all right? All right is not good enough for you.'

He was bang on and I really didn't have an answer so I accepted it, and, despite being livid and more than a little pissed off at being subbed, I took it on board and vowed he would never be able to do that to me again. Which was exactly the effect he hoped to achieve.

I was on the bench on the Saturday, but the following Monday when we headed to Pittodrie to play Aberdeen, I was up front with Kevin Thomas. My first thought was, 'Right, I'm not getting taken off tonight!' I was wrong, but this time it was for the right reasons as I scored two, laid on the third for Kevin and ran myself in to the ground, so much so that I got cramp with ten minutes left and hobbled to the changing room exhausted.

The following day Aberdeen put in a £30,000 bid for me. Having watched my performance and thinking that I wasn't in the plans, they would be more than happy to take me north. The gaffer had thought about it but told me he was turning it down as I was still part of his own plans. It was a harsh but well-meant lesson that Heggy had dished out to me about standards and perceptions. I used that to kick on once more, but still I could not get back into the team as the semi-final approached. On the day itself, once more I found myself on the bench but ready to do whatever it took to get us back to a final.

Like every other Hearts fan that watched the match, I was nervous. We had continually failed at this stage, and the semi-final defeats from St Mirren, Celtic, Rangers and Airdrie (twice), as well as League Cup semi-final losses to Dundee Utd and Rangers, still haunted us. The game was full of long bangers, the ball finding itself up in the air, and at half time the gaffer told everyone, and especially the younger ones, that they had to seize the opportunity as finals did not come along every season. They had to be prepared to push on more and have some belief. He stuck to his favoured 3-5-2 formation that saw Bruno have the two young lads either side and Lockie and Disa as wing-backs. Mackay, Johnston and Fulton were the midfield three with JC and Nipper his front two, and that left Kevin Thomas, Big Dave and me on the bench.

With nothing really happening at either end, Aberdeen summoned Duncan Shearer from the bench with twenty minutes to go. Just four minutes later, Big Dave and I were brought on for Nipper and Stevie Fulton as we switched to a 4-3-3 formation. With ten minutes to go, we took the lead. Disa floated in a corner, Big Dave knocked it down, and after my first flick was blocked, I managed to scramble it home and over the line, much to the delight of the Hearts fans. It looked as if that would be enough as we retreated to defend our goal and see out time, but it was never going to be that simple. With just three minutes left, Aberdeen were level as a sublime Shearer header from a free kick floated over big Gilles to make it 1–1.

The Celtic semi-final flashed into my head. Could it really happen again? But this time it was a happy ending as Gilles knocked a long ball out, and, after Disa had flicked it on, I collected it wide and decided right away to just whip it into the box. To my delight, Magic Johnston arrived on cue and headed home, and our semi-final hoodoo was finally over. We would be back in May to meet Rangers, led by the imperious Brian Laudrup and Paul Gascoigne.

We also signed Colin Cameron who had been a fantastic player for Raith Rovers, and, although cup-tied, everyone knew he was a shrewd piece of business. The changes kept coming. Indeed, our League form had been good since the turn of the year and we gave ourselves a boost by beating Rangers 2–0 at Tynecastle in a run of five wins and two draws from our last seven games. This saw us finish the season in fourth spot, missing out to Aberdeen on goal difference and the Old Firm, who were a distance ahead of everyone else. Rangers were top of the League once again, notching up their eighth title in a row.

The build-up to the final was a quiet one as the gaffer and Billy wanted it low key so we could focus on what we needed to do well as a team. We needed to replicate our win at Tynecastle a few weeks earlier, and if we concentrated we had a fair chance of winning as we had been in good form to finish the season. It was pretty obvious that, despite starting that victory over Rangers, it was unlikely that the gaffer was going to change the team much for the final.

As we went over the shadow play and set pieces it was clear that we would go with the 3-5-2 system, the only real change being that Big Dave would be playing at wing back with Lockie in central midfield, and Allan Johnston would partner JC up top. Although disappointed, I'd had a feeling that would be the case, but, like the semi-final, I was ready to come on and do what was required to help win us the Cup. As an experienced pro, I had to help keep the younger lads calm, focused and as nerveless as possible, which for Lockie in particular was a tough ask. As a dyed in the wool Jambo, you could see as the day got closer that he was getting more and more excited. His dream of not only winning a trophy with Hearts but being the man who ultimately, if all went well, would be lifting it first as captain, was within touching distance.

Sadly, it was not to be. Lockie did his cruciate after just seven minutes in, and his dream was over. We went behind to a very good finish from Laudrup but we were still well in the final at half time. As we took Lockie off, I had a feeling that the gaffer would drop Magic back into midfield and put me up front with JC. While that indeed was his move with Magic, it was Nipper Lawrence that was summoned to replace him. That left just me and substitute keeper Myles Hogarth on the bench. Although hugely disappointed, I kept thinking that, like the semi, I had a part to play if required and that it was about the club winning the trophy and everyone doing their bit to get us there.

Big Gilles had been a revelation since joining us. I had got on great with him and Pasquale Bruno from the off and the gaffer had pulled a real coup with him. The big man had two caps for France and had shown why, with a string of fine performances since taking over from Henry Smith. He was already a firm favourite with the Hearts fans alongside the new cult hero and resident hard man Bruno, but what happened just four minutes into the second half, you would not have wished on your worst enemy.

As an innocuous Laudrup cross floated harmlessly into our box, Gilles stooped to collect it but somehow it squirmed through his hands, then through his legs and trundled over the line without even reaching the net. Suddenly and unexpectedly it was 2–0 to Rangers and there was a mountain to climb. It left Gilles wanting the ground to swallow him up and everyone knew that there was no way we were coming back from it against a Rangers team with their tails up. Gordon Durie went on to score a hat-trick, and despite JC pulling back one at 3–0, Rangers went on to win 5–1.

I had come on just before Jukebox made it 3–0 but it made little difference. We were well beaten and had a captain with a busted knee and a keeper with a busted heart. Even with thousands of fans singing his name outside the George Hotel on our return, there was no consoling the big man. But he vowed he would make up for it and he most certainly kept that vow.

23

The Real Thing Final and the Man Who Cancelled Christmas

I had finished top goalscorer again but with only fourteen goals and, while I was not exactly happy with that total, I had seen that the gaffer was still bringing in players in all positions to create competition. Up front he had used various players and combinations and I knew once more that he would bring in forwards as he wasn't entirely happy with the balance of the front men. He'd played JC, Nipper Lawrence, Allan Johnston, Hans Eskilsson, Kevin Thomas and me, and there was still a feeling that he wanted the last of the old brigade to be moved on. But, to be fair, Gary Mackay, JC, Big Dave and I were still doing as well as the new players being brought in, although it looked as though if the right replacements were found then we would be the ones to be moved aside.

And so the battle was on to stay ahead of any prospective new players and, of course, the young guns coming through the ranks. Once more I made sure that I was as fit as I could be for pre-season, knowing the gaffer and Billy always seem to have a keener eye on my fitness than the rest of the lads. I didn't mind that as it had been the same since day one with Alex MacDonald.

We had more arrivals with Davie Weir coming from Falkirk in defence and the experienced Jeremy Goss in midfield. Neil McCann had been recruited from Dundee for £200,000 for the wing, before the obligatory new striker, this time Darren Beckford, was unveiled. All this was in August and with the late season signing of the already settled and impressive Colin Cameron, we seemed to have a strong squad assembled.

As we started the games in pre-season, I had got myself on to a total of 194 League goals and knew that, with this being the last year of my current contract, I needed thirteen more to break the club record of 206 held by Jimmy Wardhaugh. That was now one of my prime aims, along with the usual one to end the drought of silverware and bring home a trophy. I was fast realising, however, that time was running out to achieve the latter.

The Republic of Ireland was the destination for a couple of matches, and we beat Dundalk 3–1 with JC, Mickey (Cameron) and I scoring in a 3–1 win. Then a completely different eleven drew 1–1 with Shamrock Rovers, with Kevin Thomas scoring. We returned to Scotland and defeated the gaffer's old club Berwick 5–1 before we were handed a lesson from FC Porto as Jardel scored twice and the visitors beat us 3–1. Kevin Thomas scored our only goal of the game as we readied ourselves for a difficult Cup Winners Cup match with the famous Red Star Belgrade. Indeed, Kevin led the line and, just like Alex MacDonald had tended to do, I was on the bench for the European away game. We battled to a creditable 0–0 draw against a good technical side in front of 28,000 fanatical fans.

The following week we had a real scare as we fell behind to an Adrian Sprott penalty for Stenhousemuir, and despite a Neil McCann equaliser we just could not get the winner. Then we missed our first penalty in the shoot out before big Gilles made two great saves and we advanced 5–4 on penalties.

The following day I was asked to go see the manager. I thought I was in for a bollocking as I hadn't played well the previous evening – being asked to go see him was always an ominous sign. To my huge surprise he had told me I had been the subject of a £30,000 bid and he was thinking it over as he wasn't sure if he wanted me to leave. If that was a shock, there was another to come as he told me the bid had come from none other than our great rivals Hibs! He told me that I was not going to be involved over the weekend as he mulled it over and so I sat out the match against Kilmarnock which the lads won 3–2.

Come the Monday, he had decided I wasn't for sale and once more I found myself on the bench for the match against Red Star Belgrade. On a perfect evening, big Davie headed us in front right on half time, only for the Serbians to equalise on the hour with a carbon copy header from Marinovic. As the game progressed, Kevin Thomas was thrown on before I was slung on with just six minutes to go and nearly nicked it for us when I flicked on a near-post corner only for it to be blocked on the line and cleared away. That, unfortunately, was that, as we once more headed out of Europe on away goals.

I remained on the bench as Aberdeen hammered us 4–0 at Pittodrie and I was there again as we travelled to Perth to face St Johnstone and the game finished 1–1. I was brought on and set up Darren Beckford for our second before scoring a really good goal myself with a turn in the box and a curling left foot shot into the top corner. However, before my evening's work was finished, I was trod on and stretchered off to receive another seven stitches in a head wound. But we were through.

I made my first League start and scored the only goal against Dundee Utd, and as we looked forward to the upcoming quarter-final against Celtic, Stefano Salvatori was signed to bolster the midfield. But before we played Celtic, we had the small matter of visiting Ibrox for a game that would hit the headlines and leave us in deep trouble for the Cup.

We lost a goal to Rangers just before and just after the break before the roof caved in as referee Gerry Evans and his stand-side linesman, Graeme Allison, took centre stage. First, Pasquale Bruno picked up two quick yellow cards and was sent packing. Then, despite appearing to be head-butted by Gordon Durie, Davie Weir followed him with a straight red for retaliation and we were down to nine. After allowing a clear offside to play on, the linesman signalled the referee over and Neil Pointon was given another red card for kicking the post in disgust.

To complete twenty minutes of madness, Paul Ritchie followed suit as once more the linesman took offence to him questioning his decision-making with some colourful language. We were now down to seven men, meaning one more man off and the game would have to be abandoned. Richard Gough was pleading with the referee to take no more action. As the mayhem continued, Chris Robinson appeared and asked the gaffer to take us off the field in protest. Rangers were content to see the game out, adding one more goal late on.

As you can imagine, there was a massive probe into the game but, more worrying for us was that all four were now suspended for the midweek cup tie against Celtic. That meant finding an entirely new back four for the game. When we trained on the Sunday, the gaffer and Billy experimented in a practice match that saw Dave MacPherson back from injury line to up with Stefano Salvatori at centre back, with Gary Mackay at right back and youngster Gary Naysmith at left back. It was no real surprise to anyone that the 'reserves' beat us 3–0.

Things were looking bleak as, by the match day, we had still not looked like solving the problem. Indeed, it wasn't until the pre-match at the Grosvenor Hotel that I saw a familiar face who had been drafted in to help us out. The gaffer had signed an emergency centre-back on a month's contract, none other than my old teammate and pal Andy Thorn who hadn't played for a while because of injury. Now he was about to be thrown in at the deep end against Celtic alongside Big Dave with Alan McManus at right back and debutant Naysmith at left back.

Andy was outstanding as he and the back four kept Pierre van Hooijdonk, Jorge Cadete and Paolo Di Canio at bay. Then, once more, we saw red and after sixty-six minutes Stefano was sent off. We hung in there, roared on by a fantastic home crowd, before the teams were level once more as Peter Grant saw red in extra time. A great Stevie Fulton ball set Neil McCann free on the left and I thought Terry would play it in early so I took off towards the middle. Sure enough, in it came and I just slowed down and let the ball run in front of me before driving it past big Gordon Marshall in goal to send Tynecastle into meltdown. Then it was back to big Gilles, Andy, Big Dave and the lads to battle away and see out the remaining minutes to get us through to a semi-final against Dundee. It was a famous victory on the night.

Two weeks later saw another landmark moment as two goals

from Mickey Cameron and a third from me saw us win the derby, made even more special with it being my 250th competitive goal for Hearts. I scored again at Raith as I edged closer toward the club League goalscoring record.

The semi-final against Dundee was at Easter Road and we were hot favourites but, given our semi-final record, no one was taking anything for granted. My night ended early as a recurrence of a hamstring strain from arthritis in my hip saw me come off just before Mickey slammed us ahead from the penalty spot. Goals from Darren Beckford and new signing (another striker) Stéphane Paille saw us 3–0 up before Jim Hamilton pulled one back for the Dee. But we were through and that meant Rangers in November at Celtic Park as Hampden was being redeveloped. Celtic's stadium also had work going on but had the biggest capacity available, so that's where we would play the final. We stayed in good form as two wins over Dunfermline and Motherwell and a 0–0 draw with Hibs saw us ready for the Coca-Cola Cup final. It was the real thing.

There was early drama as the match was in doubt because of heavy snowstorms in Glasgow which meant the pitch and the surrounding areas were snowbound. But the game got started and it was Rangers who were out the traps as Coisty rapped in a double. We looked down and out, with us barely laying a glove on them. Somehow we found a way back in as Stevie Fulton hammered home right on the stroke of half time.

The gaffer was calm and told us this was a time for no regrets and that the next goal was huge. If we got it, we could go on and win the match and deliver the trophy. Now we had to show how much we wanted it.

The first twenty minutes of the second half saw us swarm

all over Rangers and Mickey was inches away from equalising as he raced onto my through ball. He got his shot away under pressure, only for Andy Goram's studs to divert it past the post. But we were on top and Neil McCann was creating havoc on the left flank as he ripped Rangers apart – so much so that they tried three different players against him, but he simply could not be stopped. On the day, he was unplayable and after sixty minutes he cut past three Rangers defenders, threw in a cross that I had gambled on and, from what was later shown as an offside position, I bundled home. We were level and suddenly sensed this was our time, only for a controversial decision to swing the final back Rangers' way.

As I was fouled on the touchline, instead of getting the free kick, Hugh Dallas awarded Rangers the throw. As we appealed, they went down the park and Gazza curled them ahead before scoring a superb solo goal just two minutes later. But still we rallied. Goram produced a good save from me before an unbelievable save from a Disa header. We kept piling forward and then Davie Weir glanced a header in with two minutes to go. But we just couldn't get the equaliser and, once more, despite a tremendous second-half performance, the cup eluded us. It was a hard one to take and, like the fans, we headed home empty handed.

We lost the next couple of games before the gaffer made another signing in December, and once more it was another striker. We paid six figures once more, this time for another Dundee player, Jim Hamilton, who was seen as one of the up and coming forwards in the country. Despite a decent run in the team, on reaching the stadium to face Kilmarnock, I was told I wasn't in the starting eleven or indeed on the subs bench.

My misery was compounded. Despite a bright debut from big Hammy, we were very poor and lost the match 2–0. Afterwards, the gaffer went nuts and told every player to report the following morning at 9 a.m. as he was going to run the bollocks off us. He had not got what he wanted.

Now, one or two of the lads were quite alarmed as the following day we were due on the midday train to Newcastle for the Christmas night out. It had been arranged with the coaching staff well in advance and we were spending the Sunday evening there before returning on the Monday for training on the Tuesday. I wasn't there to hear it, as the door was locked when I got down from the stand, but the gaffer had told the dressing room that the night out was cancelled and we could forget it.

The following day as we waited in the dressing room, most of the lads were still asking if they thought the gaffer would stick to his threats. And, to be fair, we thought he would probably run us into the ground and then say right, off you go. He came in, ordered us onto the pitch and proceeded to get everything he could out of us as we were subjected to three 4-minute runs then an increased demand where he ran us for thirty seconds then jogged thirty, then ran us for a minute, jogged thirty, ran us a minute and half, jogged thirty. He did this all the way up to four minutes and back down before doing 150-yarders in relay fashion and finishing with runs up and down the steps of the new stand, where one or two of the lads were reintroduced to their breakfast. After two brutal hours we were sent back to the dressing room for a meeting with the gaffer.

Again we thought, right he has punished us, we had reached the cup final and were doing all right in the League so he would surely come in, berate us again but then tell us to go to Newcastle and enjoy our night out. But no, the gaffer came in, hammered us as a squad, said he was not prepared to accept what he was getting and that we could go 'fuck ourselves because we were not going to Newcastle'. Christmas was cancelled and anyone that went to Newcastle would be fined severely and subjected to double sessions all week. He was definitely not happy and, with that, he stormed out the door and left us sitting there.

Now we had a decision to make as the young lads were already at the station waiting on us and nobody had told them that the night out was no more. So we agreed to meet up at Montpeliers to decide what we were or were not going to do.

Understandably the young lads were gutted and felt it was unfair on them. The mood amongst the first team lads was that we had been punished and that was enough so we should go out, not to Newcastle, but stay in Edinburgh. The gaffer had said we couldn't go to Newcastle but he hadn't technically said we could not go out and we had a fairly substantial kitty burning a hole in our pockets. And so it was decided that we either all had to agree to go out or none at all and within seconds it was decided we would stay in Edinburgh but have our night. With that, and a couple of calls to local publican Jim Brown, we arranged for him to open up the Blythe Spirit in Rose Street and ordered in some pizzas. So we had our Christmas celebration with everyone prepared to stand together. We had a great day, with some notable singing from the young lads with a particular 'performance' from a young Robbie Neilson that earned him the early nickname of 'Sick Boy'!

The following day, with some lads a little under the weather, we headed to Heriot-Watt from Tynecastle where Billy was waiting for us. He started us with his pressing game of everyone over the halfway line to score and if we dropped the pace, he would just restart the clock on the duration of the game that he had set at forty minutes, although everyone knew it would be longer as we had been promised tough double sessions all week. It was going fine until about twenty minutes in when Baggio (Fulton) started to limp, and this got worse until Billy stopped the game and asked him what was up? It was then we froze with horror as the vague memory of Baggio running along Rose Street and banging his leg on a bollard resurfaced. We silently hoped he would blame it on an injury in the Killie match but he blurted out the truth and the gaffer went off on one, demanding to know who was out!

All of us came to Stevie's rescue. In response to the gaffer saying we had not been allowed out, we replied saying we'd only been told we couldn't go out in Newcastle! To be fair to Billy Brown, he did back us up as he realised that we had stayed as a group. He just calmed the gaffer down and then barked that he was starting the game from zero. We got on with the game as Baggio headed back to the ground for treatment, leaving us with another forty minutes of torture ahead.

That afternoon we were hammered round the track at Tynecastle and the gaffer stuck to his threat as we did double sessions every day including the Friday. On the Saturday we played Rangers at Tynecastle where I pulled us back into the game from 2–0 down before the legs almost literally fell off us and we lost further goals to Albertz and Gazza as we went down 4–1. But we won the next four games, including mauling Hibs 4–0 at Easter Road in Jim Duffy's first game. I also scored another five which got me even closer to the goals record, and when I scored against Dundee Utd, I was only one goal behind.

It was midway through January and there were plenty games left to beat the record – a record that no one thought would ever be broken.

Hammy had come in and I had immediately struck up a great relationship with him on and off the pitch; and Colin Cameron and I had developed a great understanding as he could run off me and I could use his timed runs to my benefit. We really seemed to start to click, and with Stevie Fulton pulling the strings in midfield and Terry causing mayhem on the flanks, we really looked like a decent side. We also now had a settled defensive line-up. The only cloud for me was a troubling knee injury. After we went out in the replay of the cup at Dundee Utd, I was told I needed an op to remove a piece of bone that had flaked off, which meant I was going to miss the next three games but be back for the derby. It was frustrating, with the record in sight, but there was no option.

On my return, we beat Hibs 1–0 thanks to a late Neil McCann goal, but I was still that one elusive goal short of levelling the record. I thought Dunfermline at home in the penultimate home match of the season offered a great chance to not only equal it but beat it, but we were poor and were trailing deep into injury time. Then a ball was thrown into the box and headed goalward where I tried an overhead kick and Kevin Thomas went to head it. It got the slightest of touches to send the ball over the line for number 206. It also saved a point for the team as we tried to clinch a Euro spot through the League.

I think from my celebrations everyone knew how happy I was. To get level with two more games of the season left made me feel hugely positive about reaching an impossible target. I was overjoyed at the prospect of getting the chance to possibly beat

Jimmy Wardhaugh's League tally and my head was swimming after the game as the realisation dawned about the magnitude of this if I could just get one more goal.

The following week, a larger than normal Hearts support headed to Tannadice to roar me on to break the record, but despite coming close twice, it was not to be, as a McSwegan goal gave United victory. I had one last chance against Rangers at home, and with nothing imminent on a new deal, I had ninety minutes to break the record and cement my name in history. The pressure was on!

Rangers had gone to Tannadice in the midweek and a Brian Laudrup header had delivered them their ninth title in a row, so they were in a jubilant mood when they arrived at Tynecastle. They had brought in a couple of their younger players in McInnes and Barry Ferguson to freshen up their side and I must admit I was nervous. My nerves weren't helped when we had a strong penalty claim turned down when a Derek Holmes shot hit Gough's hand but the appeal was turned away by referee Jim McCluskey. With the game meandering towards a goalless draw and chances scarce, I just couldn't see anything happening. Then with ten minutes left, I worked a one-two with Terry but his pull-back was just too strong for me. Fortunately, it was perfect for Mickey and he slammed it home. Before the celebrations had even died down, McInnes had levelled.

A long clearance was then missed by Gordan Petrić and I got on the end of it, knocked it into the box and, as I was going away from goal, I thought it best to slow down and see if Petrić was alert. He wasn't, so I just stopped and let him clatter into the back of me. I knew on the way down that a penalty was on its way and, to my relief and the delight of the fans, he pointed to the spot. Jim Hamilton raced over with the ball and then, for the first time ever, I got nervous taking a penalty for Hearts. This was it – an opportunity to break the record and suddenly I was nervous. I thought, 'Just blast it down the middle.' Dibble, in the Rangers goal, was sure to dive but then . . . no, I thought, 'don't be silly, stick to your routine – low and hard, keeper's right, your left'. My mind was racing. I was desperate to score but now I couldn't slow everything down. My heart was racing too, and the adrenalin was coursing through me as I placed the ball on the spot.

The next part was a blur as I just ran up and placed it home, to my huge relief and the delight of the fans. Chris later told me that he was worse than me with nerves as he sat in the stand with my family, witnessing the drama. Incredibly, with the pressure off, just two minutes later I got the break of the ball, ran through from halfway in the Rangers half and, as they kept backing off, I eventually got into the box and curled home another to smash the record and clinch the game. With it we got fourth spot for the club in the League, I had nineteen goals for the season, but now, most importantly, from a personal point of view, I had 208 League goals, a new record for the club. It was a little piece of history and not bad for someone who had been told he was too small, too fat and too slow!

I must admit that after the game I shed a few tears as I celebrated with my family. It had been something that had been hanging about, and with the uncertainty of whether there would be a new deal for me or not, the pressure had been on. I got a fantastic letter from the Wardhaugh family congratulating me on my achievement and saying that they were delighted for me. I thought that was incredibly classy of them and it made it feel so much more special. But, again, I was saddened by the fact that my dad had not seen me achieve this. I could only imagine how he would have felt to me become Hearts' leading League goalscorer of all time. I just wanted to say to him that I had done it for him and that I hoped he was proud, and I am sure he would have been as he was a Hearts fan. I wanted my dad to be there so I could throw my arms around him and say that this was for you, Dad. Privately, of course, I dedicated it to him and shed a few more tears.

I had done something many thought impossible and, at that moment, I couldn't imagine ever finding a greater feeling of achievement. But, as it turned out, I was wrong. There was still one more moment to come, and this one would top the lot.

24

Fans From Hell
and Fans From Paradise

I knew from the off that season 1997/98 could well be my last. It was clear from the number of forwards that had been brought in by the gaffer and Billy that they wanted a younger and more dynamic-looking forward line. But I had finished the previous season well clear at the top of the scoring charts and, while I was fast approaching my thirty-third birthday, I still felt I was the best finisher at the club. I was at an age where I could pass on my experience to the likes of Jim Hamilton, Kris O'Neil and the rest, and still perform well. Neil McCann and I had struck up an almost telepathic link with Mickey Cameron and I felt I was still the best link-up player for the lads at the back to hit so we could get up the park. The arthritis in my hip was there but it was not stopping me playing.

I knew more than ever that my pre-season would be closely scrutinised to see if I was keeping up with the younger lads. We had brought in another striker who was quick, mobile and looked like he had an eye for goal. Frenchman Stéphane Adam was brought in on big money; the club had done a deal with him to run his contract down instead of paying the reputed fee of around £300,000 that his side had wanted in January. The rumour was that he was on over £3,000 a week, which was double what anyone else at the club was on. And, with those figures in mind, I didn't see the gaffer or Billy bringing him in to be sitting on the bench. Having also paid big money for Jim Hamilton and Neil McCann, it seemed pretty obvious where they saw the future of the forward line coming from. But I had never shirked a challenge and I knew and felt I still had the necessary skill set to compete with the young guns. So, once again, I made sure I got myself in the best possible shape to survive pre-season and be ready for the challenges ahead.

The gaffer and Billy had organised our first ever training ground which was down at Pinkie School in Musselburgh, an area they both knew well, being from neighbouring Wallyford. It was great at long last to have a designated area to come and change and train on, along with the area known as the Lagoons a short distance away. It certainly beat the scratching about that the club had done for years. Since joining in 1981, we had trained at Roseburn Park, Saughton Park, Saughton Enclosure, Heriot-Watt playing fields, Dreghorn Barracks, Paties Road, Ford's Road, the barracks at South Queensferry, George Watson's rugby pitches, Meggetland, Wester Hailes pitches, Forrester High School – you name it, we had been there. That was the way it was, with all our gym work done upstairs in the Brown gymnasium at the stadium.

So this at long last felt like the club were looking to improve the facilities and help the players by having a dedicated base. It gave us a big boost and, for the first time in sixteen years, we were not reporting directly to the stadium then jumping in cars to drive to training, or walking round Russell Road to Roseburn or S**tburn as it was known due to the amount of dog excrement that needed to be cleared before we could train.

Alongside Stéphane, the gaffer brought in another European player in the shape of Thomas Flögel, an attacking midfielder who, to be fair, looked as if he could play anywhere. And with the emergence of Davie Weir from the year before as a huge leader at the back, there was no doubt there was competition in every department of the team. We had a very strong nucleus; the younger players were maturing more and more and were now bona fide first team regulars.

The gaffer and Billy had us doing the Queen's Park and Braid Hill early but we also had lots of little runs around Musselburgh and our new base to keep us in tip-top condition. I felt I linked up well with Stéphane in the small-sided games so I felt confident enough that I could be in with a shout of forming a partnership with him or Hammy come the season start. In pre-season, the gaffer mixed it up with Stéphane and Hammy starting against Blyth Spartans (0–0) and again against Hull City (3–2) before Hammy and I got the nod. I scored one and he got two in a 3–0 win over Berwick, and we started in a testimonial game for big Dave MacPherson against Rangers who we beat 3–2. Hammy got a hat-trick, before Stéphane and Hammy started at Grimsby in a 2–0 defeat. We then prepared for our opening game at Ibrox live on TV on the Monday evening.

The gaffer and Billy had been looking at various formations, but they had plumped for a 3-5-2 that saw Davie Weir flanked by Grant Murray and Paul Ritchie, with Stevie Frail and Disa as wing-backs. Salvatori sat centrally, with Fulton and Flögel pushing on. That left the front two of Hammy and, surprisingly, Neil McCann. That decision meant that Stéphane Adam dropped to the bench alongside Mickey Cameron and young defender Robbie Horn and there was no place for myself or Big Dave. To be fair, he had hobbled off in his testimonial game and wasn't quite one hundred per cent fit so it was too risky a decision to include him for such a big opening game.

A crowd of just under 50,000 turned up as Rangers started their quest for ten in a row. I was naturally gutted not to make the fourteen but, with a big squad and a battle for places, some players were going to be left out. It was a signal that no one was guaranteed a place and selection would have to be earned, which was fine by me as I still retained the utmost belief that I could provide the standard and the goals to secure a regular start. We defended well enough in the game and looked stoic at the back without providing any great threat up front. It looked as if we would make it to the interval unscathed when Marco Negri forced the ball over the line after Rangers had hit the post. Before we had time to recover, Laudrup sent a defence-splitting pass through and Negri chipped it over big Gilles to double their lead. To lose those goals in the run-up to half time was a blow and Rangers grew in confidence. They could have scored more but we hung in, and it was six minutes from time when Alec Cleland made it 3–0 before Mickey pulled one back at the death. That was that, so Dave and I made our way down from the main stand to the bus and waited for the lads before the quiet trip back to Edinburgh.

The next day the players who started the game had the day off so the subs plus the lads that didn't play trained at Pinkie as normal under Heggie. It was a tough session with running and high-intensity games, but very enjoyable. On the Wednesday the first team starters returned and we had a similar session under the watchful eyes of the gaffer and Billy. As any player will tell you, it's normally not the day after a game that you feel stiff or any knocks are felt, but the day after that. When it came to the intensity games at the end, it was clear that the side that had the majority of the lads who had played on Monday were not quite as sharp or as fresh as the other team.

During this game, I was on fire along with Mickey as we got seven or eight goals between us in a short spell. This was too much for Billy who blew the whistle, pulled everyone in and went mad, especially at the team who were getting beaten. When he was finished, the gaffer had a go too and also laid in about the performance against Rangers, explaining that that level of performance would not be accepted.

While he was doing this, I switched off as I knew he was not having a go at me. Over his shoulder in the distance, I got distracted by a guy training his greyhounds and I was watching how he was getting them to chase some device and how it was only for about ten or fifteen seconds, then next thing I got a tug on my shirt from Davie Weir saying the gaffer was talking to me.

The gaffer asked if I heard what he had just said and I probably could have got away with it by saying he was right, we had to be better and we had to train better and raise our performances. But I honestly had not heard a thing he had said after the first couple of words. So I just apologised and said I had become distracted and had assumed he was not addressing me as I'd been training well and had not played the other evening. I also said that I hadn't heard him because of the greyhounds in the distance.

Unfortunately for me, this got a couple of giggles and the gaffer exploded and then hammered me, saying this was the reason the club had won fuck all for thirty years, that attitudes like mine were part of the reason and that I had been here too long and won nothing. I was fizzing. There was no real reason for him taking out his frustration on me as I had not played, but it was clear he was having a piece of me and once more singling me out. I cracked and replied back, 'Oh yeah, is that right? It's all my fault? I don't recall us winning anything when you played and captained us!'

It was out before I realised it and the next thing was Big Davie stepping in front of me as the gaffer came forward before he was pulled back. It finished with him telling me to fuck off and train with the reserves at the bottom end of Pinkie, a good six hundred yards away. As I walked off he told me to take off my bib and to tell Kevin Thomas to come over and take my place for the rest of the session. I was raging and just about in tears with anger but just walked the distance across despite calls to hurry up by Billy. When I got to where the reserves were training, I saw Kevin sitting at the side of the pitch.

'Legend, you all right?' I asked him as he sat there, and he said he was struggling with a migraine. 'Ah, right,' I said. 'Well, it's going to get worse as you have to take my place with the first team squad,' and handed him my bib. As he took it and jogged off, I said, 'Oh, by the way, you have to take your time going over as they are having a meeting.'

'Okay,' he said and started to walk, much to the chagrin of Billy who roared at him from the distance. Heggy asked what happened and when I told him he just sighed and said, 'Well, get involved here and get your head down and finish the session.'

With Thursday being a lighter session, I was once more banished to the reserves and told I was to get my agent Bill McMurdo in for a meeting the following day. The gaffer was not happy and wanted action. I had already phoned him to explain what had happened and that it looked like that was that. To be fair to Billy, he said we needed to get on with it and end it there, which wasn't a problem for me. But as I left I felt there was no way back anytime soon.

When we travelled to play Meadowbank-Livingston in the League Cup I was, unsurprisingly, left out the squad. Two goals from Terry gave us victory and I was still with the reserve squad on the Monday evening as we played a friendly at Newtongrange Star. I got a couple but remained with the young lads for the rest of the week until fate played a hand. Both Kevin Thomas and Hammy picked up knocks in training and I surprisingly found myself in the fourteen-man squad for the Saturday against Aberdeen at Tynecastle. Even more surprisingly, I was selected to start with Stéphane to the right of me and Terry to the left in a three-man attack.

We started well but found ourselves down 1–0 after just ten minutes as Mike Newell put the Dons in front. It was a blisteringly hot day, but our football matched the weather as I equalised from the spot and then set up Baggio for the second after neat link-up play, before setting up the third for Mickey Cameron. That one was all down to instinct as Steve Frail played a great ball in towards my feet. With two Aberdeen defenders around me, looking to see where my touch would take the ball, I just dummied the ball through my legs knowing that Mickey, without even a word between us, would have made his trade-mark run. Sure enough, as it took both defenders out the way, the wee man didn't even break stride and dispatched it with aplomb.

We finished the half on a high and although it was more of the same in the second half, we just couldn't find the net due to desperate defending and great goalkeeping. It was my replacement, Thomas Flögel, who put a much fairer reflection on the performance by adding a fourth at the death, but I had made my point. I was more than capable of playing a part.

Despite starting the Cup win at Raith the following midweek and a win against Hibs at Easter Road, I was soon back on the bench. I did have the honour of scoring the first Hearts goal in front of the newly completed Gorgie Road stand with the winner against Dundee United, however, but it was clear and understandable that the gaffer saw Hammy, Stéphane and Terry as his front three; and the competition increased even more with the arrival of José Quitongo. However, we scored the goals in another derby victory over our rivals as part of a six-game winning run that saw some of the best football at Tynecastle for many a season. That included an Adam hat-trick in a classic 5–3 victory over Kilmarnock as we maintained a challenge at the top of the table despite once more going out the League Cup at Dunfermline after extra time to ex-Hearts player Allan Moore's late goal.

I had to admit it was good to watch and I was doing plenty of that as the guys were playing well. The front men were on fire, so I had few matches, although I did score again against Rangers in a rare start. It was proving difficult to force myself into the team due to the form of Stéphane, Hammy, Terry and José, but in another rare but predictable start against Hibs, we let a two-goal lead slip in a game where we could easily have avenged the infamous 7–0 drubbing of the 1970s. Two Fulton goals gave us the lead inside ten minutes before we squandered numerous chances to be five or six ahead at the interval. We were made to pay as Hibs pegged us back in the second half. I then had a great chance at the death to win it for us only to see my miss-hit shot blocked. I should have scored.

I had to be content with sub appearances against Clydebank (2–0) and Albion Rovers (3–0) as Hammy, Stéphane and Terry continued to score, and even José chipped in with a dramatic late equaliser against Celtic. I was seeing very little game time, and, with that in mind, the gaffer came to me and said I needed to go out on loan for a month and that there had been enquiries from Raith Rovers and Dundee. Both teams were in the First Division at this point and after speaking to each manager, I decided that Dundee would be the better option to let me get four games under my belt before returning for the remainder of the season in April and May.

I met up with my new teammates on the Tuesday evening for the first time as we headed to play Partick Thistle at Firhill and I nearly scored after just fifteen seconds, heading just past before two Eddie Annand goals gave us a 2–1 win and extended the lead at the top of the table to five points. On the Saturday I set up James Grady for an early goal against St Mirren that ultimately was enough and, again, I was unlucky not to get a couple of goals. But while the victory took Dundee six points clear at the top, it was not enough to placate the 'Derry' section of the home crowd who were baying for more. Considering Dundee had a lot of young lads in their side, I thought it was a bit strange, only to be pointed to the fact that they were always like that. And so, after a brief chat with manager Jocky Scott, I asked if it was okay if I had a little bit of a pop at the fans. He just smiled and said, 'You know what you are doing, so on you go.'

So I trotted along to the press and they asked what I thought and I came out all guns blazing, asking what did the Dundee fans want from their team? They had just won again, extended their lead at the top and all they could do was slaughter the team for not scoring more goals. I said that this would affect the young lads in the run in and if they wanted to hurl abuse, hurl it at me as I could take it. Just lay off the young lads and help them out. I said that in my opinion they were the 'fans from hell'.

On Monday when I walked in, the players were delighted but warned me that the Derry section would not like it and that I would get pelters on Saturday in the match against Morton. I just shrugged my shoulders. Jocky Scott said I was bang on, but did I realise what I was stirring up? At the end of the day, I said, as long as they lay off the rest of the team then it was job done. Sure enough, the Derry seemed to have filled up slightly quicker than normal and my entrance to the warm-up was greeted with loud booing from under the Shed. I admit I continued to goad them by cupping my ear as I was fully aware that I wanted them to have a go at me.

It was the same when the game started, as every touch I made was booed. They slaughtered me but they cheered every touch from the rest of the team, so the ploy was working, and the game ended in a 3–0 victory. It was indeed job done. I had played well enough and was more than happy with how the game worked out. At the end, even the Derry begrudgingly applauded me off with five minutes to go as another two points were racked up.

The following week I got the winner in a 2–1 result against

Hamilton at Cliftonhill that saw me celebrate the arrival of my wee girl Jade to complete the set of scoring after the birth of every one of my children. I was actually cheered off the park by the Dundee fans in the away end as they saw their side go another point further ahead at the top with just a handful of games remaining.

After a light session on the Monday, I returned to Tynecastle on the Tuesday to join training for a massive match the following Saturday. While I had been away on loan, I had returned to Tynecastle (as I was cup-tied) to see Hammy score twice in a 4–1 win that saw us face Falkirk at Ibrox in the semi-final of the Scottish Cup. As Rangers and Celtic were slugging it out at the top of the League, the pressure was getting to both of them, and we were right on their tails. And they hadn't even noticed. The cup game saw me sitting in the stand as the gaffer went with his tried and trusted formation and it looked to be going the way we wanted as we led 1–0 with an early Stéphane Adam goal. Despite the best efforts of Kevin McAllister for the Bairns, we looked strong enough to hold on to that until, with eighty-five minutes showing on the scoreboards at Ibrox, he scored a truly great goal with a solo run and stunning finish. It looked like our semi-final hoodoo was back, but thankfully, in the last minute, José set up Stéphane again to put us in front. With Falkirk throwing everyone forward, we hit them on the break again and Terry finished it off. We were through in a rather flattering 3–1 victory but we deserved it over the ninety minutes.

It left us with six more league games before we faced Rangers in the final, and what was to be the swansong for the great Rangers team led by the equally great manager Walter Smith. To say we missed an opportunity is evident now but wasn't so much then. If you look at those last six matches, we drew 1–1 at home to Motherwell and St Johnstone, lost 2–1 at Easter Road, lost 3–0 at home to Rangers, drew 2–2 at Aberdeen before beating Dunfermline 2–0 at Tynecastle in the last game of the season.

It is not until you break it down and see that we took just six points from those eighteen with one win, two losses and three draws, yet finished just seven points behind eventual winners Celtic and five behind Rangers! It is no understatement that we should have beaten Motherwell and St Johnstone as well as Aberdeen in the drawn games, and the Hibs match could have gone either way at 1–1. Even the 3–0 loss to Rangers would not have deterred us had we stayed the course, but we didn't. And it was in the Hibs match during that last half-dozen games that I knew my time at Hearts would be over shortly.

If ever there was a fixture I revelled in and showed my worth to Hearts, it was the derby. So when I found out I wasn't starting, my heart sank. Even though I knew that this would be my last season, I was always sure of being a starter against Hibs, but as we ran out for the warm-up, I was on the bench with big Davie MacPherson and José Quitongo. It was April, but there were snow flurries as we approached the fourth and final derby of the season with us still in the thick of the title race. At the end of the match, deep down I knew that both the title challenge and my career at Hearts was nearly over. As we'd headed down to Easter Road earlier in the day, I was more hopeful than confident that I would get the nod to start. I had got the match practice required, had done well and was feeling sharp, but it was not to be. Hammy and Stéphane got the nod, but I was right behind them and geeing them up for the game and getting round the rest of the lads as we were still in a battle at the top and Hibs were struggling. If we won, this would be a fatal blow to their slim chances of staying up and I reminded the players that it was a derby and that we were expected to win.

The first half was a non-event as Hibs retreated and made it difficult to play through, and Mickey Cameron and Neil McCann were being starved of the ball, so it was no real surprise that it ended goalless. Then as the second half settled down, Barry Lavety fired Hibs ahead in the fifty-sixth minute in a rare attack. Three substitutes were ordered to warm up by the gaffer, and, as we did, Big Dave said to me to get going quickly as I'd be on first. It was a thought shared by everyone in maroon but, to everyone's surprise, it was a good ten minutes before Dave and José were recalled to the bench and told to strip and replace Grant Murray and Stefano Salvatori. A minute later I was signalled in and came on to replace Stéphane Adam. With just under twenty minutes left, there was more than enough time to make an impact and turn the game around. That impact arrived within seconds as Terry was crudely chopped down just outside the box. I decided I was hitting the free kick and with my first touch curled it over the wall and high into the net. We were level, much to every maroon-clad person behind the goal's delight.

We had two excellent chances after that as Terry saw a great run and a shot well saved by Bryan Gunn before Hammy hit a volley that got trapped between Gunny's legs. We sensed the match had turned, but, incredibly, Hibs broke down the park and Kevin Harper fired them in front with nine minutes remaining. Once more, Hibs had Gunn to thank as I hit one that looked like sneaking in but was palmed away. Then right on full-time, Paul Ritchie bulleted a header down low, but the big keeper turned it away. Victory went to the green half of the city that time, and with defeat to Rangers the following week, our title ambitions had gone.

There was the small consolation that our city rivals had indeed been relegated, but, deep down, I felt that was a shame as the derby was always a great game to look forward to. And given the total dominance that Hearts had enjoyed since returning to the Premier League, I felt it was going to be a miss.

The gaffer told me I would be starting in the last game at home to Dunfermline and that it might be a good idea if I brought family and friends along as it 'might' be my last appearance at Tynecastle. He also mentioned that he wanted me to play a different role as he was looking at a formation change for the cup final and wanted to look at it in this match. He explained that he wanted me to play behind the main striker and just in front of the midfield two, in what is now the modern number 10 role.

In what was to be my last appearance at Tynecastle, 13,888 fans were there. I played in the deeper role and did well and we rounded off the League campaign with a solid 2–0 win, with Stéphane and Derek Holmes getting the goals that saw us win more comfortably than the score line suggested. I was given a fantastic ovation by the fans as I was replaced by my mate Neil Pointon with twelve minutes to go, and I knew deep down that this was it for me in a maroon jersey. I was tearful, but it was more through gratitude at the reception I was receiving from the fans as they sensed that this was it for John Robertson. And after 513 League games and 214 League goals that was it in terms of the domestic campaign. However, there was still one more game left – the Scottish Cup final.

The day after the Dunfermline game we flew down to England to stay in Stratford-upon-Avon to prepare for the final against Walter Smith's recently dethroned champions. The Sunday was a golf day and we played at the magnificent Forest of Arden course. That evening, the gaffer called us all into the bar for a few drinks and outlined the plan for the rest of the week. The Monday morning was free (the gaffer wanted another game of golf) then we would train at 2 p.m. at the pristine NFU fields. We'd then train on Tuesday, and then on Wednesday morning, the bus would take us home. On Thursday we would train at Tynecastle at noon and do the press ahead of the game, and on Friday, we would train at Tynecastle again before heading to our hotel for the night ahead of the game. He explained that we would be playing a 4-2-3-1 formation and that we would use every session in England to work on the shape and to make sure that everyone knew their job. We were going to surprise Rangers with this new set up. We had played them four times that season with three defeats (3–1; 5–2; 3–0) and a solitary draw. We'd had attacking intentions but only the 2–2 draw at Ibrox had brought us our solitary point.

As we arrived to do the first session, the gaffer pulled me aside and my heart sank. It was touch and go if I was going to make the fourteen on the day of the final. He sat me down and said right away that I would not be involved in the starting line-up. I felt numb when I heard the words 'not involved' as I thought at that moment I was going to be left out of the squad entirely. But he then said, 'Look, I want you to know that you will be on the bench as I don't want you worrying all week if you are going to be involved, and I need you to tell the players how big this is and what it would mean to them, the fans and the club to win some silverware.'

To say I was relieved was an understatement and I thought it was a classy touch from the gaffer. He also said that Mickey was still struggling with injury and that I was to watch his position closely as, if he didn't make it, I would be playing in the deeper role that I had filled against Dunfermline because that was where he wanted Mickey to play.

The sessions went well. The gaffer explained that this was a real opportunity and we went through every possible scenario of what we were required to do when we had the ball, when we didn't have the ball, and for set plays. The team looked comfortable and relaxed. We realised that defensively, when Rangers had the ball, we were going to drop off and let them have it at the back and sit off them, making it hard to play through us. We'd also be giving them no room to play over the top. Attacking-wise, when we had the ball, Neil McCann and Thomas Flögel were to keep as wide as possible to pull their full backs out and allow Stéphane to stay central and run into the gaps between the centre-backs and full-backs, or allow wee Mickey to run in there.

Baggio and Stefano were to back them up, with only Baggio allowed to get forward. Stefano was told to screen the back four, the full backs being told on no occasion to get forward but to sit and defend. So when we attacked, five stayed and five went forward, but we had to be disciplined defensively with Mickey making it a 4-5-1 when we lost the ball. Hour after hour we worked on it to get it right.

The press day went well and I was asked if I thought I would be involved. The gaffer had sworn me to secrecy, so it was still very much a case of saying that I was feeling confident if I was given the opportunity. We were there to have a go and had the belief to beat Rangers, who we said may be feeling a bit low having lost the chance to win their tenth title in a row the week earlier.

Celtic had pipped them on the line and there was a sense amongst the lads that we could beat them as we had played well in the Coca-Cola Cup final the previous season and could have won it. There may well have been a bit of bravado, but there seemed to be an air of confidence as we left for the game at Parkhead on a blisteringly hot Saturday, 16 May.

The task that lay ahead was huge and even though it had been announced that this was to be Walter Smith's last game in charge, Rangers were still a formidable side. Ever since the arrival of Graeme Souness they had spent big and dominated Scottish football as title after title arrived, with no shortage of League and Scottish Cups too. They were packed with quality, season after season, and when you looked at their team sheet and saw that the likes of McCoist and Durrant were on the bench, it showed how deep their squad went. The only small bonus for us was that Jörg Albertz, he of the thunderous left foot that had flattened many a wall in Scottish football, had been sent off the previous week, and such were the nuances of Scottish football at the time, that meant he missed the cup final. Nonetheless, their team was still formidable as they lined up.

As expected, wee Mickey had recovered and so we lined up with the new formation for the game.

The gaffer had sacrificed Hammy, who had been the top scorer that season, for an extra midfield player. We were in buoyant mood and all seemed fine, but you could sense there were a few nerves as we approached kick-off time. We were getting round each other and the gaffer reminded us of the way we played in the last cup final here at Parkhead. This was a chance for us to become legends and make history.

As we were about to go, I went round the players wishing them the best of luck and to go enjoy it – by winning it. I left big Gilles until last. He had, as you would expect, taken a fair bit of stick all week as the press had dug up the 5–1 final and he had been reminded that not only had he lost nine goals in two finals, but his mistake in the previous cup final had been seen as a howler. I grabbed his hand and said good luck and that he had nothing to prove to anyone in the dressing room or to the thousands of fans in maroon in the stadium or back in Edinburgh. I told him he would be fine out there, and he looked down over me and, with his little stutter, said, 'Ttthank you, RRobbbo.' As he walked away, I shouted, 'Hey, Gilles,' and as he looked round I said, 'Mind and keep your legs shut though!' He burst out laughing and mumbled something in French, but his shoulders were back and his head high as he joined the lads in the tunnel for a day of destiny.

And what a start it was. Within the first sixty seconds Baggio had burst forward and was brought crashing to the ground. Willie Young pointed to the penalty spot and we couldn't believe it, even more so when the TV pictures suggested it might have taken place just outside the box. But we were not complaining – you need every bit of good fortune you can get on these occasions. Wee Mickey hammered it home and we were ahead and, to be fair, we settled well and kept Rangers at arm's length for most of the half, with big Gilles only really having a couple of bog standard saves to make as Rangers struggled to break down our defensive formation. The attacking side of it had not really come to anything but we didn't care as we trooped up the tunnel 1–0 to the good at the break.

The gaffer and Billy got to work on what was needed to get a bit more out of our attacking play while remaining as solid as we had been as a unit defensively. Once more I got round the players, geeing them up, reminding them of what was at stake and how well they had done and that one last big effort was needed.

The second half was only seven minutes old when we were in dreamland. A long ball over the top saw Amoruso hesitate momentarily and that was all Stéphane needed as he knocked the ball on, steadied himself and, despite a strong hand from Andy Goram, smacked it home to put us 2–0 ahead. Rangers had brought on McCoist for Stensaas at half time and then Durrant replaced McCall to add energy to the midfield. Rangers went for broke and with the heat of the day now beginning to take effect and the desperate waves of pressure coming from Rangers, it was no surprise that we were pushed back towards our own penalty area.

With twelve minutes to go, Hammy replaced Stéphane with the strict instructions of chasing balls into the corner flag and keeping the ball up the pitch, but, almost immediately, Rangers put Amoruso up front, so Hammy was signalled to play as a centre-back to mark him.

With three minutes left, Coisty (who else) cracked one home and it was game on. Big Gilles, who had made three great saves, was asked again to thwart Rangers' advances as they poured forward. The big man was plucking crosses out the air, then disaster struck as Coisty picked up a flick on and was brought down by Paul Ritchie. Referee Willie Young pointed to the spot and a penalty.

My striker's instinct immediately made me look to the linesman to see if he was onside, and as the rest of the dugout dropped their heads, I saw the official had his flag up. 'Offside! He's offside,' I was shouting and everyone looked. But he wasn't signalling offside; he had signalled it was a free kick and that the foul had been inches outside the box. And that was when our other stroke of luck kicked in. As Rangers had lost Albertz, and this free kick would have been tailor-made for him, we waited with dread to see who would take it and what would happen next. It was a rollercoaster of emotions when up stepped Lorenzo Amoruso to hammer it high into the stands.

It had been plain to see in the last ten minutes that Mickey had run his race due to his injury and he looked tired, but what a shift he had put in. His fitness was incredible, and alongside him, Baggio was burst, too, with the heat and the pace of the game. So the gaffer told Grant Murray and me to get ready. There were only a couple of minutes left and our roles were simple, Grant was to replace Baggio and sit in midfield with Stefano. I was to replace Mickey but to try and run the channels and the clock down. Then, as we were about to go on, Gary Naysmith got a boot in the face. After treatment, Alan Rae informed the gaffer that he thought he was fine but might have a slight concussion and that we needed to keep an eye on him. So it was decided that we would leave the substitution. If he wasn't right, then Baggio would have to go back into that position and, by now, we were deep into injury time as we hung on grimly.

When Gary motioned to the bench that he was fine, the gaffer started looking at the change, but for the next two minutes the ball would not go out. Then he said we couldn't change now. He was right; the lads were just a white shield. After an eternity, the whistle blew, it was over. We had won. The Scottish Cup was ours; it was coming back to Tynecastle. That was all that mattered as we rushed onto the park to grab every single one of the lads and celebrate. I was in bits as the tears flooded out and pure, unbridled emotion took over. I have never felt a sporting emotion like that as we celebrated before going over to commiserate with the Rangers players who sensed what we had achieved and, in fairness, took it very well. Many of them were international teammates over the years and they knew what it meant to us as a club and, in particular, to myself as a Hearts player.

The celebrations were slowed as we watched the best Rangers team in history collect their runners-up medals and I decided I was going to wait until last to go up for mine. I knew Lockie and Baggio were going to collect the trophy and I thought last up before the gaffer and Billy would do me fine as I took in the roars of delight, the relief and the almost disbelieving looks from the fans. As each player took their turn, eventually, it was me. To be honest, I haven't a clue what was said to me by the presentation committee as all I wanted was to get my hands on the Cup and raise it aloft. As I did, I heard the huge roar and instinctively put my hand on my heart and made my own personal tribute to my dad. I had thought about this before the game and had told my family that if we won, I would do something to honour our dad as this would have been another day of days for him. And as I did it, I firmly believed that he was with us in the sunshine in Paradise to see his team secure the Scottish Cup at long last.

Walking around, soaking it in and seeing the unbridled joy of the Hearts fans was just incredible. It was a sensational moment as it dawned on me just how special winning the trophy had become to everyone who was connected to Hearts. And the tears of joy were not contained to the pitch but were there for Hearts fans everywhere. For the players, the mix of elation and relief meant that the win had still not really sunk in.

The fans who were there that day, in the stadium back in Edinburgh and around the world had realised a dream of seeing us win something. Having been so close so many times, many had begun to feel that they may not see Hearts win anything ever again. We'd spurned a number of opportunities but as we made our way to the end with the Hearts supporters, it was incredible to see that large swathes of Rangers fans had also stayed behind and continued to applaud us as we made our way past them. This act, while a bit of class from Rangers fans, also added to the sense of how big this achievement really was.

Back in the dressing room, it was mayhem as we celebrated with obligatory champagne and the sponsor's lager, joined by the rest of the players, staff and medical team. It was then that I thought I would sneak out and get a souvenir and was actually heading to get one of the logo corner flags when I saw that the referee's dressing room was open. Willie Young and Co. were long gone, and there, lying in the middle of the floor, was the bag of match balls. With the construction work going on, this had been the first final with the multiple ball system and so I thought that would do me just fine. And so one of the match balls made its way into my possession – to be joined by 2006 and 2012 balls later on for good measure. Into my bag it went, as if a winner's medal wasn't enough!

The press was a blur, but I vaguely remember the journalists asking if I had been upset at not getting on, to which I told the truth: 'It wasn't about me getting on, it was about Hearts winning the Cup. Seeing those maroon and white ribbons on the trophy was everything I had wished for.'

I even jokingly quipped that by ninety minutes, 'I didn't want on; I was scared I might jinx it!' And anyway, I had a winner's medal in my pocket and felt incredibly fortunate. So many of my friends, teammates and colleagues over the years had missed out on this day.

We eventually made our way to the bus, but there was a long delay as the numbers pulled out for the drugs tests were Gilles and Baggio. While Gilles took a couple of minutes to provide the sample, having run about for more than ninety minutes, Baggio was severely dehydrated and was finding it a tad more difficult to provide the sample required. Indeed, by the time he joined us on the bus, he was half-cut as he had politely declined the offer of water in favour of the sponsor's brew to help him provide the necessary amount to satisfy the authorities.

The bus journey back was sensational with everyone taking the mickey out of everyone else, songs galore and plenty more champagne and beer. Every single vehicle seemed to be bedecked in maroon and white and there were various banners at the fly-overs as we finally reached the outskirts of the city and along the Calder Road toward Tynecastle. As we passed the fire station, they were out on the engines, blue lights flashing. Along past the prison to Chesser, we saw more and more fans waving, shouting and cheering. It was then that some of the younger lads and the foreign lads realised what a big deal this really was, and I told them, wait till you hit Gorgie Road. They could not believe it when, just past Luckies bar, the bus virtually came to a halt as the road was swallowed up by Hearts fans as they celebrated the return of the Scottish Cup to Gorgie Road for the first time since 1956. It took us a happy eternity before we finally arrived at the stadium to disembark, although one or two of us nearly did that earlier as we had punched through the skylights to get on to the bus roof, which was great until our driver, Alan 'Scooby' Scott, took a bend a bit quicker and we nearly flew off.

The evening was surreal as we were reunited with our families and everyone was in great form. It just felt like it was impossible to get drunk as the adrenalin and importance of the occasion finally started to kick in. I just kept glancing in my pocket to look at the winner's medal and knew I was one of the lucky ones to have won it. As the evening wore on, there was no sign of the party slowing down. Around midnight I phoned my business partner Jim Brown, with whom I'd just opened up Robertson's Bar, and we headed off there and kept going, before finally heading home with a few of the lads as house guests ahead of the parade the following morning.

I got off to a bad start the next day. While taking my tracksuit for the parade, I had forgotten the T-shirt, socks and trainers, so, having slept in my suit, I just had to keep it on, despite the blistering temperatures. I was roasting, but, to be honest, I didn't care. Nothing could take away from the pure joy of that day.

We had a great reception with the Lord Provost, Eric Milligan, at the City Chambers before heading onto the open top bus. If the day before had been crazy, then this is when it really hit home for the foreign lads. As we snaked our way down the Mound towards Princes Street and they saw the crowds waiting, they were stunned. It was the same as we headed past the West End and along to Haymarket before turning into Dalry Road. As thousands waited thousands more tagged along behind the bus.

Then it was on to one of the most amazing sights, one that will live with me forever. As we turned from Dalry Road into Gorgie Road, the bus had to stop. Before us, the road from the bank past Robertson's Bar and under the bridge to the Tynecastle Arms was rammed solid with fans. And as you looked up Ardmillan Terrace, it was the same, right to the top and on to Slateford Road. Behind us at Angle Park Terrace and up to Diggers, it was packed as well. And also on Dalry Road as far as the eye could see. In all four directions, it was just a swarm of maroon and white. When we eventually made it to the stadium, 17,500 people were waiting inside and the party continued there. As the sun blazed down on this most perfect of perfect weekends, we took the Cup around a couple of our local watering holes. And it continued to shine the following day, too, as the maroon half of Edinburgh nursed the biggest of hangovers. But, for once, nobody cared.

25

And Now the End Is Near

It was a few days later that I got the call to go in and see the gaffer and Billy, with Bill McMurdo. To be honest, as we met in Gorgie for a cup of tea, we had absolutely no idea what the outcome of the meeting was going to be, and as we talked it over beforehand, I had a feeling that it was going to be a no. I was now within seven goals of Willie Bauld's overall goal scoring record, but with Hammy, Stéphane, José and Neil McCann on the roster, and youngsters Derek Holmes and Kris O'Neil in the background, I couldn't see a new deal being offered.

That was basically how it went with the gaffer and Billy. They felt that having won the cup, maybe it was best to leave on a high and as a winner. And so it was decided that I would be, in footballing terms, 'freed', and allowed to leave the club. The following Monday, I headed into Tynecastle as a player for the last time to collect my boots and kit. It was a strange feeling. When I'd arrived before Christmas 1980, there was no one there to greet me as I walked in through the doors with Dave Bowman. And on the day I was leaving, it was the very same as the stadium was empty apart from the groundsman working away. I walked out the door with a black plastic bag with my belongings, and that was that. I was no longer a player for Heart of Midlothian Football Club. It was over.

When I walked in there at sixteen years old with wide eyes and dreams aplenty, I had no idea that years later I would walk out as the club's top League goalscorer on 214 goals, the top European scorer with seven and the top Scottish Cup scorer with twenty-nine. Particularly satisfying was that other stat that I was also the top derby scorer with twenty-seven goals, which earned me the moniker 'the Hammer of Hibs'. But, like so many before me, it was now time to leave. I walked over the stunning mosaic of the magnificent club crest in the foyer, through the front doors and out into the afternoon sun.

The game was over and the fat striker would no longer score in maroon, but there were new adventures to be had. Within a couple of weeks, I would start a new chapter in my career, one that would briefly allow me to continue to play, with the plan of moving into the management side of the game firmly in my sights. It would bring many more stories, many more great games and many more memories, but those are for another day. My playing career that had so many highs and lows, and so many goals for Hearts, was a dream come true.

Thank You

I would like to offer my thanks to everyone at Black & White Publishing for their hard work in making this book possible.

Many thanks to my sister, Jan Robertson, unofficial Robertson family historian, for the use of family photos. Also to Robert 'Bert' Renton, official photographer HMFC and founder member of the Prestonpans Hearts Supporters Club for the use of photos, along with Gordon Hanratty Chairman PHSC, Wallace Hanratty founder member of PHSC, Alan Owenson Honorary President PHSC: thank you, all.

Also many thanks to Scot Gardiner and John Brown at The Longest Forty for all the hours they have put in for the last year.

To my teammates, managers and coaches, I would have been nothing without each and every one of you and there are no words that adequately sum up what you all did for me. Thank you.

And finally to the fans – thank you for all the encouragement, love and support you gave me then and continue to do so today. Every goal meant as much to me as I hope it did to you.